PATTON'S THIRD ARMY IN WORLD WAR II

Michael Green and James D. Brown

Inspiring | Educating | Creating | Entertaining

© 2010, 2013 Zenith Press
Text © 2010, 2013 Michael Green and James D. Brown

This edition published in 2017 by Crestline,
an imprint of The Quarto Group
142 West 36th Street, 4th Floor
New York, NY 10018 USA
T (212) 779-4972 **F** (212) 779-6058
www.QuartoKnows.com

ISBN-13: 978-0-7858-3496-0

Maps by: Philip Schwartzberg, Meridian Mapping

On the cover: General George S. Patton. *Margaret Bourke-White / Time & Life Pictures / Getty Images;* U.S. Army runs through
smoke filled streets in Wernberg. *National Archives*

On the frontispiece: An M4 Sherman supports troops of the Third Army on approach to the heavily fortified and
German-occupied city of Metz in the Lorraine region. *National Archives*

On the title page: An M4 Sherman of the 8th Tank Battalion, 4th Armored Division, splashes through a shallow canal as
the division drives hard across France. *National Archives*

On the contents page and back cover: *National Archives*

10 9 8 7 6 5 4 3

Printed in China

To all the military personnel

who served with Patton's Third Army.

CONTENTS

List of Maps   viii

Acknowledgments   ix

Introduction   1

CHAPTER ONE   Patton and Operation Overlord   5

CHAPTER TWO   Patton and Operation Cobra   33

CHAPTER THREE   Third Army on the Offensive   63

CHAPTER FOUR   Third Army's Advance Continues   95

CHAPTER FIVE   The Lorraine Campaign   125

CHAPTER SIX   Battle of the Bulge Opening Moves   155

CHAPTER SEVEN   The Road to Bastogne   183

CHAPTER EIGHT   Closing the Bastogne Area   211

CHAPTER NINE   Finishing off the Reich   241

Appendix: Weapons and Vehicles   270

Selected Bibliography   283

Index   284

MAPS

Patton's Third Army from Normandy to V-E Day   x-xi

Operation Cobra Breakthrough   45

Operation Cobra: The Breakout from St.-Lô   52

The 4th and 6th Armored Divisions: Breakout into Brittany   74

Patton's Third Army Breakout   82-83

Closing the Falaise Pocket and Patton's Race to the Seine   107

Pursuit to the German Border: Patton's Advance to the Moselle   120

The Lorraine Campaign   148

The Battle of the Bulge   174

4th Armored Division Attack to Relieve the 101st Airborne Division   184

The Reduction of the Bulge   230-231

The Rhineland Campaign   243

Crossing the Rhine to V-Day   256

ACKNOWLEDGMENTS

SPECIAL THANKS ARE DUE to the staff of the U.S. National Archives still-picture branch and the General George Patton Museum for help in locating images for this book. Thanks are also due to the U.S. Army Armor School Research Library at Fort Knox, Kentucky, and the various division associations that served under Patton's Third Army. Individuals who made an extra effort in helping out on this book include Charles Lemons, Martin K. A. Morgan, Candace Fuller, Chun-Lun Hsu, Randy Talbot, and Dean and Nancy Kleffman.

For those who wish to seek out more information on Patton, the man, one can visit the websites of the Patton Museum Foundation or the Patton Society.

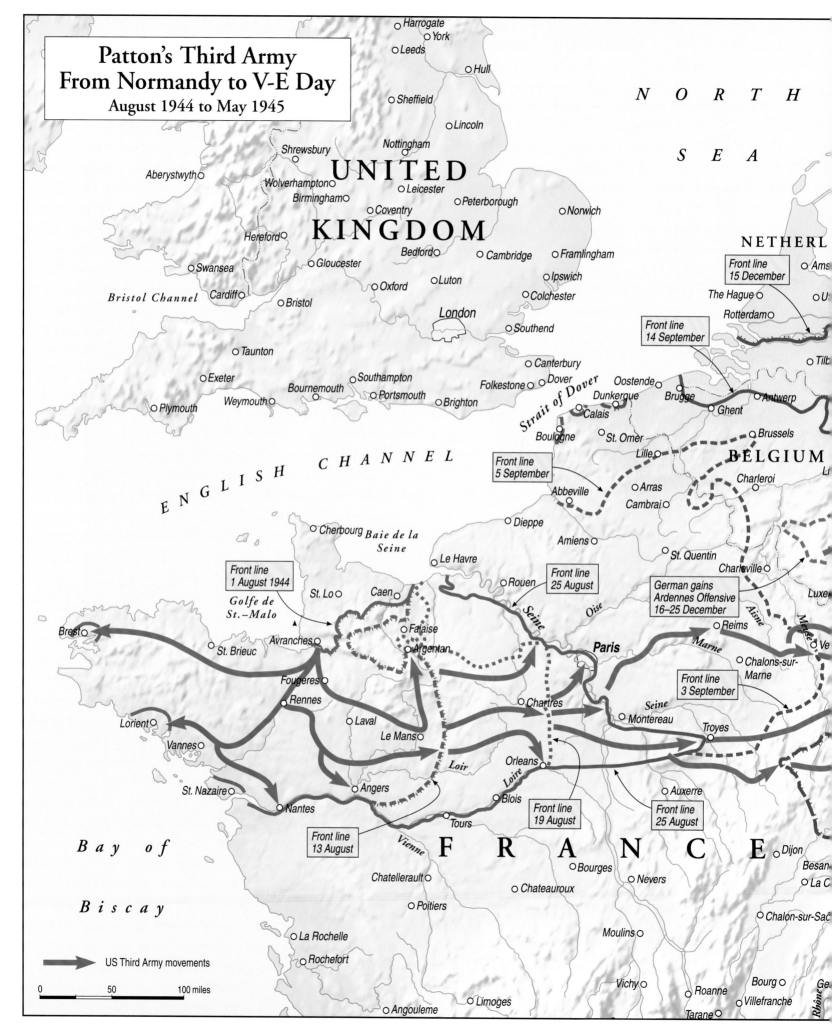

Patton's Third Army
From Normandy to V-E Day
August 1944 to May 1945

N O R T H

S E A

NETHERL

Front line
15 December

Front line
14 September

UNITED

Harrogate
York
Leeds
Hull
Sheffield
Lincoln
Nottingham
Shrewsbury
Aberystwyth
Wolverhampton
Birmingham
Leicester
Peterborough
Norwich
Coventry

KINGDOM

Hereford
Bedford
Cambridge
Framlingham
Ipswich
Gloucester
Swansea
Cardiff
Oxford
Luton
Colchester
Bristol
Canterbury
Bristol Channel

The Hague
Rotterdam
Amst
U
Tilb

Taunton
Southend
London
Dover
Oostende
Dunkerque
Brugge
Ghent
Antwerp

Exeter
Southampton
Folkestone
Calais
Strait of Dover
Boulogne

Bournemouth
Portsmouth
Brighton
Weymouth
Plymouth

Brussels
BELGIUM
Charleroi
Li

Lille
St. Omer

Front line
5 September

Abbeville
Arras
Cambrai

E N G L I S H   C H A N N E L

Dieppe
Amiens
St. Quentin
Charleville

German gains
Ardennes Offensive
16–25 December

Luxe

Cherbourg
Baie de la
Seine
Le Havre
Rouen
Seine
Oise

Aisne
Meuse
Ve

Front line
1 August 1944
St. Lo
Caen
Front line
25 August

Reims
Marne

Chalons-sur-
Marne

Golfe de
St.–Malo
Falaise
Paris

Front line
3 September

Brest
St. Brieuc
Avranches
Argentan
Chartres
Seine
Montereau
Troyes

Fougeres
Rennes
Marne

Lorient
Laval
Le Mans
Loir
Orleans
Auxerre
Front line
25 August

Vannes
Loire

Angers
Blois
Front line
19 August

St. Nazaire
Nantes
Tours

Front line
13 August
Vienne

F R A N C E
Dijon
Besan
La C

Bay of
Chatellerault
Bourges
Nevers

Biscay
Chateauroux
Chalon-sur-Sac

Poitiers

La Rochelle
Rochefort
Moulins

Bourg
Villefranche

US Third Army movements

Vichy
Roanne

0   50   100 miles

Angouleme
Limoges
Tarane
Rhone Ge

American generals of the Western Europe campaign: Front row (left to right): George S. Patton, Omar Bradley, Dwight D. Eisenhower, and Courtney Hodges. Second row: Keen, Charles H. Corlett, J. Lawton Collins, Leonard Gerow, and Elwood "Pete" Quesada. Third row: Allen, Hart, and Tjoraon. *National Archives*

INTRODUCTION

THE UNITED STATES THIRD ARMY IS NO MORE. Never vanquished in a major campaign, the proud Third Army now exists as the Coalition Forces Land Component Command (CFLCC) for U.S. Central Command (CENTCOM), with responsibilities in North Africa and in Central and Southwest Asia. Despite the prosaic name change, the official CFLCC logo still incorporates a miniature Third Army patch and the motto "Patton's Own!"

Third Army's best-known achievements were made in a ten-month period beginning with the breakout from Normandy in July 1944 and ending deep in Nazi-occupied Czechoslovakia the following May. The real story of Third Army's history-making sweep across Europe begins, however, in Louisiana in the summer of 1941.

The U.S. Army was still an infantry-centered organization in the late 1930s. Theoreticians in both Europe and America had been looking for a key to avoid the numbing stalemates brought about when infantry forces dug themselves into elaborate trench systems to survive massive artillery concentrations. The solution proved to be not merely the invention of new weapons, but also a fundamental change in the concept of mobility. In earlier conflicts, mobility was seen as a means of redistributing forces laterally along a linear battlefield. Once units were set into position, like so many pieces on a chessboard, the grisly mathematics of attrition could be set in motion. In the 1930s mobility emerged as an end in itself; it was redefined as both a tactic and a strategy to avoid the appalling losses of the Great War (World War I) by precluding the establishment of fixed positions and linear defenses. The idea was to keep one's opponent reeling back, never giving him the opportunity to reform a defensive line, reposition his forces, reconstitute his supplies, or rest his troops.

The Germans were the first to put this new thinking to practical application, and Nazi forces gave the world a lesson in mobile warfare in Poland and France. However, the Americans were not far behind in embracing mobility as the central concept of warfare. In the summer of 1941, the U.S. Army conducted a massive training exercise, called the Louisiana Maneuvers, for the purpose of examining every aspect of the military art and science, from the tactical interaction of infantry, tanks, artillery, and aircraft, to the functioning of larger formations, such as divisions, corps, and field armies. Nineteen divisions, including nearly a half-million troops, participated in what would prove to be a dress rehearsal for World War II. These maneuvers validated the concept of an armored division, which united infantry, tank, and artillery organizations with the common attribute of increased mobility. More importantly, the outcome of the Louisiana Maneuvers imbued leaders at all levels with the understanding that keeping the enemy reeling back and never allowing him to set up a prepared defense was the only way to avoid a recurrence of the muddy meat-grinders of the Great War.

Third Army's most noted leader was champing at the bit to lead the D-Day invasion. But Dwight D. Eisenhower, commanding general of Allied forces in Europe, took shrewd advantage of George Patton's earlier indiscretions—such as the infamous slapping of the soldier—and subsequent disfavor, and turned it to the Allies' advantage. Patton was placed in command of the mythical First U.S. Army Group (FUSAG), a decoy organization intended to deceive the Germans as to the time and place of the actual main invasion effort. So successfully had Patton commanded earlier actions in North Africa and Italy that the Germans were sure that the main invasion would be signaled by his presence.

Nearly seven weeks after the initial Normandy landings, Patton got his chance to take Third Army into battle. Exploiting the breakout created by the First Army, Patton began a rampage whose pace was limited as much by his own logistics as by the Germans. That run across France and into Germany is the core content of this book. No part of that combat record is more remarkable than Third Army's execution of a turning movement at the Battle of the Bulge.

Individual ships and aircraft, even when maneuvered in large formations, are able to change their direction of attack as easily as turning a steering wheel or nudging a joystick. Land armies can't. Unlike air and sea routes, which are amorphous, movement patterns on land must conform to the geography. A column of tanks moving along a valley seldom has the luxury of just climbing up over the hills at will to travel to another valley. The logistics trains that follow the tank column are even more constrained by having to traverse readily negotiable terrain in order to keep up. Adding to the difficulty of land-force maneuvers is that the routes used have a limited carrying capacity and may already be occupied by refugees or following military forces.

To understand the significance of Third Army's turn to relieve the Bulge, imagine a morning rush-hour commute in a large city. Add to the problem a severe snowstorm. Now imagine what would happen if everyone in the gridlock received a new job in a different town while on the way to work. Further imagine that all the gas stations and restaurants along the new route are closed, because they didn't expect the morning traffic. Imagine that everyone in the traffic stream slept in his car the previous night, and most hadn't slept in a real bed for over three months. Lastly, imagine that everyone had to arrive at his new job in the order in which he started for his original destination. You have only scratched the surface of understanding what it takes to turn an army in the middle of a battle.

As you read through this book, look into the eyes of the soldiers in the photos, and try to imagine yourself in their places. They are the ones who endured hardship and privation, who kept pushing when they needed to, who kept the Germans rocked back on their heels when it might have seemed easier to stop and rest. They are the ones who supplied the "Blood and Guts" that gave their commander his nickname. They are the ones who took the concept of mobile warfare off of the planning charts of the 1930s and into the history of the 1940s. They are the ones who proudly sum up their military service with a simple, "I was with Patton in Europe."

Before Third Army: Lt. Gen. George S. Patton, in command of Seventh Army, strategizes with Lt. Col. Lyle Bernard, CO, 30th Infantry Regiment, near Brolo, Sicily, 1943.
U.S. Army Signal Corps

A key issue was resolved in a series of late-1943 meetings, conducted in Tehran, Iran, by Allied leaders (seated, left to right) Winston Churchill, Franklin D. Roosevelt, and Joseph Stalin. The Americans and British committed themselves to invading northwest France, in an operation code-named Operation Overlord, in May 1944, to relieve some of the pressure on the Red Army. *National Archives*

I

PATTON AND OPERATION OVERLORD

★ ★ ★ ★ ★

ORIGINAL PLANS FOR OPERATION OVERLORD (the invasion of Europe) had General George S. Patton's Third Army arriving at Normandy shortly after General Omar Bradley's First Army initially landed on June 6, 1944. The job assigned to "Patton's Own" was to seize the Brittany peninsula, with its many harbors, and exploit the breakout of Bradley's First Army from the Normandy beachhead.

Third Army had existed as an administrative and training cadre since the end of World War I, but was reactivated to combat status on December 31, 1943, and shortly thereafter to Patton's command. The first thirteen officers and twenty-six enlisted men of Third Army headquarters staff arrived in England on January 28, 1944. The remaining headquarters staff followed on March 21, 1944.

The military unit called an army has no fixed composition, and so it is not shipped overseas as a complete unit. Rather, the component elements, such as the main army headquarters, corps headquarters, divisions, separate battalions, and independent companies, arrived in England independently of each other; divisions were the largest integral units to be shipped from the United States. Commanders assembled their armies and corps from these elements as they became available. Slowly, Patton's Third Army grew as the convoys from the United States reached

A 2cm FlaK 38 (antiaircraft gun), part of Germany's defensive line as its forces dug in. By late 1943, it was clear to the German military forces that there would be no more grand offensives for them. They were on the defensive everywhere and would be hard-pressed to hold on to what they had. *National Archives*

Massive concrete gun emplacements would serve, Adolf Hitler believed, as both physical and psychological deterrents to the Western Allies. Assuming that the Allies would enjoy air and naval supremacy, he ordered such defensive positions to be built along France's coast as early as August 1942.
National Archives

England. By the end of May 1944, Third Army consisted of four corps, the XV, VIII, XX, and the XII, which divided seven infantry divisions and six armored divisions among them. The total personnel strength of Patton's Third Army gradually rose to 250,000 men.

Patton code-named Third Army "Lucky." His forward command post was always referred to as "Lucky Forward," a harbinger of the aggressive, lead-from-the-front leadership style that Patton himself exercised and that he expected of subordinate leaders.

PATTON'S SPEECHES

Patton believed that troop morale improved when troops saw their commanding officers, and he made it a point to visit as many of his new units as possible. During his many visits to units in England, the always immaculately uniformed Patton gave very similar, profane pep talks to his men, because he felt this was the level on which the common enlisted man spoke. Patton once stated, "You can't run an army without profanity." One of his inspirational addresses began, "I want you men to remember that no bastard ever won a war by dying for his country. He won it by making sure the other dumb bastard dies for his country. All this stuff you've heard about America not wanting to fight, wanting to stay out of this war, is a

A German unit conducts a training exercise in France with a former French army vehicle modified to mount a German 7.5cm PaK 40 (antitank gun). The German military began to strengthen its forces in France beginning in late 1943. However, the constant drain on resources by the war on the eastern front made it very difficult to assemble a first-rate force that could defeat an Allied invasion of France. *National Archives*

lot of horseshit." He normally ended his pep talks with "I'm not supposed to be commanding this army. I'm not even supposed to be in England. Let the first bastards to find out be the God-damn Germans. I want them to look up and howl, 'Ach! It's the God-damn Third Army and that son of bitch Patton again!' All right, you sons of bitches, you know how I feel. I'll be proud to lead you wonderful guys into battle anywhere, anytime. That is all!"

Most Third Army soldiers heartily enjoyed Patton's somewhat vulgar speeches. Because Patton's boisterous reputation and off-color speeches garnered so much attention from the press, Eisenhower made a point of telling him that he was not to make any public speeches without the commander's express permission. He ordered Patton to guard all his statements so there would be no chance of misinterpretation. Eisenhower had been forced on earlier occasions in North Africa to smooth over problems caused by Patton's inability to keep his opinions to himself. Eisenhower obviously did not want to see Patton commit any verbal blunders that might attract the attention of the American public, Congress, or the press.

General Dwight D. Eisenhower arrived in London, England, on January 14, 1944, to take up his new duties as Supreme Commander of the Allied Expeditionary Force. The success or failure of Operation Overlord was now entirely on his shoulders. It would be only another twenty weeks before the invasion of France. National Archives

DWIGHT DAVID EISENHOWER

DWIGHT D. EISENHOWER graduated from the U.S. Military Academy at West Point in 1915. Much to his disappointment, he spent World War I training new recruits rather than leading troops into combat.

In the interwar period Eisenhower came to the attention of two prominent U.S. Army officers, Douglas MacArthur and George C. Marshall, who both thought very highly of Eisenhower's skills as a staff officer. MacArthur would write in an early 1930s fitness report on Eisenhower, "This is the best officer in the army. When the next war comes, he should go right to the top." MacArthur was Chief of Staff of the U.S. Army, and Eisenhower was his aide.

In March 1941 Eisenhower became a full colonel and by September 1941 received the single star of a brigadier general. That December he reported to Marshall for duty on the War Department staff.

Rising through a variety of important positions at the War Department, Eisenhower received his second star in February 1942. Shortly after, Marshall sent Eisenhower to England to report on the Allied efforts to plan an invasion of Nazi-occupied Europe. On his return from England, Eisenhower wrote a report detailing the goals for a new senior American command position known as the commander, European Theater of Operations, U.S. Army (ETOUSA). On completion of the report, Marshall appointed Eisenhower to the position and assigned him to carry out the goals stated in the report. After returning to England to assume his new post, Eisenhower received his third star as a lieutenant general in July 1942.

Before the invasion of Nazi-occupied Europe, it was decided that the Allies would confront the German military in North Africa in late 1942 as part of Operation Torch, which Eisenhower oversaw. He learned how to manage a multinational coalition and received his fourth star as a general in February 1943. Other officers received accelerated promotions as the American military establishment gathered itself for the war effort, but Eisenhower's rise from colonel to four-star general in a shade over eighteen months indicates how much confidence Marshall placed in him.

During the successful conclusion of the fighting in North Africa, Eisenhower oversaw the invasion and conquest of Sicily in July and August 1943 and the invasion of mainland Italy in September 1943. The experience Eisenhower gained from these operations would stand him in good stead for the planned 1944 cross-channel invasion of France, now referred to as Operation Neptune/Overlord.

There was some thought of Marshall becoming the supreme commander, Allied Expeditionary Force (SHAEF), for the invasion of France. However, President Franklin D. Roosevelt said he couldn't sleep with Marshall out of the country and, impressed with Eisenhower's reputation, appointed him as SHAEF. As commander of SHAEF and ETOUSA, Eisenhower was responsible for everything concerned with the invasion of France. Through in-depth planning and his bold decision to launch the attack on June 6, 1944, the invasion of France was a success, and Eisenhower was promoted to a five-star general of the U.S. Army in December 1944. Once on the continent, he oversaw the broad-front advance on Germany that resulted in the Nazis' surrender in May 1945.   *National Archives*

Patton apparently decided to ignore Eisenhower's order, however. On April 25, 1944, while in England, he made a public speech to a British women's club. Though Patton believed that his remarks would be off the record, portions of his speech (which referred to the joint destiny of the Americans and British to win the war, but said nothing about the Russians) leaked to the press and caused a furor in the United States and overseas. It was at this point that both Eisenhower (who, as Supreme Commander of the Allied Expeditionary Force, was responsible for harmonious relations among all the Allied powers) and General George C. Marshall (who was both Chief of Staff of the U.S. Army and Chairman of the Joint Chiefs of Staff) were ready to fire Patton, stripping him of his combat command.

Patton observes a firepower demonstration on a firing range in England prior to taking command of the Third Army in France. The first-generation M4 Sherman medium tank is armed with a low-velocity 75mm main gun. The tank sports extra welded armor on its hull. *Patton Museum*

PATTON'S THOUGHTS ON THE DUTIES OF AN OFFICER

OFFICERS ARE responsible not only for the conduct of their men in battle, but also their health and contentment when not fighting. An officer must be the last man to take shelter from fire, and the first to move forward. Similarly, he must be the last man to look after his own comfort at the close of a march. He must see that his men are cared for. The officer must constantly interest himself in the rations of the men. He should know his men so well that any sign of sickness or nervous strain will be apparent to him, and he can take such actions as may be necessary.

—*War As I Knew It*,
"Letter of Instruction No. 2"

Patton had to wait only two days in England before the first small elements of the Third Army staff began arriving. However, the bulk of the Third Army formation, such as the corps headquarters and the divisions they would command in battle, did not arrive in Britain until May 1944. *Patton Museum*

At the last moment, Eisenhower had second thoughts about sacking one of his most aggressive generals. Instead, he made a crucial decision to keep Patton in command of Third Army. In a letter to Marshall, Eisenhower explained why he decided to retain Patton, stating, "The relief of Patton would lose to us his experience as commander of an army in battle and his demonstrated ability of getting the utmost out of soldiers in offensive operations." Eisenhower also wrote to Patton informing him that his job was safe "solely because of my faith in you as a battle leader and for no other motive."

Two American soldiers hone their marksmanship skills at the rifle range prior to heading into battle. The rifle was officially designated as the Rifle, Caliber .30, M1. Most soldiers knew it as the "M1." Patton called it "the greatest weapon ever made." *National Archives*

Among the many German defensive measures on Omaha Beach encountered by American troops on June 6, 1944, was this dug-in prototype VK. 3001 tank turret armed with a short-barreled 75mm howitzer. *National Archives*

Sleeping accommodations were snug on the ships pressed into service for American military personnel heading overseas. The American buildup in Britain involved the overseas movement of almost 1,700,000 military personnel by June 6, 1944. Also delivered by sea to England were more than 14,000,000 tons of cargo. *National Archives*

OPERATION FORTITUDE AND OPERATION OVERLORD

Prior to the invasion of France, the Allies came up with a deception plan called Operation Fortitude. The goal of Operation Fortitude was to convince the Germans that the Pas de Calais area, rather than Normandy, would be the main invasion site of Operation Overlord. Fortitude also contained elements specifically designed to convince the Germans that any other landings in France would be merely feints to draw their attention away from Pas de Calais.

The first part of the deception was easy; Calais was a mere twenty miles away from the English coast and, thus, the most easily supported invasion point from the logistical point of view. The Germans were already predisposed to believe the deception, because Calais was where they would have mounted the invasion had their roles been traded with the Allies. The second part, convincing the Germans to hold their reserves in the Calais area even after they saw the massive Normandy landings develop, was much tougher. In some respects,

An American M2 60mm mortar crew during one of the frequent training exercises that kept the troops sent to England sharp before D-Day. An assault training center was set up in April 1943 to assist American combat troops in acquiring the skills they needed to overcome the German beachhead defensive positions. *National Archives*

Patton delivers one of his famous pep talks to the 2nd Infantry Division at Armagh, Northern Ireland, on April 1, 1944. On the far right is Maj. Gen. Wade Haislip, commander of XV Corps. On the far left is Brig. Gen. Hobart Gay, a member of Patton's Third Army staff. *Patton Museum*

A German Focke-Wulf Fw 190 fighter, part of the once-vaunted Luftwaffe. Although in decline late in the war, German air strength and its possible impact on Operation Overlord were still among the many concerns of the Allied planners. Estimates of the enemy's air strength varied greatly, but it was generally believed that the German air force could generate between 1,000 to 1,800 sorties on D-Day. *National Archives*

Eisenhower's biggest gamble wasn't in committing the invasion force; it was a bet he placed squarely on a soldier who would not even participate in the initial landings.

Well aware of the high regard the Germans had for Patton's command skills, Eisenhower correctly deduced that they believed Patton would, no doubt, be leading any invasion of France. Eisenhower, therefore, made Patton commander of the phantom 1st Army Group and saw to it that known enemy agents received information on the status of Patton's forces.

Eisenhower's staff had created the mythical 1st Army Group, which had up to thirty divisions in its organization. This phantom force was supposedly located near Dover, England, just across the Channel from Pas de Calais. To fool the occasional German reconnaissance plane, Allied planners used construction crews to build dummy military bases and dotted the bases with inflatable tanks and other vehicles. They also anchored a large number of inflatable rubber landing craft in the Thames River estuary. The deception plan was so detailed that it even included the release of sports scores of teams from the

An inflatable dummy tank sits beside a real M4A1 Sherman medium tank in a training exercise. It was critical to mislead the Germans about the actual invasion landing sites for Operation Overlord. The Western Allies came up with a very elaborate deception plan, code-named Operation Fortitude, which created dummy armies, one of which was supposedly headed by Patton. *National Archives*

various nonexistent units, as well as engagement and marriage announcements of U.S. soldiers with local women. Bogus radio stations were set up throughout the British Isles, carrying the usual amount of logistical and housekeeping traffic expected from a widely dispersed military establishment.

The real Allied invasion force of 5,000 ships with 130,000 Allied soldiers stood off the Normandy coast as dawn broke on June 6, 1944. The Allies' main strategy, in Eisenhower's words, was to "land amphibious and airborne forces on the Normandy coast between Le Havre and the Cotentin Peninsula and, with the successful establishment of a beachhead with adequate ports, to drive along the lines of the Loire and the Seine Rivers into the heart of France, destroying the German strength and freeing France."

The seaborne assault was under the overall command of British General Bernard Montgomery, who also commanded the 21st Army Group. This command became the

American soldiers carefully load a jeep into a Waco CG-4A glider. The Waco glider had a two-man flight crew and a wingspan of 83 feet 8 inches. It could carry four soldiers and a jeep or thirteen soldiers with no jeep into combat. During World War II American factories built almost fourteen thousand Waco gliders. *National Archives*

American B-17F bombers were a crucial part of Allied air support for Operation Overlord. Air support was given a high priority shortly before D-Day; the first targets were the German coastal batteries capable of interfering with the invasion armada, and second in line were the German beach defenses. *National Archives*

Eisenhower talks informally with U.S. Army paratroopers before they load up onto their transport aircraft for Operation Overlord. In the weeks before D-Day, Eisenhower spent much of his time visiting Allied units and observing their training maneuvers and exercises. Like Patton, Eisenhower firmly believed that a commander should show himself to his troops. *National Archives*

Antilanding obstacles litter Normandy beach prior to D-Day, as seen from a low-flying Allied plane. German Field Marshal Erwin Rommel felt the Allies' almost complete air superiority would make it impossible to use mobile formations against the Allied landing in France and that any invasion would have to be stopped on the beaches. *National Archives*

A chaplain conducts a service on the loading docks for the men heading toward Normandy as part of Operation Overlord. On May 8, 1944, Eisenhower set D-Day for sometime in early June, depending on the weather. In a high-level meeting on June 4, 1944, Eisenhower decided that June 6, 1944, would be the start of the operation. *National Archives*

Casualties were high among the American paratroopers of the 82nd and 101st Airborne Divisions. Reports that Allied paratroopers were dropping from the skies over Normandy in the early morning hours of June 6 were the first warning to the German high command that something was amiss. *National Archives*

PATTON'S THOUGHTS ON MILITARY CEMETERIES

DO NOT PLACE military cemeteries where they can be seen by replacements marching to the front. This has a very bad effect on morale, even if it adds to the pride of the Graves Registration Service.

—*War As I Knew It,* *"Reflections and Suggestions"*

controlling headquarters for the two Allied armies scheduled to make the invasion. The British Second Army, under Lieutenant General Sir Miles C. Dempsey, was to assault on the left; the U.S. First Army, under recently promoted Lieutenant General Omar Bradley, was to be on the right.

The Overlord invasion began on a broad front against fifty miles of French coastline. Aerial bombardment of beach defenses and a two-division glider and airborne drop began after midnight, and the naval bombardment started shortly after sunrise. At 0630, the first waves of assault infantry and tanks landed on the invasion beaches.

By nightfall on D-Day, five American divisions, the 1st, 4th, and 29th Infantry Divisions and the 82nd and 101st Airborne Divisions, had a foothold in Normandy. Also ashore were advance detachments of the headquarters of Maj. Gen. Leonard T. Gerow's V Corps and Maj. Gen. Joseph "Lightning Joe" Lawton Collins's VII Corps.

Anxious American soldiers in a small landing-craft vehicle, personnel (LCVP) approach Omaha Beach on D-Day. The invasion force did much better than expected in penetrating the German positions, except for on Omaha Beach, in the American sector, where terrain most favored the defenders. *National Archives*

FIRST ARMY ROADBLOCK

By the end of the first week after D-Day, the Allied beachhead in France was fairly secure. The German coastal defense system had fallen apart. These accomplishments came with a high cost. In the first ten days of fighting, Bradley's First Army had 3,282 dead, 12,600 wounded, and 7,959 missing.

The VII Corps of Bradley's First Army quickly began moving in a northwesterly direction to seize the port of Cherbourg, at the tip of the Cotentin Peninsula. The capture of Cherbourg was very important to the Allies because they hoped to get a major port into full operation before the end of the summer. Without a major port, the Allies feared that bad weather would prevent supplies from being unloaded across the open invasion beaches.

The VII Corps, with three divisions, forced the surrender of Cherbourg on June 27, after stiff fighting. The drive up the Cotentin Peninsula cost the VII Corps twenty-two thousand casualties, while the Germans had thirty-nine thousand soldiers taken prisoner and suffered an unknown number of dead and wounded. The seizure of Cherbourg with its port facilities proved a hollow victory. German engineers thoroughly demolished the port and insured that it would take months before it was suitable for use again.

On D-Day, Eisenhower was pleased that his forces moved past the German beach defenses, such as this captured pillbox on Utah Beach. However, the failure of the American V Corps (at Omaha Beach) and the American VII Corps (at Utah Beach) to link up their beachheads on D-Day was a great concern. *National Archives*

An American landing barge (nicknamed a rhino) lands at Utah Beach. Eisenhower's planners expected to have 107,000 troops and 14,500 tons of supply ashore by the first day after D-Day, but only 87,000 troops and a quarter of the supplies had made it ashore by then. *National Archives*

The crew of an American landing craft that struck a mine and sank are helped ashore on the western end of Omaha's Fox Red beach by army engineers and other personnel. *National Archives*

The Allied military leaders had planned to control the whole of Normandy and Brittany by July 6. Having acquired this area, the Allies would have had access to more than five hundred miles of French coastline and many port facilities. The Allies could then bring in all the men and materiel needed to build up their forces. In addition, the area under Allied control (known as a lodgment, in military terms) would allow maneuver room for the ground troops and suitable terrain for the building of at least twenty-seven airfields. The Allies had hoped to have sixty-two fighter squadrons in operation on these airfields.

By early July, almost a million Allied troops, 500,000 tons of supplies, and 150,000 vehicles had landed in France. Bradley's First Army had thirteen divisions, including two armored and two airborne, divided into four corps: the V, VII, VIII, and XIX. (The VIII Corps headquarters actually belonged to Patton's yet-to-be-activated Third Army. The headquarters was temporarily attached to Bradley's First Army until it would pass to control of Patton's Third Army.) These four corps held a front some fifty to fifty-five miles long. Despite these impressive figures, the Allies still found themselves confined to a very small part of France. In

An American soldier looks over an abandoned German beach gun position. The British invasion beachheads had linked up with the American V Corps at Omaha Beach on June 8. The American VII Corps from Utah Beach and V Corps at Omaha Beach finally linked up their respective positions by June 14. *National Archives*

some areas, the Allied lines extended less than four miles into France, an area less than one-fifth the size they had planned on controlling by early July.

The real benchmark of the Allies lack of progress, however, was not the unexpectedly small amount of terrain they had secured; it was their failure to capture an intact, working port. Most of the Allied troops and materiel still had to come across the original landing beaches. This not only limited the types of ships that could be used, but the tidal cycle on the English Channel limited when ships could come and go. There was a real fear among some Allied leaders that the opposing 650,000 German troops could still shove the Allied invasion forces back into the sea.

Fortunately, the Allied ground forces in France were within range of both air and naval support, which did much to keep German forces from overrunning the beachhead. Allied air-power broke up all German military ground movement during the daylight hours and even made movement at night difficult. The long range and accurate fire of Allied warships also proved a surprise to the German forces.

As VII Corps advanced northwest up the Cotentin Peninsula toward Cherbourg, other elements of the First Army center sector slowly headed southward. There was little progress

The First Army's VII Corps seized the port of Cherbourg on June 27, but German destruction of the port facilities meant most supplies still had to come over the artificial harbors (Mulberries) built at Omaha (seen here) and at the British beach code-named Gold. *National Archives*

A German paratroop mortar crew armed with an 8cm (81mm) Schwere Granatenwerfer 34. Stiff enemy resistance from crews like this brought V Corps' advance on the town of St.-Lô to a halt. *National Archives*

An American soldier crouches behind one of the hedgerows that crisscrossed the Normandy countryside. The hedgerows, up to fifteen feet high, were built upon earthen dikes averaging about four feet high and four feet thick and covered with tangled hedges, bushes, and even trees. *National Archives*

for a number of reasons, including Bradley's desire to commit most of his resources to the VII Corps' drive and the difficult nature of the terrain leading southward out of the beaches.

Without question, the key terrain obstacle faced by Bradley's First Army was the Normandy hedgerow country. For centuries, Norman farmers followed the practice of enclosing their land with thick hedgerows. (The French term for hedgerows is *bocage*, meaning "grove," and the Americans used the terms interchangeably.) The hedgerows began right behind the original First Army landing beaches and extended up to fifty miles inland in some areas. They couldn't have made a more effective defensive obstacle had they been intentionally designed as such. They also made excellent defensive positions, providing cover and concealment to the German defenders. Finally, the hedgerows restricted observation, making the effective use of tank guns or artillery almost impossible.

Like the terrain, the weather also affected Bradley's operations in Normandy. Constant rains during June and July hampered the efforts of the First Army. The early summer of 1944 was the wettest since 1900. The marshlands of Normandy turned into muddy swamps.

An American soldier fires a 2.36-inch M1A1 bazooka over a hedgerow. First Army completely underestimated the difficulty presented by the hedgerows, and General Omar Bradley described the hedgerow-covered landscape as the "damndest country I've seen." *National Archives*

Low visibility and cloud ceilings hampered the fighter-bomber support the army needed and that the aerial observers needed for artillery support. To add to the First Army's problems, a major storm struck the invasion beaches between June 19 and 22, damaging the temporary harbors, called Mulberries, and the breakwaters the Allies had installed, severely curtailing the movement of supplies onto the mainland. As a result, shortages of key supplies, such as ammunition, hampered the First Army operations during the battles in the hedgerows.

PATTON'S ARRIVAL AND FIRST ARMY'S PLANS

In the weeks following the invasion and before Patton's arrival in Normandy, the general's biggest concern was that the war would end before he had a chance to take part. Patton wrote in his diary, "I have a feeling, probably unfounded, that neither Monty [the nickname for Gen. Bernard Law Montgomery] nor Bradley are too anxious for me to have a command. If they knew what little respect I have for the fighting ability of either of them, they would be even less anxious for me to show them up."

BERNARD MONTGOMERY

BERNARD MONTGOMERY served in a variety of roles as an officer with the British army in World War I. As commander of the 3rd Division, he confronted the German army during its successful invasion of the Low Countries and France in the summer of 1940. Forced to withdraw back to the French port of Dunkirk and then England with his troops under unrelenting enemy pressure, Montgomery went on to be appointed a corps commander.

Sent to North Africa in charge of the British Eighth Army in August 1942, he rebuilt that army and lead it to victory against the German and Italian armies by May 1943. From there, he led his forces in both the invasions of Sicily and Italy until December 1943, when he returned to England to take command of the 21st Army Group, which would oversee all the Allied ground forces intended to take part in the invasion of France in June 1944.

After the successful Allied invasion of France, the number of American divisions grew, and there reached a point when it proved politically impractical for Eisenhower to continue having a British officer in charge of so many American ground troops. Eisenhower then took over that role for himself on September 1, 1944, something that the Allies had agreed to before D-Day. This shift in command left Montgomery very unhappy, although he retained control of the 21st Army Group, which included British and Canadian ground forces and, later, some American forces. British Prime Minister Winston Churchill promoted him to the rank of field marshal, a higher rank than corresponding Army Group commanders had.   *National Archives*

In the original invasion plans, Patton's Third Army should have been in Normandy by D+10, the tenth day after D-Day, June 16. As is the case in most military campaigns, however, the plans for Operation Overlord proved to be too optimistic. Patton finally flew to Normandy on July 6, in a C-47 transport plane escorted by P-47 fighters. His personal transport plane landed on an airfield very close to Omaha Beach where, one month prior, Allied troops had stormed ashore to free France of its German oppressors.

A German Panther Ausf. A medium tank moving at high speed through the hedgerows. German hedgerow tactics often involved leaving front-line positions lightly manned and having the bulk of combat troops formed into counterattacking reserve units, backed up with tanks. Once an attack began, the tanks would move though the hedgerows to attack into the American flanks. *Patton Museum*

An American M1 60mm mortar team takes part in hedgerow fighting. The hedgerows boxed in every French field and orchard, some of which were larger than a football field. Observation of indirect fire in the hedgerows was generally restricted to a single field at a time, especially in the flat grounds of the beachhead areas. Thus, each hedgerow field became a separate battleground. *National Archives*

Patton's Third Army headquarters staff traveled to Normandy in a U.S. Navy Landing Ship Tank (an LST—or as the troops referred to them, "large, slow targets"), arriving on the same day as their boss. Headquarters for Third Army were set up in an apple orchard about ten miles behind the front lines of Bradley's First Army. Between August 1944 and the end of the war in May 1945, Patton's headquarters would move nineteen times.

Eisenhower ordered that there be no publicity for Patton's or Third Army's arrival in Normandy. The Germans still firmly believed that Patton and his fake 1st Army Group were ready to invade the Pas de Calais area of France and that the landings at Normandy were only a sideshow from the main assault yet to come. As long as this deception could be maintained, the Germans would keep many of their seasoned divisions away from the fighting in Normandy.

Following Patton and his headquarters staff to Normandy were three of his four corps headquarters units. The XV Corps headquarters arrived in Normandy on July 15, while the XX Corps headquarters followed on July 24. The XII Corps headquarters involved itself with helping Third Army units get from England to Normandy, then helped the units move off the original invasion beaches into the lodgment area. Part of the XII Corps headquarters reached Normandy on July 29, and the remainder arrived on August 7. To give close air support to Third Army, Brig. Gen. Otto P. Weyland's XIX Tactical Air Command (TAC) also moved from England to Normandy. Weyland's headquarters staff set up very close to Third Army headquarters.

With Cherbourg securely under First Army control, Bradley prepared his forces to advance southward once more. Bradley's orders, as received from Montgomery on the last day of June, were twofold. The first part involved increasing the size of the lodgment area, while the second part involved pulling German forces away from the British sector of Normandy by beginning offensive operations against the German Seventh Army. If Bradley's July offensive achieved both its goals, the First Army would be facing eastward toward Paris, and its right flank would be

A German paratrooper armed with a FG42 automatic rifle and hand grenades watches Allied aircraft flying overhead. The Germans trained in the hedgerows before Operation Overload and often cut very elaborate foxholes, trenches, and individual firing pits into them. The dense bushes atop the hedgerows provided concealment for machine gunners and riflemen. *National Archives*

M4A2 Sherman medium tanks in British army service, armed with a mix of 75mm and 17-pounder (76.2mm) main guns, preparing for battle. The terrain in the British sector of Normandy proved to be a wide expanse of gently rolling pastures and cultivated fields suited for mechanized warfare. It was here that the Germans felt the main Allied thrust for Paris would be made, so they positioned the bulk of their armored units in France. *Patton Museum*

First Army tried using explosives to blow holes wide enough for tanks to pass through the hedgerows, but the strategy proved impractical. The next attempt involved M1 bulldozer blades mounted on M4 Shermans, such as this destroyed and abandoned example. *National Archives*

As there were not enough bulldozer blade–equipped tanks in First Army to support large-scale operations, the army needed another method to overcome the hedgerows. The most successful came from Sgt. Curtis G. Cullen Jr., who devised a hedgerow-cutting device from leftover German beach obstacles and welded the devices to the front of light and medium tanks, such as this M4A1 Sherman. *National Archives*

near the entrance into Brittany. At this point in the operation, plans called for Patton's Third Army to become operational and move south and west to seize Brittany and its many ports. Once those ports were in American hands, Patton's Third Army would be free to turn east to join Bradley's First Army. In the meantime, First Army, in conjunction with the British and Canadian forces on its left, would be advancing eastward to the Seine River and Paris.

An important goal of Bradley's First Army early July offensive was the high ground around the town of Coutances, roughly twenty miles inland from the existing First Army positions. As things turned out, Bradley had to settle for something far short of this goal. Heavy rains delayed Bradley's offensive operation until July 3. When the operation finally commenced, it began with three of Bradley's corps advancing on a broad front, where they quickly ran into heavy German resistance.

An intermediate objective of the First Army's drive southward was to capture the high ground around the town of St.-Lô and the road that led to Coutances. Saint-Lô was a German communications center as well as an important road center. Roads ran in almost every direction from St.-Lô. Both sides recognized that whoever controlled the city would control much of the road network in the hedgerow area of Normandy. The defense of the city and the surrounding heights were entrusted to the Luftwaffe's II Parachute Corps. (Owing to earlier power plays within the Nazi leadership, airborne forces came under Luftwaffe control, rather than army control, as in almost all other armies in the world.)

The original Allied invasion plans called for the capture of St.-Lô by June 16. The First Army's 29th Infantry Division launched an attack to capture the town on June 15. Despite some of the toughest fighting of the Normandy campaign, over the next three days, the Americans managed to get within only five miles of the town.

U.S. Army paratroopers load themselves onto a transport plane prior to going into combat. One of the important decisions made by Eisenhower for Operation Overlord, despite some early skepticism, was the use of airborne forces that were to land behind the Normandy invasion beaches on D-Day and provide support for those coming in by sea. *National Archives*

An American M1 57mm antitank gun and crew in position. Incorporating lessons learned from early fighting in the hedgerows and increased training in combined-arms warfare by the tankers and infantrymen of First Army allowed the Americans to push through the heavily defended hedgerows and take the road center of St.-Lô on July 19. *National Archives*

THE BRITISH ROLE

In contrast to the difficult terrain fought in by Bradley's First Army, Montgomery's British Second Army sector was a relatively open, flat, and dry expanse. It stretched from the old French university town of Caen to Paris, 120 miles away. This made the area a nearly perfect place to use tank units and build airfields. British forces planned on the capture of Caen, which lay about ten miles inland from the British invasion beaches, on June 6. Due to stiff German resistance, Caen did not fall into British hands until July 10.

Once the Allies made their successful landing in Normandy, Hitler and his generals convinced themselves that Paris was the primary objective. The Germans felt that the British Second Army would carry the main weight of the Allied advance. They further surmised that the American First Army, under Bradley, would fulfill only a secondary role in protecting the western flank of the British advance. A complication, which still weighed heavily in German planning, was that the eventual commitment of Patton and the mythical FUSAG to the invasion was still an unknown factor. Consequently, most of the best German units, especially the panzer (tank) divisions, sat concentrated against Montgomery's British Second Army during most of the Normandy campaign.

An American soldier armed with an M1928A1 Thompson submachine gun. The main goal of Bradley's First Army offensive operations in July was to take some of the pressure off the British and Canadian forces on his left flank and have his army facing Paris. Meanwhile, Patton's soon-to-be-activated Third Army, on his right flank, was to be facing Brittany, so it could seize its various ports. *National Archives*

FIRST ARMY'S ADVANCE ENDS

After heavy losses on both sides, Bradley's offensive ground to a halt on July 19. St.-Lô, now a complete ruin, had come under American control the day before, but would remain under German fire for another week. The road outside St.-Lô that led to Coutances remained in German hands. In some areas, Bradley's First Army advanced less than four miles. In that time, it suffered more than 40,000 casualties, of which 90 percent were infantrymen. In the fifteen days of fighting around St.-Lô, the 30th Infantry Division alone suffered 3,934 casualties.

There was a great deal of disappointment shared by Bradley and other First Army commanders about their failure to capture Coutances. As Bradley's First Army regrouped for a new attempt, there was little realization that the July offensive had actually achieved some significant results, the most important of these being the wearing down of German forces in Normandy.

An American soldier armed with an M3 submachine gun uses a field telephone. Upon activation of the Third Army on August 1, 1944, Bradley would turn over the command of First Army to Gen. Courtney Hodges and become 12th Army Group commander, overseeing both First and Third Armies. *National Archives*

Bradley and the other Allied leaders were not really aware just how close the German forces in Normandy had come to complete disintegration by mid-July. *Generalfeldmarschall* (Field Marshall) Guenther von Kluge, commander of all German forces in France, was well aware of the serious difficulties facing his men. On July 13, Kluge called *Generaloberst* (General) Alfred Jodl, chief of operations of the German army, at Hitler's headquarters. Kluge wanted more tanks to stiffen the infantry units, which he feared could not hold on much longer. Kluge also asked Jodl to tell Hitler that the Normandy situation was "very serious." Hitler mistrusted nearly all of his generals, however, so Kluge's warning went unheeded. Kluge's assessment of the situation was validated when Operation Cobra broke through German defensive lines a few weeks later.

American soldiers hug an M4 Sherman medium tank as they enter an enemy-held town. Before the armored and motorized infantry units of Collins's VII Corps could reach Coutances, they had to take the French towns of St. Gilles and Marigny. St. Gilles fell on the afternoon of the July 26, and Marigny fell the next morning.
National Archives

2

PATTON AND OPERATION COBRA

AS EARLY AS 1942, top Allied military planners began to envision a major advance southward into Brittany and then eastward to Paris, the capital of France, following the successful landing in Normandy. Both the terrain and military considerations, such as the

French road network, favored such an operation. A major advance due south from St.-Lô toward the Loire River and with a turning movement to the east at the base of the Cotentin Peninsula would have numerous advantages. Such an attack would cut off the German land forces in the Brittany peninsula and would also shut down U-boat pens from which German submarines had been savaging Allied convoys coming across the Atlantic. It would also give the Allied armies advancing on Paris a secure right flank on the Loire River and allow the Allies to force the Germans back against the Seine River. The Germans would have to retreat northward through the hilly country lying between British forces in the north and the American forces in the south instead of using a more favorable southward escape route. A retreat southward would allow the Germans to join with their units in southern France or in the Alsace region of France.

Shortly before D-Day, the staff of Montgomery's 21st Army Group, with Eisenhower's approval, formalized plans for a major advance on Brittany and then an eastward drive toward Paris. Bradley's First Army (still under 21st

A destroyed German Panther medium tank in a French hedgerow, representative of high German losses in men and equipment during the battle for Normandy. The slow progress made by Bradley's First Army through the hedgerows—from both the terrain and German defenders—as of mid-July 1944 remained the most serious concern among the senior Allied leadership. *National Archives*

Front-line casualty stations in France struggled with the high number of casualties, mostly infantrymen, suffered by First Army in overcoming the Normandy hedgerows. By the middle of July 1944, First Army requested that twenty-five thousand infantry replacements be sent as quickly as possible. *National Archives*

Dead German soldiers lie by their 2cm FlaK 38 (antiaircraft gun). Between June 6 and July 11, 1944, the German losses in France totaled almost 2,000 officers and 85,000 enlisted personnel. By July 17, these losses went up to 2,360 officers and 97,640 enlisted personnel. The Germans were unable to replace more than 12 percent of their manpower losses in France. *National Archives*

Army Group control) received the assignment. But before the First Army could begin the advance, it had to break out of the Normandy hedgerows. When Bradley initially launched his First Army southward toward Coutances, he envisioned a quick collapse of the German lines. This belief stemmed from overconfidence in American military strength and misleading intelligence reports. According to many of these reports, the German units facing the First Army suffered from both poor morale and serious shortages of men and equipment. This information may have been true during the last week of June, but was no longer accurate by the first week of July. In that very short time, the German units had reorganized and been resupplied and strengthened. It was these rebuilt German units that had stopped Bradley's July offensive.

On July 11, the German Panzer Lehr Division launched a major counterattack against the XIX Corps of Bradley's First Army. Alerted by intelligence intercepts of German cipher traffic (referred to as ULTRA), Bradley's troops managed to repel the German attackers by that evening. Despite all the valuable information provided by ULTRA, the unexpectedly heavy German resistance facing First Army in early July made top Allied leaders fear an apparent military stalemate in Normandy. To overcome this possibility, they considered a number of options, including an amphibious or airborne landing behind German lines. For various reasons, however, these options proved to be dead ends. Instead, it fell to Bradley on July 11 to come up with an acceptable concept to end the Normandy stalemate. Two days later, his First Army adopted one of Patton's ideas (without giving him credit) and made a plan that became known as Operation Cobra.

An American soldier prepares to fire a Mk II fragmentation rifle grenade over a hedgerow. The serious plight of the German forces in Normandy was unknown to the senior Allied military leadership in mid-July 1944. They only knew their plans for progress in France seemed to have been stymied, and they needed a breakthrough idea. *National Archives*

American soldiers look over an abandoned German Sd.Kfz. 8 half-track prime mover. In mid-July 1944, senior German military leaders in France decided that their forces could withstand the continuing Allied offensive operations for only a few more weeks. With Hitler's approval, the German high command started thinking, as early as July 23, about an eventual withdrawal from France. *National Archives*

OMAR NELSON BRADLEY

OMAR NELSON BRADLEY graduated from the U.S. Military Academy at West Point in 1915, the same year as General of the Army Dwight D. Eisenhower. Like Eisenhower, Bradley wanted to lead troops into combat during World War I, but spent the time training recruits instead.

As the army shrank in size after World War I, Bradley, who had reached the temporary rank of major in 1918, reverted to his permanent rank of captain. In the years between the end of World War I and the beginning of World War II, Bradley spent most of his time as either a student or an instructor in army schools. While serving as an instructor at the Infantry School in 1929, he greatly impressed the commandant, George S. Marshall, who became the chief of staff of the U.S. Army shortly before the United States became officially involved in World War II.

Bradley made the grade of lieutenant colonel in 1936. Due to his outstanding work as Marshall's assistant in the chief of staff office, in early 1941, Marshall promoted Bradley to a one-star brigadier general, skipping over the rank of colonel, and then sent him off to the Infantry School as its new commandant.

In February 1943, Marshall was ready to make Bradley a corps commander overseeing several divisions, but his West Point classmate, Eisenhower, needed Bradley to help him in the Battle for North Africa. Eventually, Bradley would replace Patton as II Corps commander on April 15, 1943, and lead the corps to victory by May 1943.

Bradley would go on to command II Corps, which was assigned to Patton's Seventh Army in the invasion of Sicily. Shortly after the successful conclusion of the Sicilian campaign, Eisenhower informed Bradley that he would command an army (composed of corps with attached divisions) and then activate an army group (composed of armies with their attached corps and divisions) in the forthcoming invasion of Nazi-occupied France.

Bradley would lead the First Army in the invasion of France. With the activation of Patton's Third Army on August 1, 1944, Bradley would become commander of the 12th Army Group, which then oversaw a total of twenty-one divisions composed of 903,000 men. By the end of the war in Europe, the total manpower of the 12th Army Group would rise to an astounding 1,300,000 men, the largest concentration of American fighting men ever assembled. Bradley would receive his fourth star as general in March 1945 and a fifth in September 1950, when he was appointed as the first chairman of the Joint Chiefs of Staff. *National Archives*

THE COBRA BUILDUP

Eisenhower enthusiastically received Bradley's plan, which called for a huge ground offensive along a very narrow front. The movement would be supported by a massive amount of airpower, which would literally and figuratively bulldoze a path through the bocage country. This type of ground offensive was a fairly new concept for the Americans. U.S. Army doctrine, as favored by Eisenhower and Bradley throughout the war, depended on a broad-front strategy, attacking the enemy forces simultaneously all along their front lines. Eisenhower knew from the ULTRA information that the Germans disliked having to deal with an enemy approaching on a broad front. Nevertheless, the perceived lack of success of Bradley's First Army's first broad-front offensive had a large influence on the decision to adopt the narrow front proposed by Operation Cobra.

Within Bradley's First Army, the hedgerow fighting produced a cadre of combat veterans that were training replacements how to survive on the battlefield. These men overcome their fear of German tanks and learned to actively hunt them with bazookas. The American soldier in the foreground is holding the 2.36-inch M9A1 bazooka and the soldier in the background the older generation 2.36-inch M1A1 bazooka. *National Archives*

Patton with members of the French Forces of the Interior (FFI) in Normandy. By early July, it had become clear to the Allied senior military leadership that the irregular forces of the FFI, also known as the French Resistance, were performing valuable services in helping defeat the Germans. *Patton Museum*

An American soldier stands ready with his Browning Automatic Rifle (BAR). During the second week of July 1944, Bradley began building upon an idea that the best way to break the Normandy stalemate was to conduct an operation combining concentrated land power and airpower along a very narrow front. This train of thought eventually became known as Operation Cobra, launched on July 14. *National Archives*

Operation Cobra, from the beginning, was designed to be only a limited attack. Its main purpose was to drive a hole in the German defenses west of St.-Lô. If that breakthrough worked, a deeper penetration into enemy territory by a large armored force would follow, thrusting deep into the German's rear, toward Coutances. When and if Coutances fell into Bradley's hands, Operation Cobra would end and be replaced by another operation aimed at the southern base of the Cotentin Peninsula, the gateway to Brittany.

While Operation Cobra plans developed, Montgomery remained in control of all ground operations in Normandy. He, in turn, allowed Bradley considerable freedom relative to plans for First Army's operations. Eisenhower and his staff shipped additional units to Normandy and sped up deliveries of ammunition and supplies.

Bradley's First Army had four corps comprising fifteen divisions on the army front. For additional backup, First Army could call upon an additional infantry division and two armored divisions. Patton's Third Army and several corps headquarters waited to become operational behind Bradley's First Army. For added assistance, First Army employed many supporting units that belonged to Third Army. These supporting detachments included engineer units, tank-destroyer units, quartermaster units, evacuation hospitals, fuel supplies, truck companies, and graves-registration units.

An American M4A1 Sherman medium tank crew works on their vehicle's engine. The main goal of Operation Cobra, originally set for July 18, was basically the same as Bradley's First Army offensive launched in early July: to break through the German front-line positions and then go on to seize Brittany and its many ports. The first step toward that goal was taking the French city of Coutances. *National Archives*

A camouflaged American M10 tank destroyer passes by a destroyed German half-track prime mover. *National Archives*

To launch Operation Cobra, Bradley's First Army had four corps overseeing fifteen divisions (both armored and infantry) facing the enemy front-line positions. Patton's Third Army headquarters had already assembled in Normandy and was ready to become operational. Communication between all these units was done by radio, as pictured, or by land lines. *National Archives*

A group of American soldiers hitch a ride into battle on an M4 Sherman tank covered with sandbags for extra protection. Patton's Third Army would not enter into combat until Operation Cobra had unfolded and Bradley's First Army had reached the base of the Cotentin Peninsula. This would provide the Third Army with an entrance to Brittany and its ports. *National Archives*

During the early planning stages of Operation Cobra, Bradley told Eisenhower that he preferred to conduct the upcoming operation without Patton's Third Army. It was not until July 28 that Bradley decided to give Patton some part in Operation Cobra prior to the activation of Third Army on August 1. Bradley directed Patton to begin forming the six divisions of the First Army's VIII Corps into two separate corps. He also told Patton to keep track of these corps during the opening stages of Operation Cobra, so that Patton would be familiar with the tactical situation when his own army became operational. The other three corps that made up First Army would remain under command of Gen. Courtney H. Hodges, assistant commander of the First Army.

An American soldier looks over a destroyed German 8.8cm FlaK 36 (antiaircraft gun). *National Archives*

In the period before launching Operation Cobra, Eisenhower (right) frequently flew from his headquarters in England to Normandy to discuss battle plans with his field commanders, like Bradley (left). All ground operations in France still remained under the control of British General Bernard Montgomery. *National Archives*

An American M4 Sherman medium tank in British army service, armed with a 17-pounder (76.2mm) main gun and designated the Sherman "Firefly" IC. To assist Bradley's First Army in Operation Cobra, the British forces on his left flank were to launch their own large-scale offensive operations at the same time Cobra was launched. *Patton Museum*

An American M8 self-propelled howitzer receives servicing by its crew. *National Archives*

As the number of American divisions grew and preparations continued for the activation of Patton's Third Army, it became more difficult for the First Army headquarters to effectively direct all the various military forces in Normandy. As a result, on July 19, Bradley recommended formation of Army Group headquarters to control both the First and Third. Allied planners for the invasion of France had long foreseen such a need, and on July 25, Eisenhower approved Bradley's suggestion. Eisenhower directed that all American ground forces in Normandy consolidated into the First and Third Armies, which would in turn come under control of the 12th Army Group, under Bradley. Bradley chose August 1 for the new command arrangement to go into effect. Hodges, assistant commander of the First Army, would assume command of First Army when Bradley became 12th Army Group commander.

An American artillery forward observer poses for the camera. Major General J. Lawton Collins's VII Corps of Bradley's First Army was chosen to push through the German lines for Operation Cobra. To make the maximum effort, Bradley increased Collins's force to a total six divisions and gave it a front line of only four and a half miles. *National Archives*

OPERATION GOODWOOD

To draw away German forces from First Army's limited attack toward Coutances, Montgomery planned for Dempsey's British Second Army to begin its own offensive toward Caen with the hope of punching a hole in the German defenses. The British advance, code-named Goodwood, began with a massive, 2,100-plane air strike on the German positions in Caen itself, followed by three Allied armored divisions attacking toward German positions east of Caen.

Operation Goodwood confirmed the German belief that the main Allied breakout lay in the British sector around Caen and not in the American sector. Unknown to the British planners of Operation Goodwood, the German defenses in the Caen area were organized in depth, with infantry forward and the tanks back, east of Caen. As British tanks advanced

PATTON'S THOUGHTS ON FIRE AND MOVEMENT

THE POLICY of holding the enemy by the nose with fire and kicking him in the pants with movement is just as true as when I wrote it, some twenty years ago, and at that time it had been true since the beginning of war. Any operation, reduced to its primary characteristics, consists of moving down the road until you bump into the enemy. It may be one road or it may be several roads. When you have bumped, hold him at the point of contact with fire with about a third of your command. Move the rest in a wide envelopment so that you can attack him from his rear flank. The enveloping attack should start first. The initial nose attack starts to move forward only when the enemy has properly reacted to the enveloping attack. Then the direct attack can go easily and fast.

—*War As I Knew It,*
"Reflections and Suggestions"

A formation of B-17 bombers in flight. First Army's plans called for Operation Cobra to begin in front of Collins's VII Corps with a tremendous air bombardment intended to obliterate the German units opposing the advance. Bradley had called for light bombs to be dropped to avoid excessive cratering. *National Archives*

toward German tank units untouched by the massive Allied aerial bombardment, which had only affected the forward positions, they came under heavy antitank and tank-gun fire. The British pushed forward long after they had lost their initial momentum, losing over one hundred tanks the first day. They lost another two hundred tanks before turning back the German counterattack that ended Operation Goodwood on July 21. If Goodwood had succeeded, it might not have been necessary for Bradley to launch Operation Cobra.

Operation Goodwood's lack of success did not stop Montgomery from ordering additional diversionary attacks to aid Operation Cobra. On the morning of July 25, a Canadian corps began an attack in the Caen area. The Canadian attack quickly bogged down under tough German resistance and a large armored counterattack. The Canadians lost more than 1,500 men and were unwilling to risk more. Montgomery called a halt to the attack the same day it had started. On July 30, Montgomery launched Dempsey's British Second Army in an operation to prevent German armored reserves from being switched to the American sector.

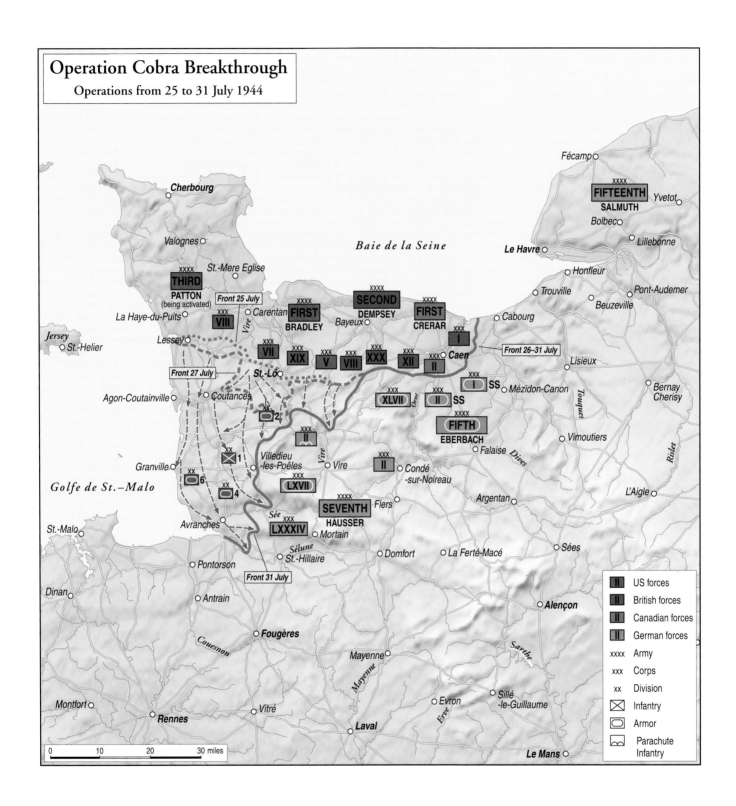

Operation Cobra Breakthrough
Operations from 25 to 31 July 1944

Fécamp

Baie de la Seine

FIFTEENTH xxxx
SALMUTH
Yvetot
Bolbec
Lillebonne
Le Havre
Honfleur
Trouville
Pont-Audemer
Beuzeville
Cabourg

Cherbourg
Valognes
St.-Mere Eglise

THIRD xxxx
PATTON
(being activated)
La Haye-du-Puits
Carentan
VIII xxx
Front 25 July
Vire

FIRST xxxx
BRADLEY
SECOND xxxx
DEMPSEY
Bayeux
FIRST xxxx
CRERAR
Caen
I xxx

Jersey
St.-Helier
Lessey
VII xxx
XIX xxx
V xxx
VIII xxx
XXX xxx
XII xxx
II xxx
Front 26–31 July
Lisieux

St.-Lô
Front 27 July
Agon-Coutainville
Coutances
XLVII xxx
Orne
II xxx SS
I xxx SS
Mézidon-Canon
Bernay
Cherisy

2 xxx
II xxx
FIFTH xxxx
EBERBACH
Falaise
Dives
Vimoutiers

Granville
1 xx
Villedieu
-les-Poêles
Vire
Vire
II xxx
Condé
-sur-Noireau
Argentan
L'Aigle

Golfe de St.–Malo
6 xx
4 xx
LXVII xxx
Flers
Sées

Avranches
Sée xxx
LXXXIV xxx
SEVENTH xxxx
HAUSSER
Mortain
St.-Malo
Pontorson
Sélune
St.-Hillaire
Domfort
La Ferté-Macé
Front 31 July
Dinan
Antrain

Fougères
Couesnon
Alençon
Mayenne
Mayenne
Sarthe
Montfort
Vitré
Evron
Sillé
-le-Guillaume
Rennes
Erve
Laval
Le Mans

	US forces
II	British forces
II	Canadian forces
II	German forces
xxxx	Army
xxx	Corps
xx	Division
⊠	Infantry
▭	Armor
⏟	Parachute Infantry

0 10 20 30 miles

An American M4 Sherman medium tank crew loads their vehicle's main gun ammunition. Once the Cobra aerial bombardment ceased, three of Collins's VII Corps infantry divisions were to make the initial breach in the German lines and keep the flanks of the corridor open while his armored units sped through the planned three-mile passageway. *National Archives*

Besides the aerial bombardment, artillery, such as this American M2A1 105mm howitzer, was to play an important part in the opening act of Operation Cobra. Bradley assigned the bulk of the First Army's artillery assets to Collins's VII Corps. *National Archives*

OPERATION COBRA UNLEASHED

The original plans for Operation Cobra called for the attack to begin on July 18. Due to poor weather, however, Bradley had to postpone until July 24. The area Bradley chose for the opening move was on the 4.2-mile front of Collins's VII Corps, which consisted of six divisions: the 1st, 4th, 9th, and 30th Infantry Divisions, and the 2nd and 3rd Armored Divisions. The 9th, 4th, and 30th concentrated for the initial assault, and the others followed closely behind a massive aerial bombardment. If they could penetrate German lines, they would create a defended corridor only three miles wide.

Down this narrow defended corridor Collins's VII Corps would push the 1st Infantry Division (supplied with extra trucks), as well as the 2nd and 3rd Armored Divisions. It should be noted that the 2nd and 3rd Armored Divisions were the only fully mechanized armored divisions in the U.S. Army. All the other armored divisions relied at least in part on towed artillery and truck-borne infantry. These two armored divisions were thus uniquely suited for employment as rapidly moving exploitation operations. The three divisions were to encircle and secure Coutances, disrupt German defenses, and be prepared for further exploitation. To protect the advance of Collins's VII Corps, the job of the VIII, V, and XIX Corps was to tie down German forces that could counterattack an Operation Cobra breakthrough. Opposing Collins's VII Corps in the initial assault were roughly three thousand German soldiers and one hundred tanks.

An American soldier climbs over a pile of Goliaths, small German remote-controlled demolition vehicles. *National Archives*

German soldiers prepare for battle. The Allied senior military leadership knew that the German units facing the planned Operation Cobra advance, barring the use of any secret weapons, were short of manpower and equipment, which made an effective defense doubtful. *National Archives*

U.S. Army medics run from the field with a wounded soldier as artillery smoke rounds cover their presence from German observation. The typical battalion aid station was normally no more than five hundred yards behind the front lines. *National Archives*

An American machine gun team guards a hedgerow position in Normandy, France. The M1917A1 .30-caliber machine gun was water-cooled; the water hose connects to the bottom of the barrel jacket. The second man of the machine gun crew is armed with an M3 submachine gun. *National Archives*

The aerial operation got off to a false start on July 24, when bad weather postponed the operation minutes before it was to begin. Due to communications problems, over three hundred American planes failed to receive the cancellation messages and dropped their bombs on the assigned targets. Human error caused a number of bombs to drop short of their targets. These bombs landed on Bradley's First Army positions, killing 25 men and wounding another 131.

The false start of Operation Cobra caused many American military commanders, including Bradley, to fear they had lost the element of surprise. But Eisenhower overruled any thoughts about postponing the operation. He was eager to see it begin. With prospects for good weather the next day, Bradley ordered Operation Cobra launched at 1100 on July 25. Fortunately, the German commanders had seen the July 24 air attack only as a ruse and had not drastically altered their defensive positions. When the real bombardment began the next day, the Germans were unprepared for the size and scope of the attack.

American military personnel gather around a knocked out German Panther Ausf. A medium tank. After the destruction and disruption of the German forces by the opening aerial and artillery bombardment of Operation Cobra, the Americans made a penetration three miles wide and one to three miles deep into enemy lines on the first day. *National Archives*

PATTON'S THOUGHTS ON DECORATIONS

WE MUST HAVE MORE decorations and we must not give them out with a niggard hand. A young soldier upon being asked by Napoleon what he desired in recompense for a heroic act said, "Sire, the Legion of Honor," to which Napoleon replied, "My boy you are over young for such an honor." The soldier again said, "Sire, in your service, we do not grow old." We must exploit their abilities and satisfy their longings to the utmost during the brief span of their existence. Surely, an inch of satin for a machine gun nest put out of action is a bargain not to be lightly passed up.

—*The Unknown Patton,*
"Patton's Quotes"

An American soldier uncovers a mine. Retreating Germans left minefields behind to hinder the American advances. American intelligence officers concluded by July 27 that the Germans forces fleeing the First Army advance would attempt to gain refuge behind a river at the French city of Avranches, south of Coutances. *National Archives*

OPERATION COBRA PICKS UP STEAM

During the second Operation Cobra bombardment, human error once again caused bombs to fall short into First Army units. More than 100 American troops died, and another 490 were wounded. Among the Americans killed was Lt. Gen. Lesley J. McNair, the commanding general of all U.S. Army ground forces.

Attacks by the 4th and 6th Armored Divisions (under VII Corps) achieved only a disappointing and partial success, but managed to enter Coutances on the afternoon of July 28. They also attracted German reserves to their area. Bradley, taking advantage of an ever-changing situation, decided to reassign the capture of Coutances from Collins's VII Corps to Maj. Gen. Troy H. Middleton's VIII Corps. Thus, when VIII Corps began its advance on the morning of July 26, it found little German opposition. By July 27, the Germans began disengaging from Collins's VII Corps front.

On July 28, part of the 2nd Armored Division drove southeast to cut off the German withdrawal. The 82nd Reconnaissance Battalion pushed through the defenses before the Germans were aware of what was going on and seized blocking positions south of Coutances. German opposition was eliminated by the combined arms team of tanks, infantry, artillery, and fighter-bombers. By the morning of July 30, the 2nd Armored Division killed 1,500 German troops and captured another 4,000, while seeing 100 of its own men killed and 300 wounded.

A column of American tanks and infantry move forward. The soldier in the foreground has a 2.36-inch M1 bazooka slung over his shoulder. Despite some enemy resistance, Collins's VII Corps armored columns captured Coutances on July 28. At that point, all four corps of Bradley's First Army where ordered to press their advances southward as the German defenses began to crumble.
National Archives

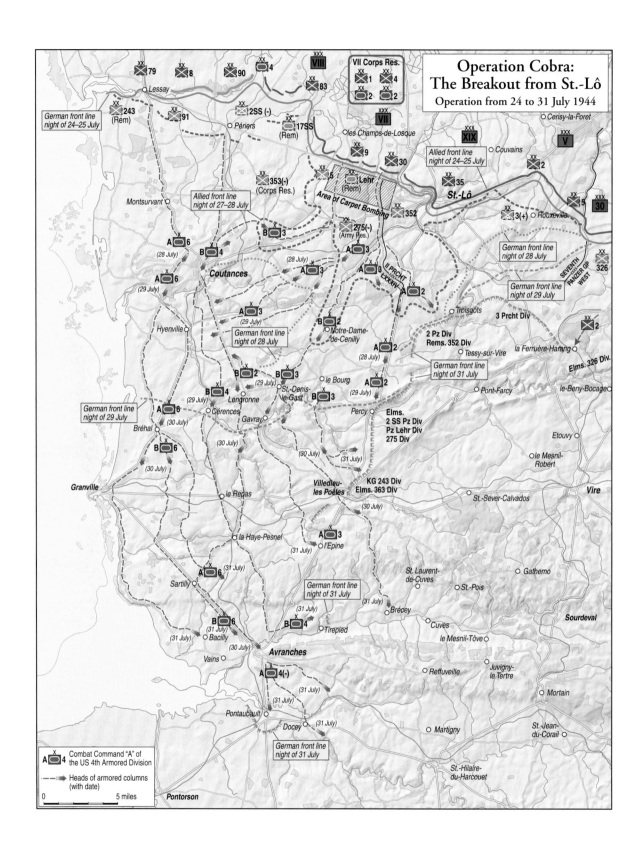

**Operation Cobra:
The Breakout from St.-Lô**
Operation from 24 to 31 July 1944

VIII

VII Corps Res.
1
4
2
2

79
8
90
4
83
Lessay

VII

XIX

V
Cerisy-la-Foret

German front line
night of 24–25 July

243
(Rem)
91
2SS (-)
Périers
17SS
(Rem)
Oles Champs-de-Losque
9
30
Allied front line
night of 24–25 July
Couvains
2

35
St.-Lô
5
30
Rouxeville

Montsurvant
353(-)
(Corps Res.)
Allied front line
night of 27–28 July
5
Lehr
(Rem)
Area of Carpet Bombing
352
3(+)

A 6
B 4
(28 July)
B 3
(28 July)
A 3
275(-)
(Army Res.)
A 3
German front line
night of 28 July

Coutances
A 3
(28 July)
A 3
II PRCHT
LXXXIV
A 2
German front line
night of 29 July
SEVENTH PANZER GP WEST
326

A 6
(29 July)
A 3
(29 July)
B 2
Notre-Dame-
de-Cenilly
A 2
(28 July)
Troisgots
3 Prcht Div
2

Hyenville
German front line
night of 28 July
2 Pz Div
Rems. 352 Div
Tessy-sur-Vire
la Ferrière-Harang
Elms. 326 Div

B 2
B 3
le Bourg
German front line
night of 31 July
le-Beny-Bocage

B 4
(29 July)
St.-Denis-
le-Gast
B 3
A 2
(29 July)
Pont-Farcy

Lengronne
German front line
night of 29 July
A 6
(30 July)
Cérences
Gavray
Percy
Elms.
2 SS Pz Div
Pz Lehr Div
275 Div
Etouvy
ole Mesnil-
Robert

Bréhal
B 6
(30 July)

Granville
(30 July)
le Repas
(30 July)
(30 July)
(31 July)
Villedieu-
les-Poéles
KG 243 Div
Elms. 363 Div
St.-Sever-Calvados
Vire

la-Haye-Pesnel
A 3
(31 July)
ol'Epine
(30 July)
St. Laurent-
de-Cuves
St.-Pois
Gathemo

A 6
(31 July)
Sartilly
German front line
night of 31 July
(31 July)
Brécey
Cuves
le Mesnil-Tôve
Sourdeval

B 6
(31 July)
Bacilly
B 4
Tirepied
German front line
night of 31 July
Reffuveille
Juvigny-
le Tertre
Mortain

Vains
(30 July)
Avranches
A 4(-)
(31 July)
Martigny
St.-Jean-
du-Corail

Pontaubault
Docey
(31 July)
German front line
night of 31 July
St.-Hilaire-
du-Harcouet

A 4
Combat Command "A" of
the US 4th Armored Division

Heads of armored columns
(with date)

0   5 miles
Pontorson

PATTON BECOMES A PLAYER IN COBRA

Originally envisioned as a limited breakthrough in the St.-Lô area, Operation Cobra managed to achieve all of its goals by July 28, when Bradley's First Army's captured Coutances. News of the initial successes was slow in reaching Eisenhower; however, he maintained that the men were fighting for all their worth and that the enemy would soon crack under the pressure. Impressed by the effects of the aerial bombardment on German morale, he felt that a concerted, intensive drive could break through the whole enemy defense system on a selected front, and that the Allies were going "to get a great victory, very soon."

American soldiers pass by a small destroyed German half-track designated the Demag 7 and mounting a 2cm (20mm) FlaK 30 (antiaircraft gun). To prevent German reinforcements from setting up new defensive lines, First Army's VIII Corps decided to capture the French city of Avranches. The city lay at the base of the Cotentin Peninsula and offered an entrance into Brittany for Patton's Third Army. *National Archives*

Two American officers enjoy a hometown newspaper that somebody mailed them. For most front-line soldiers in World War II, their knowledge of the world around them was restricted to a few thousand yards around their current position. *National Archives*

Bradley ordered Patton, whose Third Army would become operational at noon of August 1, to "supervise" the advance of Middleton's VIII Corps on the coastal flank. This command arrangement would establish a useful continuity between the Operation Cobra breakout and future operations in Brittany. Patton immediately took over the planning of the VIII Corps advance, adding to the attack plan with his own brand of audacity. He withdrew his infantry spearheads and replaced them with two armored divisions, the 4th and the 6th. Patton once wrote: "The primary mission of armored units is the attacking of infantry and artillery. The enemy's rear is the happy hunting ground for armor; use every means to get it there."

An American Jeep passes by a German corpse at the side of the road. *National Archives*

American soldiers take aim with their M1 Garand rifles. Until the armored phase of Operation Cobra would begin on July 26, the infantry divisions of Collins's VII Corps, assigned to keep the breach open in the German lines for the tanks, faced a lot of hard fighting. Although the enemy troops were disorganized, their morale was still high. *National Archives*

American soldiers climb over a French FT-17 light tank that had been pressed into German service. *National Archives*

The 6th Armored Division, attacking south along the coast, was to make the main effort. It soon managed to advance more than eight miles a day against weak German opposition. The main effort now shifted from Collins's VII Corps to Middleton's VIII Corps as the flow of the battle overtook the original Operation Cobra plans. By the evening of July 28, the local German corps headquarters lost effective control of its units. Most of the survivors were trying to escape to the southeast. American fighter-bombers discovered a large traffic jam of fleeing German troops and destroyed more than five hundred vehicles.

In the original plans for Operation Cobra, Coutances was the pinnacle of success for Bradley's First Army. After its capture, and with the entire German Seventh Army on the run, the town of Avranches now became the primary objective of the First Army and Patton's soon-to-be-activated Third Army. Avranches was the gateway to Brittany and probably the only way out of Normandy for the remaining German forces.

One of the biggest problems facing the divisions of the VIII Corps as they advanced southwest toward Avranches was the large number of captured German soldiers. As there was no time to process them, most prisoners were sent to the rear without guards. *National Archives*

American engineers prepare to erect a treadway bridge. By July 29, the 4th and 6th Armored Divisions of the VIII Corps were pushing southward toward Avranches against a disorderly German withdrawal that showed no sign of abating. American bridging parties faced only sporadic fire from enemy self-propelled guns. *National Archives*

American soldiers look over a captured Russian Army 152mm gun-howitzer M1937 that has been pressed into German military service. As the armored columns approached Avranches, the VIII Corps commander decided that 4th Armored Division was in a better position to take the city. The 6th Armored Division would capture the towns of Brehal and Granville. *National Archives*

On July 29, the 4th and 6th Armored Divisions of Middleton's VIII Corps began moving southward again, with the aim of capturing Avranches. Another objective was the securing of the bridge leading to Pontaubault, four miles south of Avranches. Part of the 4th Armored Division advanced eighteen miles on July 30 to capture Avranches, the vital point in the area for both attack and defense. On the late afternoon of July 31, a task force of the 4th Armored Division seized the bridge, as well as the important road intersection immediately south of it, despite minor German resistance. Together, the 4th and 6th Armored Divisions captured more than four thousand prisoners on July 31. The

two infantry divisions following the armored divisions rounded up an additional three thousand prisoners. In contrast to these figures, the total casualty count for Middleton's VIII Corps between July 28 and July 31 numbered fewer than seven hundred men.

The Operation Cobra breakthrough was complete. By the evening of July 27, Bradley had already concluded that Cobra would be a breakout his forces could exploit. For the Germans, the situation had become a *Riesensauerei* (giant pigpen). The commander of Germany's Seventh Army telephoned Hitler's headquarters on July 31 to say, "[I]f the Americans get through at Avranches, they will be out of the woods, and they'll be able to do what they want."

After enduring a German rear-guard delaying action, which caused forty-three casualties and the loss of eight half-tracks, like this M3A1 half-track with a towed M1 57mm antitank gun, advance elements of the 4th Armored Division entered the undefended city of Avranches in the early evening of July 30. *National Archives*

German weapons captured in battle, including 8.8cm FlaK 36 antiaircraft guns, were simply gathered in a field for storage. Seizing Avranches was just the first step in providing Patton's Third Army an unhindered entrance into Brittany. The single road from Avranches running westward into Brittany had to be secured. *National Archives*

A young girl watches the American soldiers of a field post office at work while the soldier in the foreground reads his mail. *National Archives*

Patton (right) with Bradley (center) and Lt. Gen. Courtney Hodges, who took over command of the First Army from Bradley on August 1. Operation Cobra had changed from a breakthrough of the German lines into a breakout. The defeated enemy forces in Normandy opened the door to an even bigger disaster for the Germans in France. *Patton Museum*

A derelict German eight-wheel armored car designated the Sd.Kfz. 231. *National Archives*

Patton exits his command vehicle. In the best cavalry traditions, Patton would unleash his armored units into Brittany without much direct oversight, as he expected his commanders to exercise independent judgment and tactical daring in obtaining their objectives. *Patton Museum*

3

THIRD ARMY ON THE OFFENSIVE

ON JULY 31, HITLER HELD an important conference with his senior staff in his East Prussian headquarters, where he confirmed that the success of Operation Cobra and a possible future breakout by the American forces could eventually lead to the withdrawal of all German forces in Normandy. Therefore, he ordered a special army staff to plan for a pullout, if it became necessary. At the same time, he ordered new defensive positions built along the French Somme and Marne rivers.

In an effort to gain time, Hitler also insisted there be no withdrawing from the existing defensive lines. He expected all ground controlled by German forces to be held with fanatical determination. Hitler knew that if France fell, the Allied threat to Germany would become immediate. If the German army high command did approve a withdrawal, all French roads, communication facilities, bridges, and railroads were supposed to be destroyed in the wake of a German retreat. French ports were to be held to the last man and then destroyed before falling into Allied hands.

On July 29, Bradley, in his role as the future 12th Army Group commander, ordered Patton and his soon-to-be-activated Third Army to drive south from Pontaubault to seize the cities of Rennes and Forgeres, then to turn westward to secure the various Breton ports, and finally to seize the remainder of Brittany. Bradley envisioned these goals being accomplished by Third Army armored

The French Forces of the Interior (FFI) numbered about fifty thousand members in Brittany and helped Patton's Third Army in its conquest of that region of France. Here, a Frenchman offers American soldiers wine and maybe some information on the Germans. Notice the Signal Corps cameraman on the hood of the Jeep. *National Archives*

American artillery forward observers view the battlefield. *National Archives*

An American-M4A4 Sherman medium tank in Canadian army service. Even before Patton's Third Army became operational, the Allied forces in Normandy increased their growing strength by adding the Canadian First Army on July 23, 1944. It and the British Second Army served under General Montgomery's 21st Army Group. *National Archives*

A destroyed French locomotive and cars. Hitler's plan for slowing down the Allied logistical system in France was twofold: First, the German forces were to defend all the French ports to the last man and then destroy them. Second, they were to destroy the French railroad system while withdrawing eastward. *National Archives*

and infantry divisions working together in an orderly advance, as had been done during the post–Operation Cobra drive to Avranches.

Patton saw little point in slowly reducing Brittany by carefully planned, set-piece operations taking place in successive phases. He knew the German forces within Brittany were weak. Patton even joked with his staff that he did not want the press to know just how second-rate his opponents were in Brittany.

Patton had already begun to see the conquest of Brittany as a secondary assignment even before he officially took command of Third Army. He knew the important battles for France and the path to Germany lay eastward, in the direction of Paris, not westward. It would take a few more days before Bradley would begin to see that Patton's opinion about the Brittany campaign was correct. Before the invasion of France, Allied planners believed it would take the entire Third Army to capture Brittany and its ports. Evidence of German disorganization in early August, however, convinced Allied leaders that they had the opportunity to seize Brittany and its ports with much smaller forces.

An American P-47 Thunderbolt fighter makes an unsuccessful landing. Air support for the newly operational Third Army came from Brig. Gen. Otto P. Weyland's XIX Tactical Air Command (TAC), which was operating as part of the IX TAC until August 1, 1944. *National Archives*

WADE H. HAISLIP

WADE H. HAISLIP graduated from the U.S. Military Academy at West Point in 1912 and saw combat during World War I. During the interwar period, he served as either an instructor or as a student at a variety of army schools, as did so many of his compatriots.

Haislip served in different staff positions before the United States officially entered into World War II in December 1941. He was then assigned to organize and train the 85th Infantry Division, which he commanded from April 1942 until February 1943. He then moved on to command the XV Corps as a two-star major general and remained in that position throughout the remainder of the war in Europe.   *National Archives*

On August 2, Bradley issued new orders for Patton, stating that Brittany and its ports were to be seized using "only minimum force." Patton was well aware of the dire situation facing the German army in Brittany. He decided to clear Brittany with only his VIII Corps, under the command of Middleton. Out of the forces available to the VIII Corps, three armored spearheads appeared. They would enter into battle with little or no infantry support. The two main armored spearheads consisted of the hard-charging 4th and 6th Armored Divisions, which spent most of the northwestern European campaign attached to Patton's Third Army.

A third armored spearhead sent into Brittany by Middleton's VIII Corps was a temporary unit called Task Force A, with a strength of about 3,500 men. It consisted of a mixture of tank-destroyer units, engineer units, and mechanized cavalry groups. The job of Task Force A was to protect a series of several bridges carrying a railroad line that generally ran along the north shore of Brittany. The railroad connected the Breton port of Brest to Rennes and then ran into the interior of France. If the port at Brest fell intact into Third Army hands, the railroad would be a quick means of moving military supplies into France in support of all American military forces. Task Force A would also assist Middleton's VIII Corps in the capture of the ports of St. Malo and Brest.

American soldiers take cover from enemy fire.
National Archives

An American M2 60mm mortar team in action.
Bradley planned on Patton's Third Army seizing
Pontaubault, located just south of Avranches,
and then continuing southward to take
Rennes and Forgeres before turning VIII Corps
westward into Brittany. *National Archives*

THE 4TH ARMORED DIVISION IN BRITTANY

Despite the very strong protests of Maj. Gen. John Shirley Wood, commander of the 4th Armored Division, he received the job of driving southwest forty miles from Pontaubault to capture the city of Rennes, the provincial capital of Brittany and an important road and communications center. Once the division captured Rennes, it was to continue its advance and seize the Quiberon Bay area sixty miles southwest of Rennes. In so doing, the 4th Armored Division would cut off the Brittany peninsula near its base and prevent the reinforcement or escape of German forces still there. There were also plans to build a brand-new harbor in the Quiberon Bay area if Middleton's VIII Corps failed to capture any of the existing Breton ports undamaged.

An American tanker observes mine damage to his M4A3(76)W Sherman medium tank.
National Archives

Wood rightly saw the movement westward of his division as a waste of valuable time. Like Patton, he knew the real campaign for Europe lay eastward, in the direction of Germany, and not westward to the ocean. Unfortunately for Wood, the plans for seizing Brittany were drawn up long before the invasion of France. Due to a great deal of strategic inflexibility among American senior commanders, the plans for the Brittany campaign were being doggedly carried out despite growing opportunities being created elsewhere. Eventually, the senior American commanders would see the error of their ways and prove Wood correct.

A problem in getting the VIII Corps out of Normandy and into Brittany was the fact that there were only two main highways running southward along the coastal sector. Both of these were littered with the flotsam of war, including wrecked German equipment. *National Archives*

An American bulldozer clears a small hedgerow. Patton's plan for taking Brittany involved cutting off the peninsula near its base to prevent the Germans from either withdrawing or reinforcing the area. He would then clear the central plateau of the region and push the Germans into pockets along the coast. *National Archives*

Wood sent his tanks around the western side of Rennes and cut all German lines of communication from the west and south. At this point, he tried to turn his tanks in a southeastern direction, but this movement was overruled by the VIII Corps commander, Middleton. He informed Wood that he must not merely cut off Rennes, but capture the city as well. To accomplish this added task, Wood brought up the 13th Infantry Regiment, riding in trucks, and a supporting artillery unit. He sent the 2nd Cavalry Group circling to the east of Rennes to prevent a German escape in that direction. Rennes finally fell to the 4th Armored Division on August 4. Despite the best efforts of Wood's troops, most of the two thousand German troops defending the city managed to escape.

WALTON HARRIS WALKER

WALTON HARRIS WALKER graduated from the U.S. Military Academy at West Point in 1912. His popular nickname, "Johnnie," was supposed to have come from his preferred brand of Scotch and was obviously a play on his surname.

In the period before World War I, Walker spent time patrolling the border between Mexico and the United States. It was during this period that he became good friends with Dwight D. Eisenhower. Walker would go on to see combat against the German army in World War I. He was twice cited for gallantry for his time in combat and was promoted to lieutenant colonel.

Like Eisenhower and Bradley, Walker served in a variety of roles during the years before the United States entered World War II, including a stint as an instructor at West Point. And in the 1930s, like Eisenhower and Bradley, Walker made a favorable impression on George S. Marshall, the future Chief of Staff of the U.S. Army.

As the war clouds loomed over the United States before the Japanese attack on Pearl Harbor on December 7, 1941, Walker was promoted to ever-more-responsible positions. He received his first star as a brigadier general in 1939 as one of Patton's subordinate commanders and went on to receive his second star as a major general in 1942. He commanded the 3rd Armored Division and later the IV Armored Corps. In 1943, IV Armored Corps was redesignated as XX Corps. Walker would take the XX Corps to England in early 1944, so it would take its future place in the conquest of Nazi-occupied Europe as part of Patton's Third Army.

In the drive across Western Europe, Walker's hard-charging XX Corps earned high praise from all his superior officers. Patton would be quoted as saying, "General Walker is always the most willing and most cooperative. He will apparently fight anytime, anyplace, with anything that the army commander desires to give to him." Walker was promoted to a three-star lieutenant general in 1945.

While serving as commander of the Eighth Army during the Korean War, Walker was killed in a traffic accident on December 23, 1950. As a tribute to him, the M41 Light Tank, then in development, was dubbed the Walker Bulldog. *National Archives*

At the same time Rennes was surrounded, other elements of the division continued driving deeper into Brittany. On the afternoon of August 3, Wood's tanks captured the small towns of Bain-de-Bretagne and Derval, thirty and forty miles south of Rennes. These elements of the 4th Armored Division represented a very effective blocking force at the base of the Brittany peninsula.

With the capture of Rennes, the next major objective of the 4th Armored Division became the port city of Lorient. Before advancing on Lorient, Wood ordered seizure of the small port of Vannes along the Quiberon Bay area. Vannes sat along a main road and railway that led to Lorient. With the help of a local French Resistance unit, the town fell into American hands on August 5. The capture took place so quickly that the German defenders were unable to destroy any of the port's facilities, including bridges and railroads. Wood's 4th Armored Division had effectively cut the Brittany peninsula at its base.

A loader in a German Tiger E heavy tank carefully cradles a round for the extremely powerful 8.8cm (88mm) turret-mounted main gun. Unlike the other four members of the tank's crew that wore headsets and throat microphone for inter-vehicle crew communications, the loader depended on verbal commands from the tank commander or gunner to determine his actions.
Patton Museum

A derelict German Panzer IV medium tank. *National Archives*

PATTON'S THOUGHTS ON THE USE OF ARMORED DIVISIONS

IN AN ARMORED division, as in an infantry division, attacks must be coordinated; and the infantry, and the tanks, and the guns must work as a unit. Whenever possible, it is desirable that the guns [artillery] operate under divisional control and with their forward observers in tanks, immediately take under fire enemy antitank guns, and either reduce them or blind them with smoke or white phosphorus. Success depends upon the coordinated use of the guns and the tanks, with the guns paying particular attention to hostile artillery, and above all too antitank guns and observation posts.

—*The Unknown Patton,* "Letter of Instruction No. 3"

The attack on Lorient proved a much harder process for the 4th Armored Division than the capture of Vannes. The Germans, numbering almost eleven thousand troops, put up a stiff fight. Advanced elements of the 4th Armored Division, reaching the city on August 7, found strong defenses that included antitank ditches and minefields covered by antitank guns and artillery. The division probed the city's defenses and decided that it could not take the port, which included the large and strategically important U-boat base, with its existing strength. On August 8, Middleton, the VIII Corps commander, told Wood, "Do not become involved in a fight for Lorient unless [the] enemy attacks." Wood was to seal off the port until relieved by other units. This wouldn't happen until August 15, when the last element of the 4th Armored Division was finally relieved of its duty to guard Lorient.

On August 10, Wood received orders from Middleton to capture the port of Nantes, located eighty-eight miles east of Lorient. Elements of the 4th Armored Division reached the outskirts of Nantes on August 11. With the help of the local French Resistance, the division captured the port on August 12. Unfortunately for the Allies, the Germans managed to destroy the port's facilities before their capture.

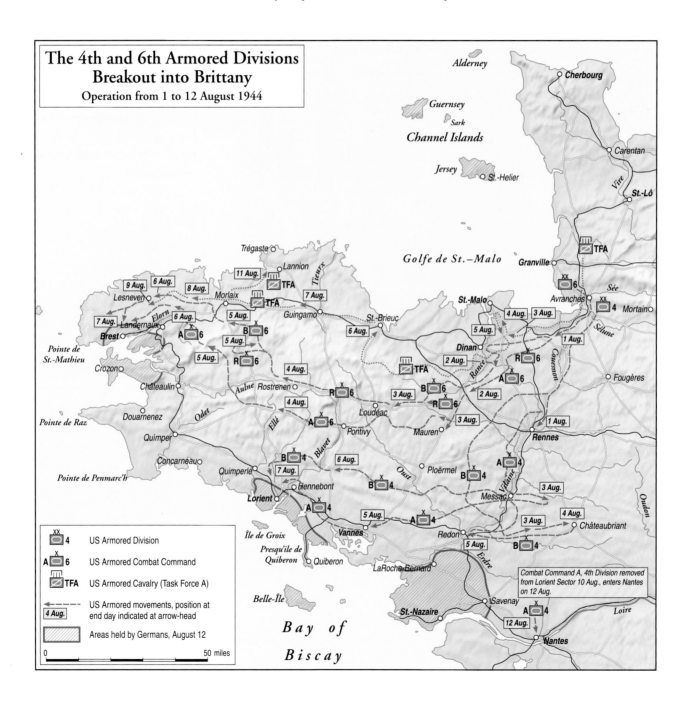

The 4th and 6th Armored Divisions Breakout into Brittany
Operation from 1 to 12 August 1944

Legend:
- **4** (XX) US Armored Division
- **A 6** (X) US Armored Combat Command
- **TFA** US Armored Cavalry (Task Force A)
- US Armored movements, position at end day indicated at arrow-head
- **4 Aug.**
- Areas held by Germans, August 12

0 — 50 miles

Combat Command A, 4th Division removed from Lorient Sector 10 Aug., enters Nantes on 12 Aug.

An American radio command Jeep. As Third Army armored units sped far and wide through the Brittany peninsula, communications between their VIII Corps headquarters and Patton himself became a serious problem. *National Archives*

A multiple caliber .50 machine gun carriage M51 with crew on alert for any sign of German aerial activity. To protect the numerous supply dumps set up by VIII Corps for its armored units in Brittany, antiaircraft units were pressed into service to protect both the supply convoys and the temporary supply sites. *National Archives*

THE 6TH ARMORED DIVISION IN BRITTANY

Major General Robert W. Grow commanded the 6th Armored Division. Like Patton, Grow was a longtime cavalryman who took up the cause of armored warfare in the 1930s. Patton described Grow as "one of the best armored forces commanders the war produced."

The advance of Grow's division into Brittany began on the morning of August 1. The original goal, as set by the VIII Corps commander, Middleton, was the small Breton town of Dinan, located west of Pontaubault. A couple of hours after Grow's division received its marching orders from Middleton, Patton showed up and told Grow he wanted his division to capture the large and important deep-water port of Brest within five days. Brest sat at the

Under fire, American soldiers hug the ground. Before the 4th Armored Division could take the major Breton port of Lorient it had to take some intermediate objectives such as the city of Rennes, the capital of Brittany. This occurred on August 4 with the help an infantry regiment. *National Archives*

An American M4A3 Sherman medium tank patrols in the ruins of a town. While the commander of 4th Armored Division wanted to advance eastward because he saw an opportunity to outflank the German Seventh Army in Normandy, Patton pushed him westward to take the town of Vannes and then the port of Lorient. *National Archives*

A captured German 15cm K. 18 artillery piece. Heavy German artillery fire took a toll on elements of the 4th Armored Division as it reached the outskirts of Lorient on the morning of August 7, 1944, and the division's advance fizzled. *National Archives*

An American soldier takes a moment away from the fighting to check his feet. Cold and wet weather could cause trench foot, and Patton ordered Third Army to take care of their feet to avoid a debilitating epidemic. *National Archives*

western tip of the Brittany peninsula and was over two hundred miles away from the division's location. In order to speed its advance, Patton told Grow to bypass any German resistance. Grow quickly stopped the advance on Dinan and began reorganizing his division into two parallel columns for the drive to Brest. That evening, Grow had to stop so his men could get some badly needed rest. He decided that his division would continue its advance to Brest the next day. This pause allowed Grow to place his mechanized cavalry squadrons at the front and on the flanks of the two armored columns.

The 6th Armored Division resumed its advance on Brest as scheduled. Meeting only minor German resistance, the division managed to push another thirty miles into Brittany. To everyone's surprise, Middleton called a halt to the advance that same afternoon. He decided he needed the 6th Armored Division to assist Task Force A and the 83rd Infantry Division in capturing the town of Dinan and the port city of St. Malo. The port lay fifty miles west of Avranches and was an important preinvasion objective assigned to Third Army. Patton considered the capture of St. Malo incidental to the entire Brittany campaign. But Middleton was much more cautious than Patton, believing the capture of St. Malo had to happen before the advance to Brest could take place. St. Malo would fall to elements of the VIII Corps on August 17, 1944.

As the disappointed staff officers of 6th Armored Division began making plans to attack Dinan, Patton arrived at the division's headquarters. He was unaware that Middleton changed the division's orders. When Patton came face to face with Grow, he angrily asked, "What in hell are you doing sitting here? I thought I told you to go to Brest." Grow explained to Patton that his advance to Brest had been halted. "On what authority?" Patton rasped. "Corps order, sir," Grow said, as he handed to Patton the actual written message from Middleton. Patton read the note and told Grow, "I'll see Middleton. You go ahead where I told you to go."

Grow assured Patton that his division could quickly continue the advance to Brest. Patton admitted to Grow that he was surprised to have found Grow's division so far into Brittany. An aide who had accompanied Patton later told Grow that Patton had to throw away several maps during the trip to the division command post. Each time he ran off one map onto another was an occasion for jubilant profanity on Patton's part.

American soldiers line up to clean their mess gear after a meal. *National Archives*

MANTON SPRAGUE EDDY

MANTON SPRAGUE EDDY saw combat in World War I against the German army and rose to the temporary rank of major by the time the conflict concluded. Upon returning to the United States, he reverted to the rank of captain. During the interwar period, Eddy was a member of the very influential Infantry Board and later became an instructor at the Command and General Staff College.

In 1942 Eddy was promoted to the one-star rank of brigadier general and assumed command of 9th Infantry Division, which fought in North Africa, Sicily under Patton's command, and Normandy. For his hard work, he was given command of XII Corps by Patton in August 1944.

Patton would write of Eddy, "General Eddy is very nervous, very much inclined to be grasping and always worrying that some other corps commander is getting a better deal than he is, but when the decision is made, he always does as he is told."

Eddy would remain in command of XII Corps until April 1945 when health reasons forced him back to the United States for medical treatment. By the conclusion of World War II, Eddy had reached the rank of lieutenant general.

National Archives

Restarting the 6th Armored Division toward Brest proved harder than Grow had hoped. The division ran into destroyed bridges and heavily mined crossing points on the evening of August 4. He decided to take advantage of a full moon and clear weather and ordered a night march. Local French Resistance groups acted as guides to Grow's armored columns. Avoiding German strong points, the 6th Armored managed to reach the town of Huelgoat, less than forty miles from Brest, on the morning of August 5. Hope arose that the division could be in Brest by nightfall, thereby meeting Patton's deadline. Unfortunately for Grow, a force of five hundred Germans, armed with artillery and tanks, near Huelgoat took several hours to clear. Unwilling to advance on Brest in darkness, Grow planned to launch his tanks at Brest on the morning of August 6. One of the two armored columns got within fifteen miles of Brest on the evening of August 6. At that point, heavy German opposition halted the American advance.

Grow remained convinced that he could take Brest by August 7 in a surprise attack. His tanks did get to within seven miles north of the port on that day before running into strong German defensive positions and heavy artillery fire. From that point on, it became clear the Germans would not give up Brest without a strong fight. Grow tried to bluff the German commander of Brest into surrendering on August 8, but the Germans rejected the offer.

The remnants of a French port that was destroyed by the Germans before withdrawing, a frequent strategy of the enemy. It would take VIII Corps until August 17, 1944, to subdue the Breton port of St. Malo. Initially, the Americans believed that the port would fall quickly. That illusion was soon shattered by the Germans, who then totally destroyed the port before surrendering it. *National Archives*

Due to its size, the barrel of the 240mm howitzer M1 required transport on its own trailer. Unable to take Brest, the 6th Armored Division commander received orders to surround the port until an infantry division and artillery could be brought up to capture the city and its facilities. *National Archives*

The 6th Armored Division had little hard information on the strength of the German defenses around Brest. The division's staff estimated that the defenders in Brest numbered no more than three thousand men. But, sensing the difficulty in capturing Brest with his existing forces, Grow requested that the VIII Corps commander, Middleton, send infantry, heavy artillery, and engineer units to his aid. Unfortunately again for Grow, most of the supporting units he needed from the VIII Corps remained engaged in trying to capture the port of St. Malo. On the evening of August 12, Grow received orders to contain Brest with one element of his division and send the rest to Lorient and Vannes to relieve the 4th Armored Division. Grow completed the relief at Lorient and Vannes on August 14.

After the capture of St. Malo, most of Middleton's VIII Corps moved to capture Brest on August 25. Despite an impressive amount of Allied support from the air, Brest did not surrender until September 20, 1944. By the time of its capture, the port facilities had suffered so much damage they were beyond any hope of immediate repair. It took almost fifty thousand troops to subdue the approximately seventy-five German strong points that made up Brest's defenses. American casualties totaled almost ten thousand men.

Why the U.S. Army devoted so much time and effort in trying to capture a port that they knew the Germans would destroy before it was allowed to fall into their hands remains unclear. Many historians and writers point out that the men and equipment involved in trying to capture Brest in September 1944 would have been much more useful in Patton's eastward advance. At the time, Bradley told Patton that success in the battle at Brest was important to the prestige of the army, and therefore, Brest had to fall at all costs. Patton later wrote, "We both [Bradley and Patton] felt that the taking of Brest at that time was useless, because it was too far away and the harbor was badly destroyed. On the other hand, we agreed that, when the American Army had once put its hands to the plow, it should not let go. Therefore, it was necessary to take Brest." Many others suggest that the battle for Brest had more to do with the strategic inflexibility of both Eisenhower and Bradley in pursuing the preinvasion plans despite ever-changing circumstances.

Two American M4 Sherman tanks; on the left is an M4A1 with a cast armored hull and on the right is an M4(105) with a welded armored hull. The opening American attack on the port of Brest took place on August 25, 1944. Over fifty thousand American soldiers would take part in the capture of Brest, and over ten thousand became casualties in the process. *National Archives*

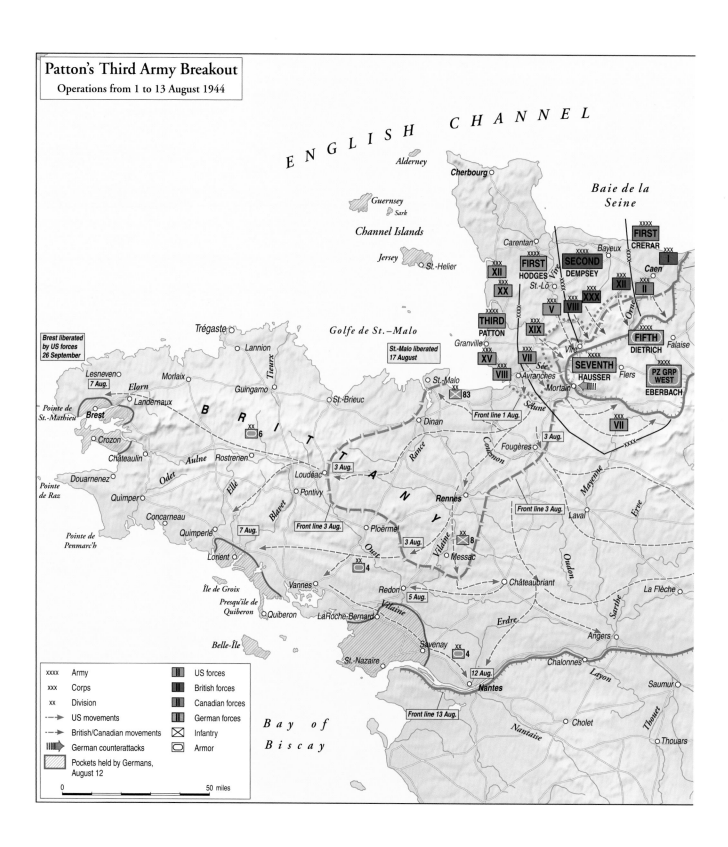

Patton's Third Army Breakout
Operations from 1 to 13 August 1944

ENGLISH CHANNEL

Alderney

Cherbourg

Guernsey
Sark

Channel Islands

Jersey

St.-Helier

Baie de la Seine

Carentan

Bayeux

FIRST CRERAR

FIRST HODGES

SECOND DEMPSEY

Caen

XII

St.-Lô

XII

I

XX

V

XXX

II

VIII

Trégaste

Golfe de St.–Malo

THIRD PATTON

XIX

Granville

FIFTH DIETRICH

Falaise

Brest liberated by US forces 26 September

Lannion

St.-Malo liberated 17 August

Morlaix

Tréeurx

Guingamo

St.-Brieuc

XV

VII

Sée

SEVENTH HAUSSER

Vire

Flers

PZ GRP WEST EBERBACH

Lesneven **7 Aug.**

Elorn

Landernaux

Avranches

Mortain

VII

Pointe de St.-Mathieu

Brest

Dinan

Sélune

Front line 1 Aug.

Crozon

B R I T T A N Y

XX **6**

St.-Malo

83

3 Aug.

Châteaulin

Aulne

Rostrenen

Rance

Couesnon

Fougères

3 Aug.

Pointe de Raz

Douarnenez

3 Aug.

Loudéac

Mayenne

Quimper

Élle

Pontivy

Rennes

Laval

Front line 3 Aug.

Blavet

Front line 3 Aug.

Concarneau

7 Aug.

Ploërmel

XX **8**

Erve

Quimperlé

Oust

Vilaine

Messac

Oudon

Sarthe

XX **4**

La Flèche

Lorient

Île de Groix

Vannes

Redon

5 Aug.

Châteaubriant

Erdre

Angers

Presqu'île de Quiberon

Quiberon

LaRoche-Bernard

Vilaine

Chalonnes

Saumur

Belle-Île

Savenay

Layon

St.-Nazaire

XX **4**

12 Aug.

Bay of Biscay

Nantes

Front line 13 Aug.

Nantaise

Cholet

Thouet

Thouars

xxxx	Army	
xxx	Corps	
xx	Division	
US movements		
British/Canadian movements		
German counterattacks		
Pockets held by Germans, August 12		

US forces	
British forces	
Canadian forces	
German forces	
Infantry	
Armor	

0   50 miles

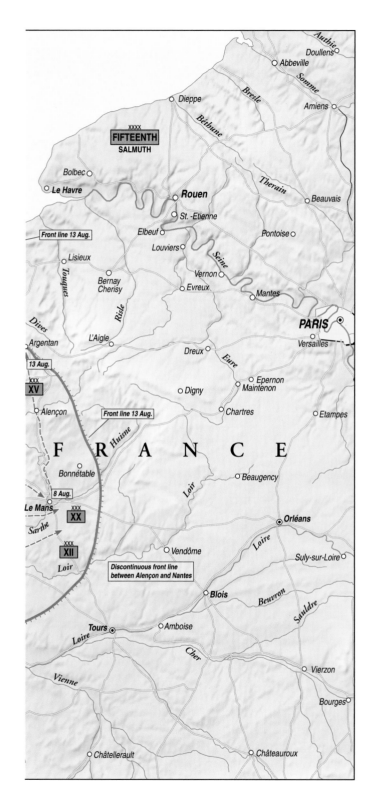

Flamethrowers, like this M1A1, were used at Brest by the U.S. Army. Brest didn't fall to VIII Corps of the Third Army until September 19, 1944. A major problem, which delayed the capture of the port, was a lack of all types of supplies, especially artillery ammunition. *National Archives*

THE REST OF THIRD ARMY COMES ON LINE

Even as the armored divisions of Middleton's VIII Corps plunged deeper into Brittany, the remaining three corps of Patton's Third Army began to line up to go into action. The first of Patton's other corps to go into action was Maj. Gen. Wade H. Haislip's XV Corps.

The XV Corps arrived in Normandy in mid-July. In the original invasion plans, XV Corps would have assisted Middleton's VIII Corps in overrunning Brittany. As it became clear to American military leaders that only a single corps needed to be in Brittany, the deployment of Haislip's XV Corps remained uncertain. Even the question of what divisions were going to become part of the corps remained up in the air. At the last moment, the corps received the 5th Armored Division and the 83rd and 90th Infantry Divisions. The 5th Armored Division, commanded by Maj. Gen. Lunsford E. Oliver, had just arrived in Normandy, while the infantry divisions came from Hodges's First Army. All three divisions went into action an hour before midnight on August 1.

PATTON'S THOUGHTS ON TANK RECONNAISSANCE

MANY TANKS are lost through the failure of the crews or the platoon leader to make foot reconnaissance. People get vehicle bound and never dismount. Before exposing a valuable tank and the lives of its crew to the danger of destruction by crossing an un-reconnoitered skyline or on emerging from cover, a foot reconnaissance with glasses should be made. Here again we have the question of haste and speed. It may seem a waste of time to take a look, but it is certain death to get on the front slope within effective range of undiscovered antitank guns or lurking enemy tanks.

—*The Unknown Patton,*
"Letter of Instruction No. 3"

The initial combat goal of Haislip's XV Corps was to establish a large protective barrier around the narrow Avranches bottleneck. If the Germans decided to counterattack the Third Army breakout, Avranches would be the logical target. By capturing Avranches, German forces could cut off supply lines to Middleton's VIII Corps. To prevent this, Haislip's XV Corps advanced in a southeastern direction fifteen miles out of Avranches to the town of St. Hilaire-du-Harcouet, where it took up a position between Middleton's VIII Corps and Hodges's First Army VII Corps on August 2. To further secure Third Army's flank, the 106th Mechanized Cavalry Group captured the town of Forgeres on August 3.

The German forces opposite Hodges's First Army continued to fight with a strong determination. In contrast, the German forces facing Patton's Third Army continued to fall apart. A large gap appeared in front of Haislip's XV Corps. Patton, as well as the other Allied military leaders, began to see a golden opportunity for an eastward breakout into central France. This new interest in a quick eastward advance differed sharply from the Allied preinvasion plans. In those plans, the Allies had not even considered an eastward advance into central France until the Breton ports were in American hands. With new opportunities presenting themselves, the importance of seizing the Breton ports steadily diminished throughout the month of August.

Patton set up Third Army headquarters in Beauchamps, eleven miles north of Avranches, on August 2. The Luftwaffe managed to bomb the headquarters on the night of August 6, but caused no casualties. At the time, the news blackout ordered by Eisenhower on the arrival of Patton's Third Army in France was still in effect. It was finally lifted on August 15, during a press conference given by Eisenhower. By that time, the Germans were well aware of Patton's arrival.

A German soldier who fell to American firepower lies in his death throes.
National Archives

PATTON'S XX CORPS IN ACTION

The Allied leaders formulated plans for an eastward advance toward Paris. At the same time, Patton's Third Army received new assignments that included securing a sixty-mile stretch of terrain and bridges along the Mayenne River, which oriented along a north-south axis. Patton also had to protect his right flank along the Loire River, which oriented along an east-west axis. To complete these assignments, Patton brought the XX Corps, commanded by Lt. Gen. Walton H. Walker, into line on August 6. The corps originally consisted of the 5th and 35th Infantry Divisions, plus the Free French 2nd Armored Division, commanded by Maj. Gen. Jacques Philippe Leclerc; the Americans had helped organize, equip, and train the French division.

An American minesweeper team works its way down a street. The first task of XV Corps was to capture St. Hilaire-du-Harcouet, located fifteen miles southeast of Avranches. Capturing this town would widen the Avranches corridor and enable XV Corps to provide a blocking position east of the corridor in conjunction with the VII Corps Hodges's First Army. *National Archives*

An American soldier compares a German bazooka, nicknamed the Panzerschreck ("tank terror"), on the left with an American 2.36-inch M1A1 bazooka on the right. *National Archives*

PATTON'S THOUGHTS ON INFANTRY IN COMBAT

INFANTRY MUST move in order to close with the enemy. It must shoot in order to move. When physical targets are not visible, the fire of all infantry weapons must search the area probably occupied by the enemy. Use marching fire. It reduces the accuracy of his fire and increases our confidence. Shoot short. Ricochets make nastier sounds and wounds. To halt under fire is folly. To halt under fire and not fire back is suicide. Move forward out of the fire. Officers must set the example.

—*War As I Knew It*,
"Letter of Instruction No. 2"

Patton received a strong warning from his senior intelligence officer that there were enough German forces on the opposite side of the Loire River to mount a serious counterattack if the opportunity presented itself. Walker's XX Corps did not have enough forces to adequately guard the entire Loire River flank. Patton, therefore, decided to use the pilots and planes of Weyland's XIX Tactical Air Command to guard the Loire River flank. Planes from the XIX TAC accomplished the job by flying armed reconnaissance missions south of the Loire River throughout the month of August. No threat of a German counterattack ever appeared along the Loire River flank during that month. Patton would later describe the relationship between Weyland's XIX TAC and his Third Army as "love at first sight."

Haislip's XV Corps began its advance on the Mayenne River thirty miles from St. Hilaire-du-Harcouet on August 5. At about a hundred feet wide and five feet deep, the river itself was a serious obstacle. All the bridges except one, at the town of Mayenne, were in ruins. If that bridge fell intact to Haislip's XV Corps, the corps could move on to capture the town of Laval. The loss of Laval would be a serious blow to the Germans, threatening Le Mans and Alencon, both important German communications and supply centers. Knowing that the fighting during the next few days might be decisive for the entire western European campaign, Haislip urged his commanders "to push all personnel to the limits of human endurance."

American soldiers plan their next target at an artillery command post. Even as VIII Corps headed into Brittany, the American senior military leadership felt that the southeastern pressure of elements of XV Corps against weak German resistance was opening a door to bigger things than Operation Overlord originally envisioned. *National Archives*

A German Tiger E tank heads toward the front lines. The weak and disorganized German resistance in front of XV Corps at the end of Operation Cobra contrasted sharply with the strong and determined German resistance still faced by Hodges's First Army. *National Archives*

An American M10 tank destroyer works its way through rubble. The original Operation Overlord plans stated that the American armies in Normandy could not head eastward toward the Seine River and Paris until all the Breton ports had been seized. Bradley changed the plan on August 3, 1944, informing the American forces in Normandy that their main mission now lay eastward. *National Archives*

Elements of Haislip's fast-moving XV Corps reached the Mayenne River by noon on August 5. They found the bridge at Mayenne intact. Brushing aside minor German resistance, the American troops quickly captured both the bridge and town. Other elements of XV Corps also reached the Mayenne River on August 5, crossing it on bridges built by its engineers. On August 6, XV Corps elements captured Laval. Even before the town's capture, Patton received permission from Bradley to send the XV Corps on to Le Mans. To reach it, the corps would have to pass through forty-five miles of highly defensible terrain and cross a major river. Without missing a beat, Haislip captured Le Mans on August 8, with only very light casualties. In the four days it took XV Corps to advance the seventy-five miles from St. Hilaire-du-Harcouet to Le Mans, it captured over seven thousand enemy prisoners and frustrated German plans to organize strong defensive positions at both Laval and Le Mans.

An American team in charge of a M2 4.2-inch mortar turns away from the launch blast as they attack enemy positions. *National Archives*

On August 12, Patton brought into line the last of Third Army's four corps: the XII Corps, commanded by Maj. Gen. Gilbert R. Cook. Seven days later, because of Cook's health, Patton replaced him with Maj. Gen. Manton S. Eddy. Patton attached 4th Armored Division and 35th Infantry Division to the newly arrived corps and assigned it the job of protecting Third Army's southern flank.

THE GERMAN COUNTERATTACK

The staff officers of Bradley's 12th Army Group began planning the next advance. Bradley knew from the ULTRA reports that the Germans were planning a counterattack aimed at Avranches. In the early morning hours of August 7, the commander of the German Seventh Army, *Generalfeldmarschall* (Field Marshal) Guenther von Kluge, launched the counterattack to regain Avranches and to reestablish German defensive lines in Normandy. Hitler saw it as a last chance to throw the Allies back toward the sea. Unfortunately for Hitler, none of his field commanders shared his conviction. Most felt the counterattack was doomed to failure before it began.

The German counterattack forces consisted of four understrength armored divisions with about 150 tanks. The division included the German army's 2nd and 116th Panzer Divisions and the 1st and 2nd Waffen SS Panzer Divisions. One of their most important targets was the small town of Mortain. If Mortain fell into German hands, the Germans could then sweep westward on to Avranches, roughly ten miles away. In the official history of the U.S. Army in World War II, this German operation became known as the Mortain Counterattack.

Patton, like Bradley, had received advance warning of the German counterattack through ULTRA. Prior to that moment, Patton had little interest in or knowledge of the information that ULTRA could provide about German military intentions. Despite the advance warning about a possible German counterattack, Patton originally believed the German effort was only a ruse designed to cover a withdrawal. After the counterattack, Patton insisted on an ULTRA briefing every morning.

As the size of the German counterattack became more apparent to Patton, he quickly realized that it could pose a threat to the narrow Avranches corridor through which all Third Army supplies flowed. He directed Walker's XX Corps to divert some forces from its planned

PATTON'S THOUGHTS ON TANK DESTROYERS

TANK DESTROYER units must be emplaced sufficiently forward to prevent enemy tanks from over running the infantry. There is a prevalent and erroneous idea, particularly in the case of self propelled tank destroyer units, that they should be held in reserve far to the rear. In such a position they will be impotent to get to the front in time to stop a tank attack before it has penetrated the infantry lines.

—*The Unknown Patton,*
"Letter of Instruction No. 3"

American soldiers take down a captured German flag. Bradley's new eastward advancing strategy envisioned the possibility of swinging the Allied right flank (Patton's Third Army) around toward Paris and trapping all the German forces west of the Seine River and destroying them. *National Archives*

American soldiers fire at enemy positions from behind limited cover. Between August 5 and August 9, 1944, XV Corps advanced eastward seventy-five miles to Le Mans. At that point, Bradley and Patton decided to send XV Corps northward behind the German forces in Normandy. *National Archives*

move south and rush those forces to the threatened area to assist the First Army in halting the German counterattack. At this time, XX Corps was already on the move with 5th Infantry Division, located some eight miles south of Vitre, and the remainder of the corps was near St. Hilaire-du-Harcouet. Walker immediately decided to use those elements nearest the threat: the 35th Infantry Division. At the same time, the Free French 2nd Armored Division was ordered to send a task force to guard the bridge at St. Hilaire-du-Harcouet. As the 35th Infantry Division moved northward to help stop the German counterattack, a part of Walker's XX Corps headquarters was moving southward to Vitre to establish an advanced command post.

Upon arriving in Vitre, General Hugh J. Gaffey, the chief of staff of Patton's Third Army, informed Walker's XX Corps headquarters of the developments and of their general's decision to use the forces remaining in the vicinity of St. Hilaire-du-Harcouet. Gaffey also directed that the corps attack to the south, toward Angers and Nantes, with the 5th Infantry Division now at Vitre. Walker's XX Corps captured Angers on August 10, thus effectively guarding the southern flank of Haislip's XV Corps during the latter's advance.

Walker's XX Corps now had two important jobs. The first was to protect the Avranches corridor against the German counterattack, now in full force; the second was to continue the drive to the south. Thus, during its first major action, Walker's XX Corps was creating military history by fighting on two fronts separated by some seventy-five miles. Hodges's First Army recaptured Mortain from the Germans on August 12. The retreating German armored divisions left more than one hundred of their destroyed and abandoned tanks in the area around Mortain at the close of the battle.

American troops look over the bodies of dead German soldiers collected together after a battle. *National Archives*

A French armored division manning American M4A2 Sherman medium tanks fills an assembly area. The XX Corps of Patton's Third Army included the 5th and 6th Infantry Divisions, as well as the Free French 2nd Armored Division, which had been trained and equipped by the U.S. Army. *National Archives*

A lightly camouflaged German Panther Ausf. A medium tank hides along a hedgerow. At the beginning of August 1944, the Germans began organizing an attack aimed at taking the town of Mortain and then advancing on to Avranches and cutting off Patton's VIII Corps in Brittany. *National Archives*

Bradley was so confident in his ability to contain the German advance toward Avranches that he wrote, on August 8, that the Mortain counterattack "had apparently been contained." As he studied his maps, Bradley quickly concluded that the Germans made a serious tactical mistake. By sending the mass of their armored forces into the area southwest of Falaise, they gave the British and American armies an opportunity to trap them between the towns of Falaise and Argentan, an area history would record as the Falaise Gap. Bradley knew if he could successfully close this gap, the 150,000 men of the German Seventh Army and Fifth Panzer Army (formerly known as Panzer Group West) would be trapped. With the approval of Eisenhower and Montgomery, he decided to change the planned eastward drive of Patton's Third Army into a northeastern advance to take advantage of the German blunder.

Americans troops recover a destroyed German Panther Ausf. A medium tank from the battlefield. While the tank-heavy German forces of the Mortain counteroffensive made some progress on the morning of August 7, Allied airpower soon made an appearance and caused heavy losses among the German tanks. *National Archives*

A Panzer IV medium tank radioman waits for the order that will send his vehicle into combat. Behind the radioman (located in the vehicle's front hull) is the vehicle commander in the turret cupola. Both men wear black panzer uniforms and radio headsets with throat microphones. *Patton Museum*

On August 9, Eisenhower wrote a letter to Chief of Staff of the Army and Chairman of the Joint Chiefs of Staff Committee, Gen. George C. Marshall, describing the change in plans. In the letter, he explained, "Patton has the marching wing which will turn in rather sharply to the northeast from the general vicinity of Le Mans and just to the west thereof marching toward Alencon and Falaise. The enemy's bitter resistance and counterattack in the area between Mortain and south of Caen makes it appear that we have a good chance to encircle and destroy a lot of his forces."

An American Jeep burns in a rubble-strewn street. The Americans managed to contain the German Mortain counteroffensive, stopping it two miles short of Avranches with the help of Allied ground-attack aircraft. Bradley organized counterattacks along the flanks of the German advance. *National Archives*

An American soldier fires his Browning Automatic Rifle. The German forces that took part in the Mortain counteroffensive took serious losses in men and equipment and by August 13, 1944, were driven out of the ground they had taken. *National Archives*

American engineers erect a portable treadway bridge. By August 25, 1944, XII Corps and XX Corps of Third Army had between them four bridges across the Seine, south of Paris. *National Archives*

4

THIRD ARMY'S ADVANCE CONTINUES

★ ★ ★ ★ ★

PRIOR TO PATTON LAUNCHING HAISLIP'S XV Corps in a northeastern direction to encircle the German Seventh Army and Fifth Panzer Army, the Canadian First Army, under the command of Lt. Gen. Henry D. G. Crerar and located north of the Germans, began a southward advance on August 8, a day after the German launched their Mortain counterattack. Crerar had planned the Canadian attack a week prior to the German operation, so the timing of the Canadian attack had nothing to do with the Mortain counterattack.

The Canadian First Army had come into existence on August 1. Half the army consisted of British troops, and it included a British-trained and -equipped Polish armored division. The Canadian advance consisted of six hundred tanks heading from Caen toward Falaise, twenty-one miles southeast. If the Canadians captured Falaise quickly, they could move on to seize Argentan. Canadian success in securing these two towns would have made unnecessary the northeastern advance of Haislip's XV Corps.

Patton's XV Corps reached its assigned goals far ahead of the Canadian First Army. Facing stiff German resistance, the Canadian tanks halted eight miles short of Falaise on August 9. They proved unable to restart their advance until August 14 and did not reach Falaise until the evening of August 16. When the Canadians finally secured Falaise, a fifteen-mile gap, which became known as the

While the terrain for the August 8, 1944, Canadian attack on the Germans was favorable for employing large armored formations, the German defenders fought hard for every mile, using a combination of self-propelled antitank guns, like this Sd.Kfz. 167 StuG IV (assault gun/tank destroyer), as well as towed antitank guns. *National Archives*

A British soldier hunkers down in the coverage provided by the wreckage of a building. *National Archives*

Falaise Gap or Falaise Pocket, still remained between them and Patton's troops located south of Argentan.

Haislip's XV Corps set off from Le Mans toward Alencon on August 10. To increase the striking power of the advance, Patton transferred Leclerc's Free French 2nd Armored Division from Walker's XX Corps to Haislip's XV Corps. Patton ordered Haislip to lead his advance to Alencon with his two armored divisions. Alencon fell on August 12. With its capture, Haislip's XV Corps had a clear shot at capturing the town of Argentan, which lay roughly twenty miles north of Alencon. At either Argentan or Falaise, Haislip's XV Corps could link up with the Canadian First Army and complete the encirclement of the German Seventh Army and the Fifth Panzer Army. Meanwhile, the British Second Army and Hodges's First Army would continue attacking along the westward front of the German forces. On the night of August 12, 5th Armored Division managed to reach the outskirts of Argentan, an important transportation and supply center for the Germans.

Kluge, the German Seventh Army commander, easily figured out what was happening. He frantically sought permission from Hitler's headquarters to make a short, sharp armored thrust at Patton's forces. But Hitler wanted to know only if Kluge could continue

Canadian soldiers inspect a disabled German Panther Ausf. D medium tank. In August 1944, while the Germans were attacking westward during the Mortain counterattack, the Canadian First Army attacked southeast toward Falaise on August 8 and cut off the Germans from the rear. *George Bradford collection*

While it was rare for American soldiers to engage in hand-to-hand combat with the enemy, it was not unheard of, as can be seen in this picture of the bodies of an American soldier (a military censor has blocked out his face) and a German soldier who killed each other with their bayonets. *National Archives*

A German armored half-track, designated the Sd.Kfz. 251 Ausf. D, burns along the roadside. By August 8, 1944, Bradley, like Montgomery, was convinced that the German Mortain counterattack could be contained and had opened the door for the German armies in Normandy to be encircled by the British and Canadians from the north and the Americans from the south. *National Archives*

PATTON'S THOUGHTS ON THE USE OF THE BAZOOKA

THE PURPOSE of the Bazooka is not to hunt tanks offensively, but to be used as the last resort in keeping tanks from over-running infantry. Since the Bazooka is unarmored, and always discloses its position when fired, it must get a hit on the first shot. To insure this, the range should be held to around 30 yards. When thus used, the Bazooka will hit and penetrate any tank that I have seen and will probably stop it. If used at longer ranges, it will probably miss and its operators will then become targets for the tank's machine guns.

—*The Unknown Patton,*
"Letter of Instruction No. 3"

his counterattack toward Avranches from Mortain. On the morning of August 11, Hitler received information that another strike at Avranches was no longer feasible. He also received an ultimatum from Kluge, stating that unless a strong attack began immediately against Patton's advancing forces, his army would be cut off and unable to withdraw from its current positions. Hitler finally gave his approval for a counterattack against Haislip's fast-advancing XV Corps on the evening of August 11. To assist in the counterattack, Hitler also granted permission for the Seventh Army to withdraw its forces eastward from Mortain. Despite their best efforts, the Germans could not muster enough men or equipment to conduct an attack large enough to stop XV Corps.

On August 13, Kluge officially canceled the planned counterattack. The remaining German resources would try to maintain a defensive line against the advancing XV Corps. On the same day, *General der Panzertruppen* (Lieutenant General) Josef ("Sepp") Dietrich, the commander of the Fifth Panzer Army, informed Hitler's headquarters, "If every effort is not made to move the forces toward the east and out of the threatened encirclement, the army group will have to write off both armies. Within a short time, resupplying the troops with ammunition and fuel will no longer be possible. Therefore, immediate measures are necessary to move to the east before such movement is definitely too late. It will soon be possible for the enemy to fire into the pocket with artillery from all sides."

An American M-10 tank destroyer carries passengers at high speed. To further his aim of encircling the German armies in Normandy, Bradley decided that 12th Army Group, which included Hodges's First Army and Patton's Third Army, would turn northward, instead of toward the east, and head toward the towns of Flers and Argentan. *National Archives*

In Bradley's plan to close a trap around the Germans in Normandy, the American First and Third Armies would act as the southern jaws of a vise, while the armies of Montgomery's 21st Army Group, approaching the same line from the north, would form the other half of the jaw. Many M4A3 Shermans would be knocked out along the way. *Patton Museum*

An American soldier poses in a captured German Sd.Kfz. 2 Kleines Kettenrad. As Bradley activated his plan to encircle German forces in Normandy in August 1944, he had Patton turn Haslip's XV Corps northward from the town of Le Mans and gave him another division for the job. He had Hodges's take his VII and XIX Corps and wipe out the German salient that had come about from the Germans' Mortain counterattack. *National Archives*

Two destroyed American M4 Sherman medium tanks have been pushed to the sides of the road to make room for traffic. Everybody knew that once the German armies in Normandy became aware of the jaws of the trap closing behind them, the Allies could either expect counterattacks by German forces from the east or by the German force within the trap and trying to flee eastward. *National Archives*

On the morning of August 13, the 5th Armored Division tried to advance north to Falaise by driving around Argentan. It quickly ran into heavy German fire from the high ground north of the town and made no progress. That afternoon, a patrol from the Free French 2nd Armored Division managed to briefly enter Argentan before German tanks forced it to retreat. Exhausted, the German defenders braced themselves for the next attack, knowing they might be unable to stop Patton's tanks. To the utter bewilderment of the German troops, the Americans did not attack.

Unknown to the Germans, a surprising order from Bradley had arrived at Haislip's XV Corps headquarters in the early afternoon, stating that the corps must stop its northward advance toward Falaise. It also ordered that any elements of the corps "in the vicinity of Falaise or to the north of Argentan" were to withdraw.

American soldiers enter Argentan. As part of Bradley's August 1994 plan to trap the Germans in Normandy, Montgomery and Bradley anticipated that their forces could meet south of Argentan to close the vise around the German forces to their west. As events unfolded, Patton's Third Army, part of Bradley's forces, reached Argentan before the Canadian First Army, part of Montgomery's forces, which couldn't make it past Falaise. *National Archives*

German prisoners are held under guard. Haislip's XV Corps reached the outskirts of Argentan on August 13. Surprisingly, Bradley told the corps to halt its advance northward toward Falaise and prepare to head eastward once again. The Canadian First Army could not restart its advance toward Falaise until August 14 and did not take the town until August 16. *National Archives*

A wounded German soldier receives aid. When Bradley halted Haislip's XV Corps just south of Argentan on August 13, the Canadian First Army was still several miles north of Falaise. This left a twenty-five-mile unguarded gap that allowed a large number of Germans to flee eastward to safety, beginning on August 16. *National Archives*

PATTON IS ANGRY

Patton protested Bradley's order to no avail. Originally, he had not been in favor of Bradley's plan to close the Falaise Gap. Patton, like Montgomery, believed that a wider encirclement to the Seine River would be a more effective means of cutting off the German forces west of the river. However, once committed to Bradley's plan, Patton could not understand why the gap between his forces and those of the Canadian First Army was not going to be closed. He knew the Germans would employ this opening to withdraw their forces from the area west of the gap.

Beginning on the afternoon of August 16, anywhere from twenty thousand to forty thousand German troops (minus most of their heavy equipment) drove through the Falaise Gap. Losses among the fleeing German troops numbered roughly ten thousand men killed and another fifty thousand taken prisoner by the various Allied armies.

Bradley, in conjunction with Eisenhower, had decided for many different reasons that he did not want Haislip's XV Corps to continue its advance on to Falaise. One reason was the fear that Haislip's XV Corps would overrun the boundary lines of the Canadian First Army coming from the other direction. To the layman, the importance Bradley attached to preserving army group boundary lines seems misplaced. To the military minded, however, the establishment of boundary lines in wartime is crucial in preventing both confusion and friendly fire losses.

A German self-propelled rocket launcher, known as the Maultier, lies abandoned by retreating German soldiers. Bradley would provide a number of reasons why he decided to stop Patton's XV Corps at Argentan and failed to close the door on the German forces west of their location. Patton saw a great opportunity wasted, and most military historians now concur. *National Archives*

An American M4 Sherman medium tank gets its engine replaced. Even before the Falaise gap closed, three of Patton's four corps where racing eastward toward the Seine River to start an even larger envelopment of all the German forces west of the Seine. *National Archives*

Patton (center) with Hugh Gaffey, his chief of staff (left), and a special intelligence officer go over operations. A prime objective of Third Army's eastward advance was designated as the Paris-Orleans Gap, which the German forces west of the Seine might use as an escape path eastward. *Patton Museum*

Another important reason Bradley and Eisenhower halted the advance of Haislip's XV Corps was the corps' overextended position. Both long flanks of the XV Corps lay exposed to German counterattacks. Haislip had expressed his concern to Patton about this problem and received confirmation that it would be addressed. Patton planned to employ two newly arrived divisions of Walker's XX Corps to provide flank protection for the advance to Argentan and Falaise. Unfortunately, for different reasons, neither of the XX Corps' new divisions arrived in time.

Eisenhower and Bradley feared that once the German forces west of the Falaise Gap realized their dire predicament, they would turn eastward and overrun Haislip's XV Corps in order to escape through the gap.

An American soldier observes the damage to the lower front hull of an M4 Sherman tank that was struck by a German antitank weapon. The sandbags placed on the front hull of the tank clearly did little to protect the vehicle from destruction. *National Archives*

American soldiers prepare to erect a portable radio antenna. Third Army's capture of Orleans, Dreux, and Chartres placed Cook's XII Corps and Walker's XX Corps within striking distances of Paris, the most vital communication center in France. *National Archives*

PATTON'S THOUGHTS ON ARMORED INFANTRY

IN USING armored infantry we should remember that it is nothing but a form of cavalry; that is, it uses its vehicles [armored halftracks] to deploy and to ploy mounted, thus saving time and avoiding fatigue. It does not use its vehicles except very rarely, for mounted charges. This function is reserved to the tanks. Further, since armored infantry is always operating with its tank elements, it does not have to hold out an infantry reserve because tanks are available, either to exploit the success of the armored infantry or to cover mistakes. Armored infantry should make a violent attack using all its men and weapons.

—*The Unknown Patton,* *"Letter of Instruction No. 3"*

German paratroopers prepare to fire an 8cm (81mm) schwere Granatwerfer 34 heavy mortar model 1934. This weapon had a fearsome reputation among allied soldiers due to its accuracy and high rate of fire with a well-trained crew. *Patton Museum*

Patton wrote that Haislip's XV Corps could have completely closed the gap, saying "[T[his halt was a great mistake, as I was certain that we could have entered Falaise and I was not certain the British would."

On August 16, Montgomery finally phoned Bradley and suggested that Haislip's XV Corps and the Canadian First Army meet not somewhere between Argentan and Falaise, but seven miles northeast of Argentan. Since the XV Corps headquarters staff had already moved east toward the Seine River (on August 15) with the bulk of the corps, there remained nobody to direct the American part of the planned meeting. The American advance, therefore, did not begin until August 19. Halsip's XV Corps finally linked up with the Canadian First Army troops on August 20, and the Falaise Gap was not officially closed until August 25.

Patton (right) with Bradley (left) and Brig. Gen. Otto P. Weyland. Patton's dog, Willie, is in the foreground. Despite the Allies' misgivings about capturing Paris, the citizens of the city were tired of being occupied by the Germans and rose up in arms between August 19 and 23, 1944, in order to force the Allies to liberate the city. *Patton Museum*

A column of American M5 light tanks pass through a heavily damaged French town. Despite the importance of Paris, the Allied senior military leaders were concerned that the fighting necessary to drive the Germans from the historical city could destroy it. Some thought that it made more sense to bypass the city and encircle it, then wait for the city garrison to surrender. *National Archives*

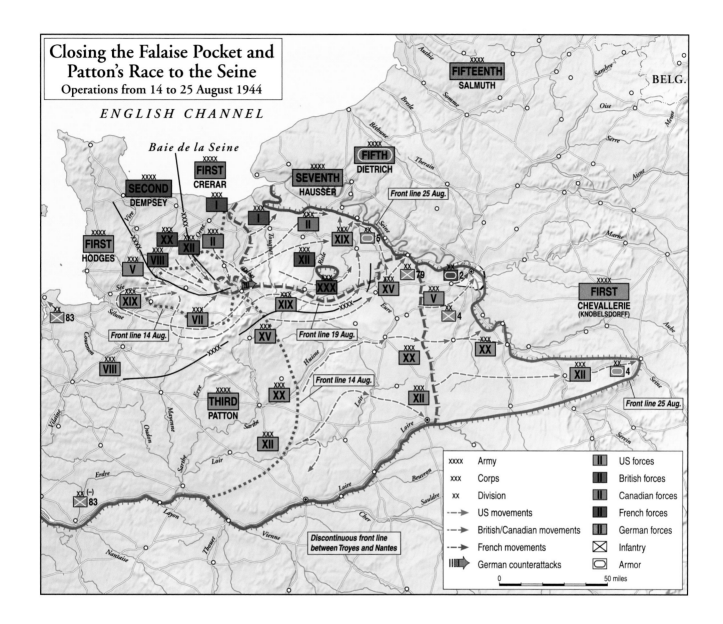

Closing the Falaise Pocket and Patton's Race to the Seine
Operations from 14 to 25 August 1944

ENGLISH CHANNEL

Baie de la Seine

BELG.

Legend:
- xxxx Army
- xxx Corps
- xx Division
- → US movements
- → British/Canadian movements
- → French movements
- German counterattacks
- US forces
- British forces
- Canadian forces
- French forces
- German forces
- Infantry
- Armor

Discontinuous front line between Troyes and Nantes

0 — 50 miles

PATTON'S DRIVE TO THE SEINE

Although ordered by Bradley to halt on August 13, Patton continued to lobby his boss to keep moving. Bradley's stand-fast order made little sense to the older general. To Patton, there existed only one tactical principle: "To use the means at hand to inflict the maximum amount of wounds, death, and destruction on the enemy in the minimum amount of time."

With Patton's prompting, Bradley issued new orders to Haislip's XV Corps on August 14, sending the 5th Armored Division and the 79th Infantry Division eastward in the direction of an area north of Paris along the Seine River. The Free French 2nd Armored Division and 90th Infantry Division remained behind in the Argentan area.

American troops do a bit of sightseeing in front of the Eiffel Tower after the liberation of Paris. Eisenhower sent the Free French 2nd Armored Division toward Paris along with American and British units on August 22, 1944. They reached the city on August 23, and the Germans surrendered the city on August 25. *National Archives*

With Haislip's XV Corps moving north of Paris to the Seine, Patton's Third Army would, in effect, be extending another trap around any German troops that managed to escape eastward out of the Falaise Gap. In addition, west of the Seine, Third Army could cut off any remaining German forces that where not trapped in the Falaise Gap. The Allies estimated, on August 19, that 75,000 German troops and 250 tanks could still be encircled west of the Seine River.

As Patton's various corps headed toward the Seine, the citizens of Paris rose up against their German oppressors. Knowing the Allied armies would head in the general direction of the city, French Resistance leaders inside Paris radioed for help before the Germans could destroy the city. Facing incredible political pressure to liberate Paris, Eisenhower gave permission for the Free French 2nd Armored Division to capture the city. In its advance, the French armored division had support from various First Army units, as well as a contingent of British troops. The German commander of Paris surrendered the city on August 25.

On its advance to the Seine River, Haislip's XV Corps met only minor German resistance, which so encouraged Bradley that he gave permission for the 79th Infantry Division to cross the Seine River on August 19. The division built a temporary Bailey bridge across the river, and the bridge opened to traffic on August 23. At the same time, the 5th Armored Division drove up the western bank of the Seine River, cutting German escape routes.

Free French soldiers gather at the foot of the Arc de Triomphe in Paris during ceremonies at the Tomb of the Unknown Soldier, following the liberation of the French capital. *National Archives*

The joy the French people felt for the Allies liberating their beloved city of Paris is clearly seen in this picture taken shortly after the German surrender. French woman have made dresses representing the United States, Great Britain, and the Soviet Union, as well as France. *National Archives*

The American 28th Infantry Division marches in a parade down the Champs-Élysées, in front of various Allied senior officers on August 29, 1944. The American presence in the French capital helped to restore civil order to the city. *National Archives*

Despite the best American efforts, the Germans managed to move twenty thousand men and some wheeled vehicles across the Seine River to its eastern bank between August 20 and 24, using ferries and boats. What the Germans could not save were their tanks. Of the roughly 2,300 tanks committed to battle west of the Seine River since the beginning of the Allied invasion in June, fewer than 120 managed to make it back to the east riverbank.

In the original Operation Overlord plans, the Allied armies planned to stop at the Seine River so they could reorganize and build up a supply base. Once reorganized, they would then continue their advance across France to the German border. This plan would be forgotten as an incredible spirit of optimism began to sweep through the higher ranks of the Allied armies.

With the 5th Armored Division pushing up the western bank of the Seine River, Bradley once again faced the problem of having to cross the boundary lines of Montgomery's 21st Army Group. Having learned a painful lesson from the failure to close the Falaise Gap, Bradley quickly asked and received Montgomery's permission to continue the 5th Armored Division's advance. On August 20, Montgomery reaffirmed his desire to push the Allied armies forward by issuing an order that cautioned "[t]his is no time to relax, or to sit back and

An American soldier takes the time to shave in his foxhole. Patton was always keen on the men of Third Army looking smart despite the rigors of war. The appearance of the M1 Carbine on the edge of the foxhole indicates that the soldier is probably serving in a rear area and not the front lines. *National Archives*

congratulate ourselves. Let us finish off the business in record time." On August 24, Bradley ordered Haislip's XV Corps transferred from Third Army to First Army command.

Before Bradley ordered part of Haislip's XV Corps eastward toward the Seine River on August 14, Patton had already ordered his other corps, Eddy's XII and Walker's XX, in the same general direction as Haislip's XV Corps, with the Seine River as their ultimate objective. The XII Corps consisted of the 4th Armored Division and the 35th Infantry Division. The XX Corps consisted of the 7th Armored Division, commanded by Maj. Gen. Lindsay M. Sylvester, and the 5th Infantry Division. Before reaching the Seine, both corps had to secure an intermediate objective known as the Paris-Orleans Gap.

The Paris-Orleans Gap lay between Paris on the Seine River and Orleans on the Loire River. It was the only land route available to the Germans that did not require the crossing of any major rivers or bridges. Allied airpower had already destroyed almost all the bridges across the Seine and Loire rivers. By securing the Paris-Orleans Gap, Third Army could deny the German Seventh Army and Fifth Panzer Army a possible escape route to southern France.

American soldiers inspect a German 88mm rocket projector, designated the Raketenwerfer 43. By crossing onto the eastern side of the Seine River, elements of Patton's Third Army could then advance along the river's banks and deny the Germans any crossing points over the Seine. *National Archives*

Not wasting time, Eddy's VII Corps captured Orleans on the night of August 16. Due to supply problems, Patton held Eddy's XII Corps at Orleans until August 21. The speed of XII Corps' advance prevented any German hopes of organizing a defense of the Paris-Orleans Gap.

To protect the southern flank, Patton again employed planes of Weyland's XIX TAC to patrol on the southern side of the Loire River and watch for any signs of German counterattacks. This use of tactical airpower in the classical cavalry screening role was one of Patton's brilliant innovations. As an added measure of security, Patton ordered Eddy's XII Corps to clear the northern bank of the Loire River and destroy any remaining bridges. On the evening of August 25, elements of XII Corps crossed the Seine River near the city of Troyes.

Walker's XX Corps, located north of Eddy's XII Corps and south of Haislip's XV Corps, received orders from Patton on August 14 to capture the city of Chartres, which lay directly in the center of the Paris-Orleans Gap. It had a population of forty thousand people and the nickname "the Gateway to Paris." The 7th Armored Division reached the outskirts of the city on

British infantrymen on the move. On August 20, 1944, Montgomery sent elements of his 21st Army Group eastward to cross the Seine with the same intention as Patton's Third Army: to trap German Normandy forces still located on the western side of the Seine River. *National Archives*

On August 20, 1944, Haislip's XV Corps of Patton's Third Army, with the 79th Infantry Division, established a bridgehead across the Seine River, north of Paris at Mantes-Gassicourt. Antiaircraft guns, like the 40mm automatic gun M1 pictured on an M2A1 carriage, were brought up to defend the portable treadway bridges XV Corps built. *National Archives*

OTTO PAUL WEYLAND

OTTO PAUL WEYLAND attended a civilian college, graduating with a degree in mechanical engineering in 1923. He later got his regular U.S. Army commission in the air service in 1924. He took flight training at Brooks and Kelly fields, Texas, and had his initial duty with the 12th Observation Squadron at Fort Sam Houston, Texas.

Promoted to first lieutenant in June 1930, he went to Hawaii as commanding officer of the 4th Observation Squadron. There he tried to promote a working relationship between the pilots and the ground troops by having his squadron take part in both ground-training exercises and coast artillery live-fire exercises.

Weyland returned to Kelly Field in November 1934 as instructor and in 1935 became chief of the observation section; he received a promotion to captain in March 1935. Weyland attended both the Air Corps Tactical School and the Army Command and General Staff School. His next duty was in Washington in June 1939 as assistant to the chief of the Aviation Division in the National Guard Bureau.

Weyland was promoted to major in March 1940 and to lieutenant colonel in December 1941. The latter promotion came while he was in Panama as commanding officer of the 16th Pursuit Group and chief of staff of the 6th Air Force. Weyland went on to be promoted to colonel in March 1942 and was back in Washington in June of that year as deputy director of air support at Headquarters Army Air Force. He achieved the rank of brigadier general in September 1943 and in November went to Europe as commanding general of the 84th Fighter Wing. Four months later, he became commanding general of the XIX Tactical Air Command (TAC). Under him, this combat unit gained fame for its air support of Patton's Third's Army in the successful drive across France.

By January 1945, Weyland had become a major general and finished the air war against Germany, participating in six major campaigns. Patton called him "the best damn General in the Air Corps."

National Archives

August 15. Early the next morning, the division raced into the heart of the city. Heavy fighting developed, and American armored infantrymen slugged it out with the tenacious students of a German air force antiaircraft training school. The corps' mechanized cavalry group swung around the town in an arc and prevented the escape of the German garrison.

Savage counterattacks drove the tankers and armored infantrymen of the 7th Armored Division back. Facing the loss of the newly liberated city, Walker quickly rushed elements of the 5th Infantry Division into Chartres. Large and still-organized German units fought from the woods south of Chartres and in the city itself. But despite their best efforts, the German garrison surrendered on August 19. Two days later, in a steady rain, Walker's XX Corps set out for the sixty-mile drive to the Seine.

PATTON'S THOUGHTS ON ANTITANK MINES

THE EFFECT of mines is largely mental. Not over 10 percent of our casualties come from them. When they are encountered, they must be passed through or around. There are not enough mines in the world to cover the whole country. It is cheaper to make a detour than to search; however, the engineers should start clearing the straight road while the advance elements continue via the detour. See that all types of troops have mine detectors and know how to use them. You must, repeat, must get through!

—*War As I Knew It, "Letter of Instruction No. 2"*

On reaching the Seine River the next day, Walker's XX Corps found the east bank of the river defended by over eighteen thousand German soldiers with a large number of artillery pieces. Documents taken from dead or captured enemy soldiers showed the Germans had hoped to delay or possibly hold the hard-charging XX Corps along the river. There was no other American bridgehead across the Seine River south of Paris. Despite repeated attempts, the 7th Armored Division could not push through the constant German artillery barrages. During the evening of August 22, air support bombed the German defensive positions.

Early next morning, Walker began a multipronged attack along the Seine River. In one area, American infantrymen crossed by either swimming or rowing abandoned boats across the river. The Germans quickly counterattacked the soldiers who made it to the shore. With the full support of corps artillery units, the American units managed to cling to their small bridgehead. In another area, two battalions of Walker's XX Corps swam and waded across a ford to rout the surprised German defenders on the east side of the river. Army engineers quickly built temporary bridges or employed small ferries to bring across additional troops and equipment.

On August 26, elements of the 5th Infantry Division swept along the west bank of the Seine River to capture the town of Nogent-sur-Seine from a German panzer grenadier division. Sadly, the bridge the division sought across the Seine River had been destroyed by the Germans prior to its arrival. In an all-night operation, the corps engineers erected a new bridge across the Seine River.

The German ground forces had over 400,000 men killed, wounded, or captured fighting in the west. More than 1,300 tanks, 20,000 other vehicles, 500 assault guns, and 1,500 field guns and heavier artillery pieces were captured or destroyed. The German air force also took a fearful beating. At least 2,370 planes were destroyed in the air and 1,167 on the ground.

American soldiers pose with a captured German MG34 machine gun. *National Archives*

THE DRIVE BEYOND THE SEINE

As Patton and Third Army crossed the Seine, Eisenhower began thinking about the future direction of the war. The Ruhr, the heart of Germany's industrial might, lay within striking distance from France and remained the Allies' primary objective. Berlin, the capital of Germany and an important political objective, lay too far east to make it practical as the next military objective.

Once Eisenhower decided that the Ruhr was his main target, he figured out which of four routes from northern France was the most suitable for his forces. Ruling out both the easily flooded flatlands of Flanders and the hilly woodlands of the Ardennes, Eisenhower chose to divide his forces into two mutually supportive groups for the advance. Due to fuel shortfalls, he also had to face the fact that the Allied logistical system could not fully support the simultaneous advance of both Montgomery's 21st Army Group and Bradley's 12th Army Group. Eisenhower decided, after much deliberation, that the main Allied effort would be with Montgomery's 21st Army Group. Montgomery's forces would advance in a northeasterly direction through the

An American M4A3(76)W HVSS Sherman medium tank armed with a 76mm main gun. To make up for the thin armor on the front of the vehicle's hull and turret, the crew of this tank has welded on additional armor plating that might have come from enemy tanks destroyed in battle. *Tank Museum, Bovington*

cities of Amiens, Manbeuge, and Liege along the northern edge of the Ardennes in Belgium. This route was both favorable to the advance of large military forces and the most direct route to the Ruhr. In such an advance, Montgomery's 21st Army Group would liberate both Belgium and parts of the Netherlands. The large and badly needed ports of Antwerp and Rotterdam would also fall into Allied hands. Most important, Montgomery's forces would overrun the German V-rocket sites. From these launching sites, Germany had unleashed its rocket weapons at England in large numbers, taking a heavy toll on British civilians and their morale.

The secondary Allied effort would consist of Bradley's 12th Army Group. The Ninth Army took on the job of capturing Brest and other French ports. The advance of the First and Third Armies also lay in a northeasterly direction, but kept to the south of the Ardennes in Belgium. The Third Army advance called for the capture of the French cities of Metz and Nancy before moving on to the Rhine River. The path to these cities was less favorable for an advance of a large military force than the route north of the Ardennes. It was also a far less direct route, since it did not lead directly to the Ruhr, but instead led to the Saar (Sarre) Basin, which had a much smaller industrial capacity than the Ruhr.

The crew of an American M16 antiaircraft half-track has their four .50-caliber machine guns at maximum elevation. *National Archives*

The very difficult decisions Eisenhower made about the future direction of the war managed to upset almost everyone. Montgomery felt that all the Allied forces should come under his command for one massive thrust into Germany. Eisenhower could not agree, since American public opinion would no longer allow the growing number of American armies to remain under British command. Eisenhower took over the job as commander of all Allied ground forces in Western Europe from Montgomery on September 1, although Montgomery retained command of 21st Army Group.

Despite Montgomery's partial demotion, both Bradley and Patton were livid over what they perceived as Eisenhower's decision to favor the British effort rather than the planned advance of Bradley's 12th Army Group. Patton was so upset that he tried to persuade Bradley that they should quit in protest of Eisenhower's decision. Bradley declined. Patton remained convinced that the threat of their resignations would have forced Eisenhower to change his mind. Since the invasion of North Africa in November 1942, Patton often voiced the opinion that Eisenhower favored the British more than his own people. At one point, Patton wrote, "Monty does what he pleases, and Ike says, 'Yes, Sir!'"

American soldiers pose with a 2.36-inch M1A1 bazooka and the M7A1 rocket it fired. *National Archives*

American engineers are laying railroad ties to rebuild the French railroad system. The Americans had expected to use the French railroad system to transport supplies from the Normandy beaches to forces inland, but the withdrawing Germans thwarted that plan by destroying the railroads. Patton and his Third Army's rip-roaring advance across France would slow down in late August 1944 when sufficient supplies could no longer be moved from the Normandy beaches to the front lines in a timely manner. *National Archives*

To replace the destroyed French locomotive fleet, the U.S. Army brought in replacement locomotives. *National Archives*

While Patton fumed over Eisenhower's decision, his Third Army's XII and XX Corps continued to enlarge their bridgeheads across the Seine River to favor Montgomery's advance. To flesh out his corps, he added an infantry division to each: the 80th went to the XII Corps, and the 90th went to the XX Corps. Patton's VIII Corps, still fighting in Brittany, was not available for the eastward drive.

On September 5, Middelton's VIII Corps became part of American Ninth Army under the command of Lt. Gen. William H. Simpson, but the 83rd Infantry Division and 6th Armored Division remained with Patton's Third Army. To make up for the loss of Middleton's VIII Corps, Bradley transferred Haislip's XV Corps headquarters from First Army back to Third Army control, but without any attached divisions. Bradley later sent the 79th and 90th Infantry Divisions, and the Free French 2nd Armored Division, to fill out the XV Corps. Due to the delay in receiving the divisions, the XV Corps did not become available for Patton's initial eastward advance. It did see action on the southern flank of Third Army from September 11 through September 20.

To reach Metz and Nancy, Third Army would have to first cross the Marne and Meuse rivers. Units of both Eddy's XII Corps and Walker's XX Corps crossed the Marne on August 28, in the face of weak German resistance. Eddy's corps breached the Meuse River three days later. Patton was now in position to attack toward the Moselle River and the French cities of Metz and Nancy. If these cities fell, Third Army would be barely one

The Red Ball Express trucking service ran twenty-four hours a day, seven days a week, along specially designated roads patrolled by military policemen. The "red ball" in "Red Ball Express" is an old railroad term for a priority freight train. *National Archives*

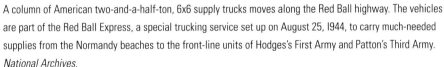

A column of American two-and-a-half-ton, 6x6 supply trucks moves along the Red Ball highway. The vehicles are part of the Red Ball Express, a special trucking service set up on August 25, 1944, to carry much-needed supplies from the Normandy beaches to the front-line units of Hodges's First Army and Patton's Third Army. *National Archives.*

hundred miles away from the Rhine. But to the chagrin of the bold commander, his tanks had no more fuel to continue the advance.

On August 30, Bradley's 12th Army Group informed Third Army that gasoline stocks were running low and that no additional fuel would be forthcoming until September 3. The lack of a strong logistical support system was finally catching up with Patton and his Third Army. To make matters worse, Eisenhower explained that all available fuel supplies would go to Montgomery's 21st Army Group until further notice. Eisenhower also informed Patton that he could not continue his advance until sufficient stocks of gasoline arrived.

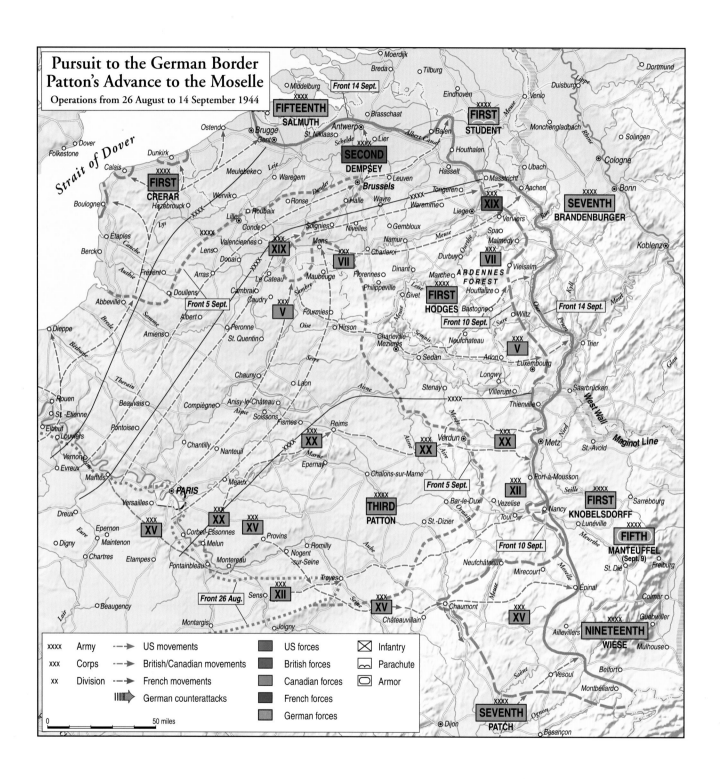

**Pursuit to the German Border
Patton's Advance to the Moselle**

Operations from 26 August to 14 September 1944

xxxx	Army	
xxx	Corps	
xx	Division	

- - → US movements
- - → British/Canadian movements
- - → French movements
⫸ German counterattacks

☐ US forces
☐ British forces
☐ Canadian forces
☐ French forces
☐ German forces

⊠ Infantry
⊡ Parachute
▭ Armor

0   50 miles

SUPPLYING THIRD ARMY

Third Army's problems with logistical support began with the turn eastward toward the Seine River on August 3. As the army chased the fleeing Germans across France, logistical considerations were subordinated to prospects of a quick victory. As a result, by the end of August, almost 90 percent of all the American supplies remained near the invasion beaches. Between these beachhead supply dumps and forward army depots (often a distance of three hundred miles), there were few stockpiles capable of supporting large units conducting sustained operations. The Allied advance was literally a victim of its own success, as even the most audacious logistics planners had failed to anticipate the tempo of the German withdrawal.

Patton would write of the serious nature of the Third Army fuel shortage:

"The 29th of August, 1944 was in my opinion, one of the critical days in this war. Hereafter pages will be written on it, or rather on the events which produced it. It was evident that at that time there were no real threats against us as long as we did not stop ourselves or allow ourselves to be stopped by imaginary enemies. Everything seemed rosy when suddenly it was reported to me that 140,000 gallons of gasoline which we were supposed to get for that day did not arrive. I presented my case for a rapid advance to the east for the purpose of cutting the Siegfried Line before it could be manned. It is my opinion that this was the momentous error of the war."

In their initial post-invasion plans, American commanders hoped to use the French railroad system to move supplies from the coast forward to their advancing armies. Unfortunately, the combination of American air attacks, sabotage by the French Resistance, and retreating Germans' destruction of the French railroad rendered the rail system almost completely useless, forcing logistical commanders to depend on trucks to supply the forward elements of the fast-moving Third Army. The commanders soon established a temporary long-distance highway system that came to be immortalized as the Red Ball Express.

Supplies for the U.S. Army at a liberated French port wait for transport to the front lines. Despite the best efforts of the Red Ball Express, Patton figured out on August 30 that his Third Army was barely getting a tenth of the fuel needed to keep its tanks and trucks moving. *National Archives*

Besides trucks, transport aircraft, such as the C-47, brought supplies to Third Army during August 1944. Despite the anxiety of many Third Army officers regarding the gasoline shortages, Patton remained optimistic that the fuel needed to keep his army running would turn up in time. *National Archives*

The Red Ball Express officially began on August 25 and lasted until November 15. Within five days of its inception, the Express reached its peak operational level, and 6,000 trucks delivered 12,342 tons of supplies to Third Army. Operating twenty-four hours a day, the truckers drove on special one-way roads that remained off-limits to all other military traffic. The roads themselves were marked with large red balls to guide the truck convoys to their drop-off points, so the truckers would not need to stop and check maps.

The most important item delivered in the early stages was gasoline. To supply enough trucks to keep the Red Ball Express rolling, many newly arrived combat troops, as well as units classified as nonessential (such as antiaircraft and heavy artillery), were stripped of their wheeled transports. In addition to the truck convoys, the Allies employed transport planes and converted bombers to move supplies forward to their various armies. Due to these planes' low tonnage capacity, a lack of support handling, and weather concerns, the amount of airlifted supplies remained fairly low.

A LUCKY BREAK FOR THE GERMANS

The Germans saw this logistically imposed pause in Third Army's lightning advance across France as a gift and quickly rushed in reinforcements to oppose any future Third Army attack. A very angry Patton wrote, "Eisenhower kept talking of the future Great Battle of Germany while we assured him that the Germans have nothing left to fight with and if we push on now, there will not be a Great Battle of Germany. . . . God deliver us from our friends. We can handle the enemy."

No one knew it yet, but the grand advance of Third Army across France, which had begun with Operation Cobra in late July, was at its end. Patton and Third Army would now face sixteen weeks of slow and bloody fighting in what military historians would refer to (unofficially) as the Lorraine Campaign. Lorraine was a French province located between the Moselle and Sarre rivers and bordering Belgium, Luxembourg, and Germany.

At the end of the war, Patton summarized his feelings about the halt of the Third Army advance: "[I] feel that had I been permitted to go all out, the war would have ended sooner and more lives would have been saved. Particularly I think this statement applies to the time when, early in September, we were halted, owning to the desire, or the necessity, on the part of General Eisenhower in backing Montgomery's move to the North. At the time there was no question of doubt that we could have gone through and across the Rhine within ten days."

Patton (left) meets with French general Henri Geraud. On August 30, 1944, Bradley's 12th Army Group informed Patton's Third Army that almost no gasoline supplies could be expected until at least September 3. *Patton Museum*

A camouflaged American M4A3 (105) Sherman medium tank armed with a 105mm howitzer waits for a fire mission. On August 31, 1944, Third Army received no fuel, even though Patton had requested four hundred thousand gallons. In response, Patton told his troops to keep moving forward until their vehicles ran out of gas. Then they should walk. *Patton Museum*

Fresh to the fight, American replacements disembark from the ship that brought them to Europe. *National Archives*

5

THE LORRAINE CAMPAIGN

★ ★ ★ ★ ★

ON SEPTEMBER 5, with gasoline once more flowing into Third Army's fuel tanks, Patton ordered Eddy's XII Corps and Walker's XX Corps into action. Eddy's XII Corps received the job of seizing the French city of Nancy, in the province of Lorraine, in preparation for an advance to the Rhine River. An important transportation center for both road and rail, Nancy lay thirty-five miles south of Metz, the provincial capitol. The 35th Infantry Division of the XII Corps was assigned to guard the southern flank of Third Army's advance until Haislip's XV Corps could arrive and once more serve in the ranks of Third Army.

At this point, Walker's XX Corps consisted of the 7th Armored Division and two infantry divisions, the 5th and 90th. Their main job involved crossing the Moselle River, and from there, the Sarre River, some thirty miles east of the Moselle. The two old fortified cities that formed the anchor position for the main German defensive line, Metz and Thionville, were to be intermediate objectives. The ultimate objective for Walker's XX Corps, like Eddy's XII Corps, remained the Rhine River, which historically separated Germany from its Western European neighbors.

On the eve of the attack, Patton (like his superiors) did not foresee any major German resistance. Patton himself expressed the opinion that the German forces in front of Third Army might make a stand at or in front of

From the window of a building, two American soldiers stand guard with their water-cooled .30-caliber 1917A1 Browning machine gun. *National Archives*

the Siegfried Line, the West Wall of German defenses, but he was confident his armor could breach the wall. Among the senior Allied military staff, many believed Patton would reach the Rhine River by the middle of December. On September 7, Patton told a group of Third Army correspondents, "I hope to go through the Siegfried Line like shit through a goose."

The lightning advance across France in August and the spectacle of a fleeing German military lulled the U.S. Army leaders into a false sense of superiority. The Germans still had a lot of fight left. Hitler began planning for a large-scale counterattack against Patton's Third Army as early as August 28.

Eisenhower (right) poses with Montgomery. On September 1, 1944, Eisenhower assumed direct operational command of all the Allied forces in northern France. He now oversaw both Bradley's 12th Army Group and Montgomery's 21st Army Group with a grand total of over two million men.
National Archives

In a series of meetings, Hitler instructed *Generalfeldmarschall* (Field Marshal) Walter Model, the German commander of the Western Front, to launch a large counterattack at the southern flank of Patton's Third Army as soon as possible. Hitler also told his commanders that he wanted the German armies to stand and hold in front of the West Wall at all costs.

Due to the static nature of the fighting on the western front, in September 1944, the German army began using land lines instead of radios for the majority of its communication needs. This change in German communication habits effectively robbed the Allies of ULTRA's valuable insights on many German plans. As a result, Allied ground operations made much less progress between September and December 1944 than they did in the period between July and August 1944, and Patton was unaware of the German buildup or plans to delay Third Army in the Lorraine sector.

Major General Manton S. Eddy, the XII Corps commander, ordered 80th Infantry Division to make a surprise crossing of the Moselle River north of Nancy on the morning of September 5. According to information provided by the local French resistance and cavalry patrols, the German defenders would be unable to put up much of a fight. In truth, the Germans were well aware of the XII Corps plans and had two strong panzer grenadier divisions deployed in the area. The Germans cut the 80th Infantry Division to pieces. By the next day, any American soldiers on the east bank of the Moselle River not killed or taken prisoner withdrew, and the attack was canceled.

PATTON'S THOUGHTS ON INFANTRY WEAPON USE

THE NECESSITY for using all weapons to their maximum fire capacity during our attacks cannot be too strongly impressed on the soldiers. Any gun that is not firing is not doing its job. In the assault where marching fire is used by the infantry, every gun, machine gun, and mortar must fire. Actual experiments have shown that using a relatively intense marching fire in an advance of over a thousand yards, that less than 35 rounds per rifle are actually expended. This is lower than would have been the case if we would have attempted to advance by rushes and taken three or four times as long reaching the enemy.

—*The Unknown Patton,*
"Letter of Instruction No. 3"

Two German half-track crews take a break in a French town. The vehicles were designated the Sd.Kfz. 250 Neu. Eisenhower's thirty-eight divisions were opposed in Western Europe by forty-one German divisions. However, none of the German divisions were at full strength. The ratio of combat effectives was approximately two to one in favor of the Allies. In tanks it was twenty to one. *Frank Schulz collection*

American soldiers inspect a P-47 Thunderbolt that made a surprisingly clean crash landing. The Western Allies enjoyed a great aircraft superiority over the Germans by September 1944, having over fourteen thousand in service compared to a German total of about six thousand for all theaters of operation. *National Archives*

An American M1 155mm howitzer crew fires from beneath their camouflage netting. Besides its roughly 90-mile-wide eastward advance, Patton's Third Army guarded 360 miles of the 629-mile-long Loire River, which marked the right flank of the Allied armies in northern France. *National Archives*

With his attack north of Nancy repelled, Eddy decided to make the area south of the city the site of the corps' main effort. He ordered the 35th Infantry Division and the 4th Armored Division to advance on Nancy from the south. However, due to the influence of Wood, the 4th Armored Division commander, Eddy modified his plans at the last minute. The 35th Infantry Division and the bulk of the 4th Armored Division still made the main effort south of Nancy, but the 80th Infantry Division also attempted another river crossing north of the city. Elements of the 4th Armored Division would stand by in reserve, ready to exploit an opportunity in either direction. If the northern crossing succeeded, Nancy would fall in a pincer movement.

JOHN SHIRLEY WOOD

COMMANDER OF the 4th Armored Division, John Shirley Wood was nicknamed "Tiger Jack" or "P" Wood. The first came from Wood's habit of nervously pacing like a caged animal. The "P," for "Professor," was a term of endearment acquired at West Point, where he spent much time tutoring his fellow cadets in their studies.

Wood trained his troops hard in the United States in order to turn them into a crack fighting unit. Before his division was shipped to England for eventual deployment to Western Europe, Wood informed his troops, "This division will attack and attack, and if an order is given to fall back, that order will not come from me."

That aggressive spirit was behind his refusal to pick an official nickname for the unit when doing so became the rage among the other divisions. Wood announced, "The 4th Armored Division will have no nickname. They shall be known by their deeds alone." This quote soon became the division's motto. The division did go on to acquire some unofficial nicknames, such as Patton's Best and the Name Enough Division.

The hard-charging Wood led from the front, as so many other great military leaders have throughout history. On one occasion, Wood was being flown over one of his units in a light observation plane during the breakout from the Normandy beachheads when the plane came across a small French town. Rather than wait for his men, Wood took it upon himself to march into the town under enemy fire. In the process, he single-handily captured a German soldier and found a path through a mined area. He then sent a note to his combat commander, ordering, "General Dager, send the infantry after me."

As the Germans tried to regroup their forces fast enough to stop the Allied breakout from the Normandy beachheads, Wood's division, under the oversight of Patton's Third Army command, kept them off balance and on the run. The division then sped across France until supply problems ground everything to a halt in October 1944. The head of the tactical air command that supported the Third Army noted that Wood frequently "out-Pattoned" Patton.

Patton himself praised Wood's division, saying, "The accomplishments of this division have never been equaled. And by that statement I do not mean in this war, I mean in the history of warfare. There has never been such a superb fighting organization as the 4th Armored Division."

Noted British military historian Liddell Hart said that Wood was "the Rommel of the American armored forces ... one of the most dynamic commanders of armor ... and the first in the Allied Armies to demonstrate in Europe ... the art ... of handling a mobile force."

Despite a sterling record of achievement during four months in combat, in early December 1944 Wood was relieved of his command and sent home. He was replaced by Patton's chief of staff of the Third Army, Maj. Gen. Hugh J. Gaffey.

The official reason was Wood's failing health, but most felt he was relieved for constantly disagreeing with his XII Corps commander, Maj. Gen. Manton S. Eddy. Eddy waged war in a methodical, thorough manner, while Wood was daring and took chances to achieve bigger goals. This was much like the problem Patton had with his superiors, who he felt played it safe rather than make bold battlefield decisions that might end the war sooner. *National Archives*

Soldiers hitch a ride on an American M4A3 (105) Sherman medium tank armed with a 105mm howitzer. On September 1, 1944, advance elements of the American Seventh Army, part of the 6th Army Group, which landed on the French Mediterranean coast on August 15, 1944, were within 175 miles of the southern flank of Patton's Third Army.
National Archives

On September 10, Bradley and Patton, working together, decided to undermine Eisenhower's decision to favor the northern advance of Montgomery's 21st Army Group. Their plan called for Patton to become so involved in operations across the Moselle River that Eisenhower would be unable to reduce their allotment of supplies for fear of an American military defeat.

On September 11, Bradley visited Eisenhower to inform him that Patton had just started to advance toward the Moselle. Bradley also told Eisenhower that if Patton's forces had not successfully crossed the Moselle by September 14, the advance would end. The next day Bradley wrote a message to Eisenhower in which he pleaded with him not to make any additional cuts in Patton's supply allotment. But Eisenhower quickly convinced Bradley that supporting Montgomery's northern advance was the logical decision. Patton was not swayed by Bradley's change of heart and asked him not to contact him until after dark on the September 19, so he could continue pushing his forces forward.

Patton inspects his troops in France. The American Seventh Army would link up with Patton's Third Army in mid-September 1944 and go on to form the right flank of the Allied armies in northern France. Its right flank would rest on the Swiss border. Switzerland was a neutral state during World War II.
National Archives

An American soldier dashes across a street exposed to enemy fire. In September 1944, Patton's Third Army began a series of operations against German forces in the Lorraine region of France. These operations lasted into early December 1944 and became unofficially known to the U.S. Army as the Lorraine Campaign.
National Archives

A young American officer holds a captured German Panzerfaust ("tank fist"), much feared by all Allied tankers. The Third Army began the advance into the Lorraine region of France with a strong feeling that the war in Europe was quickly nearing its end. Unbeknownst to them, the Germans intended to defend Lorraine to the last man. *National Archives*

On September 11, the 35th Infantry Division managed to cross the Moselle River against stiff opposition and establish an infantry bridgehead south of Nancy. The lead elements of 4th Armored Division's main effort chose not to wait for heavy pontoon bridges to be constructed. Instead, the lead tanks improvised a crossing of the drained canal flanking the Moselle, forded the river, and established contact with the 35th Infantry Division while engineers constructed bridges behind them. Poor roads, rather than German resistance, proved to be the main impediment to the 4th Armored Division's drive toward the rear of Nancy.

North of Nancy, the 80th Infantry Division mounted a successful river crossing on September 12. The Germans reacted quickly with strong counterattacks, but to no avail. Despite heavy German resistance, elements of 4th Armored Division rushed through the 80th Infantry Division bridgehead. American tanks intended to execute a deep attack, and the objective for the day focused on the capture of the important road center at Château-Salins, some twenty miles distant. The tanks met little opposition until they reached Château-Salins the next day. The northern elements of Eddy's division drove southward to the vicinity of Arracourt, cutting the German lines of communication to Nancy in the process. From the area around Arracourt, the northern elements were to continue southward until they could link up with the elements of the division advancing from the south.

On September 15, the northern elements of 4th Armored Division linked up with the southern elements of the division. The raid forced the German division defending Nancy to withdraw, allowing the 35th Infantry Division to occupy the city against little opposition.

To the officers of the 4th Armored Division, there was no question about the reunited division's next move. The most obvious path of action was to exploit the advantage immediately and keep the Germans on the run. The road to Germany was open. Eddy, however, rejected the division's request to continue its advance, because there were no provisions to support a continued armored advance. Instead, Eddy directed the armored division to turn around in order to assist the 35th and 80th Infantry Divisions in mopping-up operations.

Eddy informed 4th Armored Division that it would be able to resume its general offensive on September 18. The attack plan would consist of the armored division and the

American soldiers inspect a small captured German mortar designated the 5cm (50mm) Leichter Granatenwerfer 36. Patton's Third Army advance through Lorraine was an important part of Eisenhower's grand strategy to advance on Nazi Germany on a wide front from the North Sea to the Swiss border. *National Archives*

The fighting edge of Patton's Third Army during the Lorraine Campaign was XII Corps, under the command of Maj. Gene. Manton S. Eddy, and XX Corps, under the command of Maj. Gen. Walton H. Walker. From left to right: Bradley, Patton, Walker, and Eddy. *Patton Museum*

The German eight-wheel armored car known as the Puma (this one has lost a wheel) was armed with a 5cm (50mm) KwK 39/1 main gun. *Frank Schulz collection*

An American M18 tank destroyer edges around a corner. The first troop list for the Lorraine Campaign, dated September 5, 1944, showed that Patton's Third Army had fifteen tank destroyer battalions. There were also eight squadrons of mechanized cavalry and 669 M4 Sherman medium tanks. *National Archives*

THE DAY I MET GEORGE PATTON

By Colonel Leslie H. Cross (Retired)

IT WAS IN SEPTEMBER 1944 that the 43rd Reconnaissance Squadron moved to a Nazi youth camp in Bettembourg, Luxembourg. We had been given a mission of occupying a twenty-five-mile front along the Moselle River. The reconnaissance troops were out in front, manning observation posts not far from the river in the daytime and then moving to listening posts at nightfall. The squadron headquarters was some ten to twelve miles from the river in approximately the center of the sector.

I was notified that General Patton, Third Army commander, accompanied by the group commander, Col. James Polk, was on his way to visit the squadron headquarters. They arrived in the middle of a pleasant morning, so far as the weather was concerned. The leading jeep dove up, and one got the impression of chrome trimmings, flags flying, and emblems blazing. Upon coming to a rather abrupt halt, two majors, looking like ex-pugilists, leaped from the jeep with their Tommy guns at the ready

and ran to a corner of the building that offered cover and observation of the road leading to the camp.

A tall big man, easily recognizable as General Patton, got out of the jeep rather briskly. I advanced promptly to report to him. "Colonel Cross commanding the 43rd Reconnaissance Squadron reports to the army commander." He returned my salute, extended his hand, and said something like, "Not a bad place you have here." He wore a well-tailored uniform with a pearl-handled pistol. I hadn't realized how tall he was, standing a full head and shoulder over me. After some small talk about parking jeeps, he said, "I'll like to see your situation map." I led the way, and after entering the building and upon opening the door to the operations office, I called attention loud enough to make the windows rattle. He seemed pleased— at least, not displeased. After he was seated at a table and had the situation map brought to him, I thought that he might have trouble seeing, since the table was away from

35th Infantry Division attacking in column. Bad weather forced the plan to be postponed until September 19 (five days after elements of the 4th Armored Division reached Arracourt). But the attack was never launched, because during the delay, the Arracourt location had become endangered. Eddy's delay had cost XII Corps the initiative. His decision to consolidate his positions proved to give the Germans a priceless gift of time, during which the German First Army concentrated reserves around Château-Salins, thus blocking one of the principal Third Army avenues to the Rhine River.

In an even more serious development, the Fifth Panzer Army began assembling forces for a major counteroffensive against XII Corps' right flank. The Fifth Panzer Army had orders to roll up Third Army's right flank with a massive counterattack, but the 4th Armored Division's sudden thrust to Arracourt surprised the Germans and threw off the

and facing the window. So I said, "Sir, maybe you'd like to move over so that you can see better." But he said, "I can see well enough."

After studying the map for a while, he pointed to the location of the squadron headquarters on the map and said, "You're pretty far back from the river." I explained that we had a very broad front for a force our size, and that one had to stay well back in order to defend the sector properly by allowing himself sufficient maneuver room. After a short, tense delay, "Believe you're right, believe you're right," was his comment. I began to feel the tension in the room as my officers and soldiers waited to see whether they or I would catch hell for something or other or come through the meeting unscathed. All the while, General Patton was studying the map. I felt my mouth go dry and I wished we could get on with it.

Finally he spoke. "I know where every German division is on my front but one. Do you think it could be over there?" he asked me, pointing to a wooded area across the Moselle River.

The tension in the room rose like a rocket. My officers and soldiers wondered what I could say or do. I was really on the spot. The thought that raced through my mind was a lieutenant colonel in my position wasn't being paid to answer that type of question. I looked at the map, studied it and thought of the actions we had been through in the past few weeks. The place was quiet as a morgue when I said firmly, "No, sir, I don't think it is there."

He immediately asked, "Why not?"

I thought, *Oh hell, I might as well tell him exactly what I think and let him make the most of it.* With the tension still running high, I replied, "Sir, the road net does not appear sufficiently extensive to facilitate supporting a division there, and further, of the numerous prisoners we have captured in the past few weeks, all have been from units previously identified."

"I don't believe it is there either," he exclaimed, as he started to get up. With that the tension was relieved, almost audibly. He stood up to his full six feet plus, looked at everybody in the room, pointed to another map on the wall and said, "I was here in 1918 and if you are going to be attacked, they will come right down that valley (pointing again) and I expect you to whip 'em!"

The visit was over and as we moved outside, the chaplain approached and asked General Patton if he (the chaplain) could take his picture with me.

"Happy to do it," the general said, straightening up to his full height and extending his hand to indicate the picture should be taken with us shaking hands. During the interval the jeeps were being lined up, and he mounted and moved out with everyone saluting and feeling very relieved as he departed.   *National Archives*

---

effort. It also forced the Germans into a series of premature, piecemeal attacks strung out over twelve days. The first of these fell on elements of the 4th Armored Division at Luneville on September 18. Reinforcements from the 4th and 6th Armored Divisions drove off the Germans. Both Eddy and his divisional commanders, believing the Luneville engagement to be only a local counterattack, proceeded with plans for another corps offensive to begin the next day. Reports of increased German activity throughout the night of September 18, however, forced Eddy and his commanders to delay their attack. What happened was the Fifth Panzer Army had simply bypassed Luneville and was moving north to strike at the exposed position of the 4th Armored Division around Arracourt. The resulting operation was one of the largest armored engagements ever fought on the western front.

At the same time the 4th Armored Division was dealing with the Fifth Panzer Army, the 35th Infantry Division faced a series of strong counterattacks by other units of the German army. The division beat back the German attacks without help on September 27 and 28, but in one last major attack, the Germans managed to punch holes in the division's front lines. Extremely worried, Eddy called a meeting of the 35th Infantry Division staff that afternoon. Also present at the meeting was Third Army Chief of Staff General Gaffey, as well as General Grow, whose 6th Armored Division now formed the Third Army reserve. Eddy, in tacit agreement with the other officers, decided to order a withdrawal of the hard-pressed 35th Infantry Division behind the Seille River. The 6th Armored Division got the job of covering the withdrawal.

The bodies of American soldiers killed in battle have been collected for burial.
National Archives

An American soldier inspects a fuel pipeline in France. By the end of August 1944, the Allied armies outran their supply system. Eisenhower allocated existing supplies to Montgomery's 21st Army Group. Third Army was first affected by logistical shortfalls on August 28, 1944. Patton quickly visited Bradley and was told there would be no appreciable gasoline until September 3, 1944. *National Archives*

American soldiers provide medical aid to a wounded German soldier. *National Archives*

A pint-sized American soldier with a big grin is armed with an M3 submachine gun. Third Army was rolling again when fuel finally arrived on September 5, 1944, but, sadly, the fuel supply lasted only ten days and then reverted to a trickle. *National Archives*

The two main targets of Patton's Third Army advance across Lorraine were the French cities of Nancy and Metz. The city of Metz was heavily fortified with both French and German defensive systems, like this captured German bunker. *National Archives*

An American Signal Corps photographer looks at a dead German soldier who was armed with an antitank rocket launcher known as the Panzerschreck. Eddy's XII Corps was assigned the job of taking Nancy, while Walker's XX Corps was tasked with the capture of Metz. Both corps would begin their assignments with little information on their objectives or their defenders' strength or battlefield disposition. *National Archives*

A well-covered American soldier takes aim with his M1 rifle. Based on past successes, Eddy decided on September 4, 1944, that the next day he would use a regimental combat team of his 80th Infantry Division to make a quick thrust north across the Moselle River and come up from behind Nancy and capture it. *National Archives*

Patton, alerted to the meeting by Gaffey, flew to Eddy's XII Corps headquarters in Nancy on the same day. On his arrival, Patton quickly countermanded the withdrawal order of the 35th Infantry Division. Instead, he told Eddy, "Counterattack with the 6th Armored. . . . Tell them [the 35th Infantry Division] to hang on." Patton then went on to the 6th Armored Division headquarters east of Nancy, where plans were made for the division to attack the next morning. On October 1, by the end of the day, the 6th Armored Division had inflicted heavy casualties and pushed the Germans back to their original positions. Americans and Germans then settled down for a long period of watchful waiting, beginning a lull in this area that would continue until November 1944.

THE ADVANCE OF XX CORPS

On the last day of August, tanks of the 7th Armored Division raced across the Meuse River on an intact bridge in the city of Verdun. The crossing at Verdun was close to the last step in a rapid, four-hundred-mile advance that Walker's XX Corps had been making since August 6. The 5th Infantry Division followed the 7th Armored Division across the Meuse River. At this point, the advance stalled five days for lack of fuel. On September 5, the refueled XX Corps once again began its eastward advance, leading with its mechanized cavalry group.

The general plan called for 7th Armored Division to bypass Metz and strike straight for the Sarre River and its bridges. The corps' two infantry divisions received the job of capturing the fortified cities of Thionville and Metz. The intricate fortifications of Metz extended many miles around the city on either side of the Moselle River.

Prior to September 5, Major General Walker had little information on the strength and disposition of the German forces along the Moselle River or the fortified positions guarding the respective cities. Early messages from the corps' mechanized cavalry group showed that the Germans were withdrawing. By the night of September 5, new information reached Walker indicating that the Germans were going to defend both Thionville and Metz. Despite this news, Walker's XX Corps staff believed that the fortified defenses around Thionville and Metz were obsolete and the Germans might not be willing to risk defending the cities.

Contrary to American intelligence, Hitler had no intention of allowing his forces to abandon the Metz-Thionville defenses. Neither would the German defenders on the west bank of the Moselle River be allowed to withdraw. To defend the Metz-Thionville area from Walker's advancing XX Corps, Hitler had roughly four and a half understrength divisions.

A knocked-out German self-propelled gun nicknamed the Hornisse ("hornet"), armed with an 8.8cm (88mm) PaK 43/1 (antitank gun). The day before Eddy's successful attack across the Moselle River north of Nancy on September 12, 1944, Eddy also launched a successful attack across the Moselle River south of Nancy with 35th Infantry Division and elements of 4th Armored Division.
National Archives

An American soldier examines a captured German MP44 assault rifle. In the foreground is a German MG42 machine gun. Eddy's initial attack across the Moselle River, north of Nancy, on September 5, 1944, was blunted by the German defenders. Eddy would launch another attack in the same area on September 12, 1944, and this attack would prove successful. *National Archives*

And the Germans had used the Allies' logistically imposed pause between August 31 and September 6 to prepare themselves for the expected American attack.

On the night of September 7, Walker launched his main attack toward the Moselle River and the northwest ring of forts that guarded Metz. From the concrete and steel fortifications, most of which lay below ground, the Germans fired antitank and artillery rounds on the advancing American soldiers. Despite heavy losses, the corps pressed its attacks until September 14. Fighter-bombers and heavy artillery failed to destroy the concrete and steel emplacements, and the German soldiers defending the area counterattacked any attempt to get near their defensive positions. The Americans soldiers had managed to occupy positions a mere thousand yards from the first line of German forts when, on corps orders, the main effort was redirected to the south of Metz.

THE XX CORPS RIVER CROSSINGS

The southern advance toward Metz, which began on September 7, also ran into fierce German resistance. Unwilling to halt their attack, American soldiers reached the Moselle River near the town of Dornot on that same evening. The next morning, supported by corps artillery, they attempted a river assault to the east side, but the Germans strongly counterattacked. In addition, the Germans pounded the bridgehead area with artillery fire. With losses mounting, the last American assault troops withdrew on September 11 under protective artillery fire.

An American soldier gives a great big smile for the Signal Corps photographer. He's manning an air-cooled MI919A4 .30-caliber machine gun from an improvised bunker. The thirty-one-pound machine gun was mounted on an M2 tripod that weighed fourteen pounds. *National Archives*

American soldiers escort German prisoners past a destroyed and still-burning American M3A1 half-track. On the evening of September 14, the northern and southern elements of 4th Armored Division joined forces behind Nancy. The city was captured on September 15. *National Archives*

A German Panther Ausf. G medium tanks prepare for action. By the time Eddy was ready to order his XII Corps to begin its eastward advance toward Germany once again on September 19, the German forces had regrouped and were prepared to counterattack his forces near the town of Arracourt. *Frank Schulz collection*

On the morning of September 10, while the Germans were busy concentrating on reducing XX Corps' bridgehead at Dornot, Walker ordered a second bridgehead at a point four thousand yards south, near Arnaville. The Germans quickly recovered from their initial surprise and launched the expected counterattacks. From across the river, Walker's XX Corps now had thirteen artillery battalions firing in support of the Arnaville bridgehead. In what amounted to an artillery ambush, the few German tanks that managed to get through the curtain of American artillery fire were driven off by bazooka fire from the infantry.

On September 11, the corps engineers prepared a ford north of Arnaville, and tanks and tank destroyers rushed across the river into the bridgehead zone. By the afternoon of September 12, Walker's engineers completed a large bridge across the Moselle. By quickly rushing additional forces to the Arnaville bridgehead, Walker's XX Corps managed to repel all further German counterattacks, the largest of which began on September 17 and was stopped only at the last moment by furious hand-to-hand fighting.

By securing the bridgehead at Arrraville and capturing Thionville, Walker's XX Corps managed to partially outflank several of the major fortresses on the western side of the Moselle River. In response to the initial success, Hitler had ordered his First Army on September 16 to reinforce the areas on either side of Metz to prevent Walker's XX Corps from encircling the city. On the same day, the 7th Armored Division and the 5th Infantry Division began an attack aimed at crossing both the Seille and Nied rivers. The ultimate goal was to reach the rear of Metz. Against heavy German resistance, neither division made much headway.

The two divisions restarted their advance to the Seille River on September 18. By the afternoon of September 20, they reached the river after stiff fighting. Two early attempts at crossing the river the next day failed. The 7th Armored Division began making plans for a major crossing of the river on the night of September 23, but it was never made. That afternoon, General Bradley ordered the division transferred to First Army control. The division quickly received orders to move north to its new location in Belgium. This move made it necessary for the 5th Infantry Division to discontinue its advance toward the rear of Metz and go on the defensive, forcing it to give up some of the ground it had fought so hard to capture.

On September 25, Bradley sent a message to Eisenhower telling him that he had ordered Patton to go on the defensive with the entire Third Army. At the same time, Bradley also informed Eisenhower that he had given Patton permission to make some minor adjustments in his present lines. Patton stretched the vague definition of "minor adjustments" to continue attacking the German positions throughout the Third Army sector, despite serious shortages of everything from gasoline to ammunition.

Patton confers with Eddy (left) and Maj. Gen. Horace L. McBride (right), commander of 80th Infantry Division. Rather than send 4th Armored Division in the direction of Germany after Nancy was captured, Eddy ordered it to assist the 35th and 80th Infantry Divisions in mopping up operations. *Patton Museum*

PATTON'S THOUGHTS ON ATTACKING PILLBOXES

PILLBOXES ARE best attacked by the use of prearranged groups. A satisfactory group consists of two Browning automatic rifles, a bazooka, a light machine gun, two to four riflemen, and two men with the demolition charge.... Before initiating an attack on a pillbox area, a reconnaissance should be made to determine which pillboxes are mutually supporting. Those in such a group must be attacked simultaneously. The best results are obtained by a silent night attack, which places the assault groups in position close to their respective pillboxes at dawn. The apertures are immediately taken under fire and silenced. When this is achieved, the demolition charge, covered by riflemen and light machine gun, is placed against the door at the rear of the pillbox, the fuse is lit, and the men withdraw around the corner of the building. As soon as the charge is exploded, riflemen throw in grenades.... Any enemy emerging are killed or captured, according to the frame of mind of the enemy.

—*War As I Knew It,*
"Reflections and Suggestions"

FORT BUSTING

On September 27, Walker ordered 5th Infantry Division to assault Fort Driant, five miles southwest of Metz. The powerful old fort with its batteries of huge guns was a thorn in the side of Walker's XX Corps. From its commanding heights, the Germans controlled the approach to Metz along the Moselle Valley. To Walker, the fort needed to be captured before a successful advance up the Moselle Valley would work.

The assault on the fort began with both air and artillery support. As the assault troops began to approach the fort, they met heavy machine-gun fire along a huge (sixty feet wide and thirty feet deep) moat. The concrete walls of the fort were seven feet thick, and barbed wire covered every approach. On top of the fort lay revolving gun turrets protected by thick steel armor. Against such defenses, the assault troops of the 5th Infantry Division stood little chance of success, and the attack stalled.

Unfavorable weather postponed further attacks against Fort Driant. American officers reviewed the lessons learned from the first attack and developed a more ambitious plan for the second assault. On October 3, planes of Weyland's XIX TAC dropped napalm on the fort. At the same time, a combined force of tanks, infantry, and engineers carrying everything

Two American soldiers look over a captured German 28/32cm Nebelwerfer 41, which could fire either a 280mm high explosive rocket or a 320mm incendiary rocket. *National Archives*

A column of American M4A3 Sherman medium tanks. *National Archives*

from flamethrowers to bangalore torpedoes attacked the fort from the north and south. The southern force succeeded in penetrating the walls on the first day of the attack. Once inside the many underground passages of Fort Driant, there began a strange, confusing fight that came to be known as the Battle of the Tunnels.

After a week's tough fighting, the American soldiers inside the German fort still had not ferreted out all German resistance. Patton commented, "If we could get the supplies we need and with three good days of weather, we could take it." He went on to say, "In fact, I am not going to let these soldiers get killed until we have something on our side." On the morning of October 10, Major Generals Gaffey and Walker and various divisional commanders decided that sufficient forces were not available to complete the capture of Fort Driant. By the morning of October 14, all remaining American soldiers inside the fort withdrew. Losses for the assault on Fort Driant cost the 5th Infantry Division over five hundred men, with little tangible result.

PLANS FOR A NEW OFFENSIVE

Eisenhower's general policy throughout the campaign in Europe was to keep constant pressure on the German ground forces all along their lines. In the middle of October, Eisenhower began thinking about giving the American armies a larger role in the Allied advance to the Rhine. On October 17, Eisenhower visited Patton to talk about restarting Third Army's advance. Patton eagerly looked forward to further opportunities to make a few "minor adjustments" in Third Army's lines. The next day, Eisenhower met with Bradley and Montgomery in Belgium to make plans for a new southern advance to the Rhine River by both the American First and Ninth Armies. The Ninth Army, under the command of Lt. Gen. Alan Simpson, having

A knocked-out German Panther Ausf. G medium tank. In a series of battlefield encounters that lasted until September 29, 1944, 4th Armored Division dealt the German Fifth Panzer Army a serious defeat in one of the largest tank-versus-tank battles between the Western Allies and the Germans. *Patton Museum*

finished mopping up in Brittany by the end of September, took over the northern sector of the First Army's front. Eisenhower's plan called for the American southern advance to the Rhine River in conjunction with the northern advance to the Rhine by Montgomery's 21st Army Group. In Eisenhower's original plan, Third Army was to play only a secondary role by advancing in a northeasterly direction in support of the main advance Hodges's First Army and Simpson's Ninth Army were making to the Rhine River. Eisenhower's plan was not a slap at Patton's ambition, but recognition that the fresher First and Ninth Armies were better suited to the task.

On October 19, Patton wrote a personal letter to Bradley setting forth his plans for a Third Army drive up to the West Wall—a drive that would take three days at the most. Patton also assured Bradley that the Germans facing his forces had all their strength in their front lines. Once they overran the German front lines, Third Army stood a good chance of breaking through the West Wall and driving rapidly to the Rhine.

On October 22, Bradley issued an order that stated, "12th Army Group will regroup and prepare for an advance by all three Armies to the Rhine River." Bradley told Patton at the same time, "If all the armies ... attacked simultaneously, it might end the war." The actual launching of the American southern advance would depend on a number of factors, the most important being the availability of adequate supplies. Another factor, almost as important, was the weather. Without decent weather, Weyland's XIX TAC could not provide

An American MI917A4 water-cooled .30-caliber machine-gun crew watches over the river. Assigned the capture of Metz, Walker's XX Corps sent out 3rd Cavalry Group on September 6, 1944, to force openings across the Moselle River and seize bridges capable of supporting tanks. Heavy German resistance put a stop to this reconnaissance mission. *National Archives*

air support for the planned American advance. Within these parameters, Eisenhower figured the combined advance of all his armies could begin sometime between November 1 and 5. It was an optimistic estimate.

By the end of the first week in November, the required supplies for an advance to the Rhine River began appearing in Bradley's 12th Army Group sector. At the same time, it became apparent that strong German resistance in the north would delay the advance of Montgomery's 21st Army Group. On November 2, Bradley visited Patton's headquarters to inform him that neither the British nor the other American armies were ready to begin the planned advance. Bradley, therefore, asked if Third Army could begin the offensive by itself. Long frustrated by Montgomery's timidity, as well as Eisenhower's perceived favoritism of the British general, Patton received the opportunity he was waiting for. He promptly answered that his Third Army would be able to attack on twenty-four-hours notice. Patton's staff had already begun planning for such an operation as early as September. Patton informed his commander that Third Army should begin the offensive as soon as the weather permitted the air forces to begin softening up the German defensive positions.

Third Army received two orders from 12th Army Group on November 3. First, it was to envelop Metz and destroy any German forces trying to withdraw from the area. Second, it was to capture the German cities of Mainz, Frankfurt, and Darmstadt. Not only would crossing the Rhine cut a vital line of German communication, but capturing the first large and inarguably German homeland cities would also be a psychological blow. If it successfully attained these two goals, Third Army was to prepare itself for a deeper advance into Germany.

American M12 155mm self-propelled guns during a fire-support mission. On September 7, 1944, Walker launched his 5th Infantry Division against the outer line of forts that guarded the northwestern outskirts of Metz. Despite artillery and air support, which lasted until September 14, the German defenses continued to hold. *National Archives*

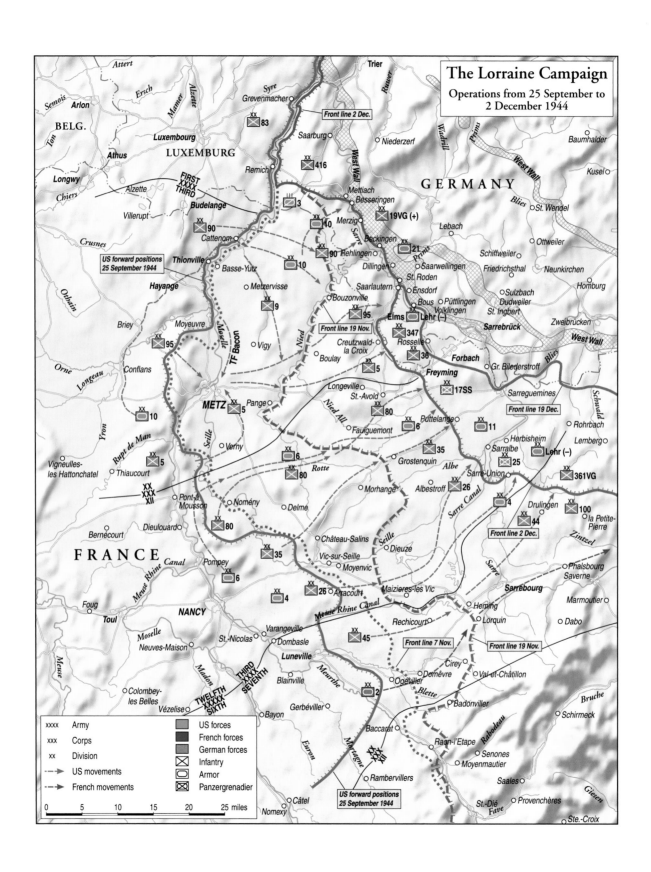

The Lorraine Campaign
Operations from 25 September to
2 December 1944

GERMANY

BELG.

LUXEMBURG

FRANCE

NANCY

METZ

Legend:

xxxx Army
xxx Corps
xx Division
US movements
French movements

US forces
French forces
German forces
Infantry
Armor
Panzergrenadier

0   5   10   15   20   25 miles

THE NOVEMBER ADVANCE

Patton began his main advance to the Rhine River on November 8, using Eddy's XII Corps to attack on a thirty-mile front. The advance started with an early morning artillery barrage that lasted three and a half hours. After lifting the barrage, Eddy's XII Corps sent the 26th, 35th, and 80th Infantry Divisions forward.

The goal of the three infantry divisions was to cross the flooded Seille River and provide maneuver room for armored divisions to exploit any holes punched in the German lines. The three infantry divisions achieved some initial success against the surprised German defenders, but could not establish the maneuver room needed for the armored divisions. Eddy ordered his two armored divisions across the Seille River anyway. Once on the eastern side of the river, the armored divisions found their progress stalled by both mud and German minefields. In eight days of fierce fighting, the various divisions of Eddy's XII Corps gained only fifteen miles. The German army group commander easily anticipated both the place and date of Patton's attack and planned his defenses accordingly.

Unlike during Operation Cobra, when the German lines collapsed after some brief fighting, the German resistance in Lorraine (aided by the heavy autumn rains) grew in strength and intensity as time progressed, adding to Third Army's toll of casualties and lost equipment. Compounding the problems of rain and mud, snow fell on the second day of Patton's advance. Bitter cold weather further hindered mobility and added to the misery of Patton's troops.

American soldiers bring in German prisoners.
National Archives

An American M4A3 Sherman medium tank drives across a treadway bridge. Another XX Corps' crossing of the Moselle River took place at the town of Arnaville, south of Dornot, on September 10. This crossing proved to be a success, and 7th Armored Division poured across despite constant German counterattacks. *National Archives*

American troops set off an explosive charge to destroy German fortifications.
National Archives

The left flank of Eddy's XII Corps guarded Walker's XX Corps, whose general advance began on November 9. Walker's corps, with three infantry divisions and a single armored division, had the job of surrounding and capturing Metz. Inside the city were roughly fourteen thousand Germans, of which about ten thousand were combat troops. After securing Metz, XX Corps was to drive northeastward toward the Saar (Sarre) River between the German cities of Saarburg (or Sarrebourg, in French) and Saarlautern. This area was referred to as the Saar-Moselle Triangle. If Walker's XX Corps could successfully seize this area, it could then continue its northeasterly advance toward the Rhine.

Walker began his advance on Metz with a classic double-envelopment attack by the 90th and 5th Infantry Divisions. The 90th Infantry Division crossed the Moselle River north of Metz, and the 5th Infantry Division crossed the Seille River to the south. Their job was to encircle Metz and prevent the escape of German forces. Assisting the northern advance was the 10th Armored Division, commanded by Maj. Gen. W. H. H. Morris. At the same time the 10th Armored Division was assisting in the encirclement, it also set armored reconnaissance columns east toward the Saar (Sarre) River to look for bridging sites. The 95th Infantry Division had the job of containing the German forces west of the Moselle, crossing the river, and capturing Metz.

Unfortunately, XX Corps' advance was plagued by the same poor weather and stiff German resistance that faced Eddy's XII Corps. It was not until November 19 that the 5th and 90th Infantry Divisions finally linked up behind Metz, effectively preventing either the escape or reinforcement of the Germans trapped inside. Most of the Germans in the city lost the will to fight on and began surrendering in large numbers. The city officially fell into American hands on November 22.

With his troops exhausted, Patton soon abandoned any hope of a quick breakthrough to the Rhine. He had to remain content with simply driving Third Army steadily forward. Patton would write: "The impetus of the attack is naturally slacking due to the fatigue of the men." At the end of November, some units of Third Army managed to push within sight of the Saar (Sarre) River, but did not cross the river. Within Walker's XX Corps area of operations, the Saar River flowed through Germany. In Eddy's XII Corps area, on the other hand, most of the Saar River flowed through France. The inability of Patton's Third Army to break through the German lines was matched by the lack of success of Hodges's First Army and Simpson's Ninth Army.

The only American military force to reach the Rhine River during the November advance was the 6th Army Group, south of Third Army. The 6th Army Group, led by Gen. Jacob L. Devers, consisted of the American Seventh Army and the Free French First Army. The 6th Army Group had landed on the Mediterranean coast of southern France on August 15 and advanced northeast to the German border, where it linked up with Bradley's 12th Army Group on September 12. On November 27, Eisenhower, acting upon a suggestion from Patton, ordered Devers to attack northward with the two American corps. Their objective was to breach the West

The business end of a gun port in a German bunker. On November 3, Walker's XX Corps tried to capture Metz once again. The city would fall on November 22, but some of the German-held forts continued to fight. *National Archives*

The rear entrance of a German bunker, with an aperture for a machine gun positioned to deter anybody from attacking from that direction. *National Archives*

A U.S. Army chaplain leads a ceremony shortly before the assembled troops head into battle. Chaplains did much to provide a degree of comfort for those soldiers who sought solace from the strains of combat in their religious beliefs. *National Archives*

Wall, thereby aiding Patton's Third Army in its drive toward the Saar (Sarre) River. Eisenhower wanted 6th Army Group's advance to attract German divisions away from other areas, making it easier for the other Allied armies to advance.

The Germans failed to fall for Eisenhower's ploy and withdrew only a single infantry division from north of Third Army's sector. Despite the help from 6th Army Group, Patton's Third Army still made little headway. On December 4, Eisenhower wrote to Marshall that the Germans "should be able to maintain a strong defensive front for some time, assisted by weather, floods and muddy ground."

On the morning of November 23, the first elements of Eddy's XII Corps crossed the Saar River (in France) north of Saarburg (Sarrebourg in French) in two locations. By the end of the month, Eddy's XII Corps cleared almost all of the remaining German positions from the west bank of the Saar (Sarre). On November 24, advance elements of Walker's XX Corps reached the Saar River in Germany. As the bulk of XX Corps approached the river, the Germans savagely defended every foot of ground, for they were now fighting on their own soil. The main goal of Walker's XX Corps was to seize the heavily defended German industrial center of Saarlautern and its vital bridges across the Saar River, where the West Wall paralleled the eastern riverbank.

DECEMBER OPERATIONS

In a surprise attack on December 4, elements of Walker's XX Corps captured one of the bridges across the Saar River. The corps rushed troops, tanks, and tank destroyers across the bridge as quickly as possible, despite strong German counterattacks. Patton wrote, "We are attacking the Siegfried Line [West Wall]. I know that there are many generals with my reputation who would not have dared to do so because 'they are more afraid of losing a battle than anxious to win one.' I do not believe that any of these lines are impregnable. If we get through, we will materially shorten the war. There is no if about getting through; I am sure we will!"

By December 6, Walker's XX Corps had two more bridgeheads across the Saar River. The fighting along the West Wall soon developed into a bitter slugging match against tenacious German resistance. Adding to the difficulty was a constant cold rain, which prevented Patton's troops from receiving any air support. On December 3, Patton wrote in his diary, "I have never seen or imagined such a hell hole of a country. There is about four inches of liquid mud over everything, and it rains all the time, not hard but steadily."

Walker's XX Corps continued its attempt to breach the West Wall until December 20. By then, the massive German counterattack in the Ardennes on December 16, 1944—an attack later known as the Battle of the Bulge—compelled Patton and his Third Army to discontinue their aggressive attacks to the east and to swing the biggest part of their forces to the north. Although Patton's Lorraine Campaign came to an abrupt and inglorious ending, without sadness, Patton embarked on a new campaign that would bring both him and his Third Army historic fame.

A couple of American artillerymen take an impromptu musical break to entertain themselves and their comrades-in-arms. The vehicle in the background is a 105mm howitzer motor carriage M7. *National Archives*

An American M1 155mm Howitzer in action during a night firing mission. The fierce fighting in the Ardennes Forest is best known to most Americans as the Battle of the Bulge, but it is more properly classified as a campaign, because it consisted of numerous battles spread over a fairly wide area at different times. *National Archives*

6

BATTLE OF THE BULGE OPENING MOVES

★ ★ ★ ★ ★

IN THE EARLY MORNING HOURS of December 16, 1944, Hitler launched a surprise offensive operation, code-named *Wacht am Rhein* (Watch on the Rhine), against the American First Army's thinly defended, eighty-five-mile-long Ardennes sector, encompassing territory in Belgium, Germany, and Luxembourg. The invading German forces numbered 250,000 men, 1,900 artillery pieces, and almost 1,000 tanks and armored assault guns.

The ostensible German military goal was to reach the Allied-controlled port of Antwerp in Belgium within a week. The more realistic political goal was to inflict enough losses on the Western Allies to set the stage for an armistice, which would allow the German armed forces to concentrate their remaining resources on the Red Army, by then on the eastern borders of Nazi Germany with over five hundred divisions.

Major General Troy H. Middleton's overextended three-division VIII Corps occupied the First Army's southern sector, where the main German attack began. A long defensive line and lack of manpower prevented Middleton from maintaining a mobile reserve to plug any gaps in an emergency. If attacked, Middleton's troops would have to rely on help from outside the Ardennes. Hitler knew this and chose to launch his forces through the Ardennes.

A German Tiger B heavy tank is poised for action. *Patton Museum*

As the German forces pushed through Middleton's front lines, the resulting disruption in communications created widespread confusion. Bradley, the 12th Army Group commander, did not receive word about the attack until the afternoon of December 16, as he sat in conference with Eisenhower at his headquarters. Eisenhower's intelligence officer, British Major General Ken Strong, told both men, "The Germans have counterattacked in the Ardennes and scored penetrations at five places on the VIII Corps front." Strong explained that the attacks began early that morning. Although the full extent of the attack was still unknown, he said, "The most dangerous penetration seems to be developing along the V Corps-VIII Corps boundary in the Losheim Gap."

An American soldier fires his M3 submachine gun, popularly nicknamed the Grease Gun. The German forces that invaded the Ardennes Forest included 250,000 soldiers and almost 1,000 tanks and armored assault guns. Although the Allies held almost complete air superiority, Hitler's plan counted on poor flying weather to compensate for the weakness of his own air force. *National Archives*

A German Sd.Kfz. 251 half-track passes a captured American M3 half-track. The German soldiers that entered the Ardennes were divided among three field armies: Sixth Panzer Army, which was intended to deliver the main blow against the Americans; Fifth Panzer Army on its northern flank; and Seventh Army defending the southern flank of both their advances. *National Archives*

American soldiers keep watch with their Browning M1917A1 .30-caliber, water-cooled machine gun. *National Archives*

After studying various maps with Bradley and Strong, Eisenhower directed Bradley to quickly dispatch elements of the 7th and 10th Armored Divisions to the aid of Middleton's hard-pressed VIII Corps. Part of 7th Armored Division, detached from Lt. Gen. William H. Simpson's Ninth Army, located north of the Ardennes, was sent to defend St. Vith. Elements of 10th Armored Division were redeployed to Bastogne from Patton's Third Army, located south of the Ardennes, officially notifying Patton of the Germans' counteroffensive.

An open-topped American M-10 tank destroyer stands guard against the German advance. On the morning of December 16, 1944, there were ninety-six Allied divisions along the western front border of Nazi Germany, which ran 450 miles from the northern tip of neutral Switzerland to the North Sea. *National Archives*

A German crew of a Granatwerfer (GrW) 42 12cm (120mm) mortar makes adjustments prior to firing. The operational goal of the German military was to push through the Ardennes and reach the Belgium port of Antwerp within a week's time. *National Archives*

Waffen SS soldiers check their map somewhere in the Ardennes. Offensive operations, such as Wacht am Rhein, should have a force ratio of at least three to one in its favor to ensure success. Hitler did not have an exact count of the Allied forces arrayed against him, and he mounted a force that was outnumbered by the Allies nearly one to four. This unfavorable force ratio was an early indicator of the desperation of the German attack. *National Archives*

TROY HOUSTON MIDDLETON

COMMISSIONED AS an officer in the U.S. Army in 1912, Troy H. Middleton would see heavy combat in World War I and rise to the rank of colonel by the war's conclusion. In the interwar period, he studied at a number of schools and served as an instructor. Middleton retired from the army in 1937 and went to work at Louisiana State University.

Middleton was recalled to army service in early 1942 and eventually given command of the 45th Infantry Division in the invasion of Sicily. While in Sicily, Middleton's division served as part of Patton's Seventh Army. Due to his skills, Middleton was given command of the VIII Corps in early 1944. Middleton's leadership served the army and Patton's Third Army through the end of the war in Europe, by which time Middleton had risen to the rank of lieutenant general. *National Archives*

American soldiers are pictured with a German 8.8cm (88mm) PaK 43 (antitank gun) that they are firing back at its former owners. The German generals of the Ardennes forces knew that the grand military objective of retaking Antwerp by plunging through the Ardennes was not realistic, and Hitler's plan for a political victory was the best that could be hoped for. *National Archives*

Patton had actually anticipated the attack and, on December 12, had even directed his staff to make "a study of what Third Army would do if called upon to counterattack such a breakthrough." Patton's intuition about the German offensive in the Ardennes area was based on the solid information being collected and analyzed by the head of his intelligence (G-2) section, Col Oscar W. Koch. Patton once said, "Oscar Koch is the best damned intelligence officer in any United States Army Command." During November, Koch had identified a number of German units leaving Westphalia (a region of Germany) and Third Army's front. Koch believed these units were regrouping somewhere. On November 23, he wrote in his daily report: "This powerful striking force, with an estimated 500 tanks, is still an untouched strategic reserve held for future employment." He concluded they might be used for a "coordinated counteroffensive."

Through early December, Koch continued to pursue information on this possible threat. On December 7, he warned of "enemy reserves with large panzer concentrations west of the Rhine in the northern portion of 12th Army Group's zone of advance." Two days later, Koch informally briefed Patton on the possibility of a German attack and their capability to mount it. On December 11, Koch again warned, "Overall, the initiative still rests with the Allies. But the massive armored force the enemy has built up in reserve gives him the definite capability of launching a spoiling offensive to disrupt Allied plans." Koch's predictions ran counter to most other higher-headquarters intelligence units.

While visiting several division headquarters on December 12, Patton decided to place the 6th Armored Division and the 26th Infantry Division in the III Corps sector near

An American soldier looks up from his meal, most likely to observe the activity of the U.S. Army Air Forces. While the pilots and aircrews of the USAAF provided valuable support to the ground forces throughout the European Theater of Operation, there were enough errant bombing raids on friendly forces that some American soldiers jokingly referred to it as the "American Luftwaffe." *National Archives*

Patton confers with five-star General of the Army George C. Marshall, Chief of Staff of the U.S. Army during World War II.
Patton Museum

Saarbrilcken. He felt that the enemy would probably attack the VIII Corps of the First Army and that he could use the III Corps to attack straight north, west of the Moselle. That day, Patton directed his staff to study what Third Army would do if requested to counterattack a breakthrough to the north. Four days later, during his normal morning meeting and while still unaware that the Germans had begun their attack through the Ardennes an hour earlier, Patton received a briefing on the German intercepts from the previous evening. They indicated that the German armored formations around Trier, Germany, were spreading out and moving to an unknown destination. The Germans had also just gone on radio silence. Patton was now certain that the attack would be through the Ardennes.

An American M4A1 Sherman medium tank with sandbags on its front hull passes a small church. As a matter of strategic policy arrived at before the German Ardennes offensive, Eisenhower favored a broad-front policy along the entire 450-mile front with Nazi Germany.
National Archives

An American truck convoy takes soldiers to the front lines. Despite Eisenhower's broad-front policy, some areas of the front were perceived to be of little strategic value to either the Germans or the Allies. One of those areas was the Ardennes, which fell within the control of Bradley's 12th Army Group. *National Archives*

PATTON'S THOUGHTS ON TANKS AND INFANTRY WORKING TOGETHER

THE QUESTION of whether infantry or tanks lead in attacking is determined by the character of the ground and of the enemy resistance. Whenever the ground permits tanks to advance rapidly, even with the certainty of a loss from minefields, they should lead. Through dense woods or against prepared positions or un-located antitank guns, infantry leads, following closely by the tanks, which act as close supporting artillery. But, irrespective of the foregoing, some tanks must accompany the infantry when they reach the objective. These tanks are for the purpose of removing enemy weapons which emerge after the passage of the leading tanks.

—*War As I Knew It,*
"Reflections and Suggestions"

Whitewash camouflages an American M4A3 medium tank in the surrounding winter wonderland of snow. Bradley, with Eisenhower's approval, took a calculated risk by deciding to use the Ardennes front as an area where war-weary divisions could recover and refit, and where newly arrived and untested divisions could acquire a little combat experience. *National Archives*

Patton asked Gen. Hobart R. Gay, his chief of staff, and Col. Halley G. Maddox, his G-3 (operations and plans chief), how they were progressing on the study that he ordered on December 12. After they updated him, he made his instructions more specific: "I want you, gentlemen, to start making plans for pulling Third Army out of its eastward attack, changing the direction 90 degrees, moving to Luxembourg, and attacking north." As if his previous achievements had not been sufficient, that statement ensured Patton's place in history as a military genius.

Patton was not overly surprised when Bradley called him on the evening of December 16, asking for 10th Armored Division to be sent northward. During their daily morning briefing on December 17, Koch reported that the Germans were continuing their attack on VIII Corps and they also appeared to be moving into the area occupied by Third Army's XX Corps.

Patton considered this new information for a moment, then said, "One of these is a feint; one is the real thing. If they attack us, I'm ready for them, but I'm inclined to think the party will be up north. VIII Corps has been sitting still; a sure invitation to trouble."

An American soldier stands guard over two German prisoners of war. *National Archives*

The American crew of an M1 81mm mortar have taken the time to provide themselves a little overhead cover from the elements. The defense of the Ardennes was assigned to two corps: V Corps, under the command of Maj. Gen. Leonard T. Gerow, and VIII Corps, under the leadership of Maj. Gen. Troy H. Middleton. *National Archives*

An American soldier cleans his M1 rifle during a break in the fighting. Each U.S. Army squad on paper consisted of twelve soldiers, including a staff sergeant who was the squad leader, and a sergeant who was the assistant squad leader. Both men were normally armed with M1s. The remaining men in the squad were armed with nine M1s and a single Browning Automatic Rifle (BAR). *National Archives*

An American soldier stands watch by a 57mm Gun M1. The gun and carriage weighed in at 2,810 pounds. Middleton's VIII Corps, located to the south of Gerow's V Corps, defended the bulk of the Ardennes front and consisted of three infantry divisions: the 4th, 28th, and 106th. *National Archives*

AMERICAN REINFORCEMENTS TO THE ARDENNES

In addition to elements from 7th and 10th Armored Divisions, Eisenhower ordered the 82nd and 101st Airborne Divisions to the Ardennes sector. Both divisions were recovering in France following their seventy-two-day participation in Operation Market Garden when Eisenhower ordered them into action. He sent the 82nd Airborne to shore up the collapse toward St. Vith. The 101st Airborne, instead of going to St. Vith as originally planned, went to Bastogne, as Bastogne had been the VIII Corps headquarters prior to the German offensive. As the 101st Airborne entered Bastogne, headquarters personnel from VIII Corps were still leaving the area. Bastogne's importance for both the defensive forces and attacking Germans centered on

The American M29 cargo carrier known as the Weasel was perfectly adapted to the frozen, snow-covered terrain in the Ardennes. *National Archives*

An American M8 armored car stands guard at the side of a building. The 14th Cavalry Group, which was assigned to 106th Infantry Division, patrolled the area known as the Losheim Gap. The Losheim Gap was seven miles wide and was the classic invasion route for German armies into France going back to 1870, during the Franco-Prussian War. It was also used as an invasion route by the Germans in 1914, during World War I, and in the summer of 1940, during the early part of World War II. *National Archives*

American soldiers, on patrol in winter gear, walk by a barbed-wire barrier. *National Archives*

A German Waffen SS soldier lies dead in an Ardennes snowbank. *National Archives*

the road network through the town. Seven major and minor roads passed through Bastogne, which would provide the attacking Germans with the ability to bypass defensive positions and isolate the Allied forces.

The U.S. Army's traditional doctrine for countering a large penetration, like the one in the Ardennes, formed the basis of Eisenhower's plan. The first step would be to hold the shoulders of the penetration to prevent the enemy from expanding the base of his salient and allowing easier access to follow-on forces. Then crucial choke points, such as St. Vith and Bastogne, would be cut off to restrict the advance of the enemy forces. The final step would be to counterattack along the flanks of the penetration to cut off and destroy advancing enemy forces. To implement this course of action, Eisenhower knew he would have to completely transform his 21st, 12th, and the 6th Army Groups from their ongoing offensive to a defensive posture in all but the Ardennes sector.

Eisenhower ordered 6th Army Group, on the southern flank of Patton's Third Army, to shift its forces so that it could move its boundary northward to cover a large portion of the Third Army sector. This would free Patton to launch an early counterattack into the southern flank of the German penetration in the Ardennes.

On December 18, Eisenhower distributed a message to his top subordinates, stating: "The enemy is making a major thrust and still has reserves uncommitted. It appears that he

American soldiers trudge through the snow with antitank mines to slow down the advancing German forces. The German Sixth Panzer Army punched through the northernmost portion of the Ardennes. The shortest path to Antwerp for the Germans was over the Elsenborn Ridge. Despite the forces arrayed against them, the American units held on to Elsenborn Ridge and could not be pushed off. *National Archives*

An American M4 Sherman medium tank has been pressed into duty as an artillery piece. A key factor in helping the Americans throw back the German attacks on the Elsenborn Ridge in the Ardennes was the large number of divisional and nondivisional artillery units. *National Archives*

will be prepared to employ the whole of his armored reserve to achieve success. My intention is to take immediate action to check the enemy advance, and then to launch a counteroffensive without delay with all forces north of the Moselle."

Eisenhower soon supplemented this message with these instructions: "The German line of advance must not be permitted to cross the Meuse River." He did not want the large number of Allied supply dumps on the western side of the Meuse to fall into enemy hands. He feared that if the German offensive operation reached these critical supplies, especially fuel, the Germans could rupture the entire Allied line.

American soldiers, most with snow capes, head out on patrol. The 28th and 106th Infantry Divisions took the brunt of the German Ardennes offensive operation and ceased to be effective fighting units after a few days. The badly outnumbered and outgunned 14th Cavalry Group, defending the Losheim Gap, was knocked out of action by December 17. *National Archives*

American soldiers in the Ardennes are talking a moment away from the rigors of combat to joke around. One of the standing soldiers is holding a 2.36-inch (60mm) Rocket Launcher M1. The Jeep has snow chains on for better traction and looks to have a parachute on its front hood. *National Archives*

In response to Eisenhower's message, Patton noted:

At the direction of the army commander [Bradley] I reported to his headquarters in Luxembourg, accompanied by G-2, G-3, and G-4 of Third Army. The situation of the enemy breakthrough, as then known, was explained.

General Bradley asked when I could intervene. I stated I could do so with three divisions very shortly. I then telephoned Chief of Staff Third Army and directed that the attack of 4th Armored and 80th Infantry Divisions be halted and sufficient transportation to move 80th Division anytime after dawn of the 19th be collected, and that 4th Armored Division be prepared to move the night 18–19 December. Also, I directed that the XIX Tactical Air Command be notified that the blitz was off for the present.

General Bradley called at 2200 hours and stated that the situation was worse than it had been at noon and directed that the troops as per previous paragraph be moved as rapidly as possible. Also that General Milliken move forward echelon of his headquarters to the front. I suggested Arlon. This was approved. General Bradley further ordered that General [John] Millikin report in person to the Chief of Staff Twelfth Army Group on the morning of the 19th; and that I, accompanied by one staff officer, meet General Bradley for a conference with General Eisenhower at Verdun at 1100 the same date.

One CC [Combat Command] of the 4th Armored moved at midnight on Longwy, followed by remainder of division at dawn. The 80th Infantry started to move on Luxembourg at dawn December 19. The G-4 of the 12th Army Group facilitated these operations by a rapid collection of truck companies from COMMZ [communications zone]."

On December 19, Eisenhower summoned his senior commanders to a meeting at Verdun, where he issued additional orders for stopping the German Ardennes counteroffensive. Before leaving for Verdun, Patton addressed his Third Army staff, saying:

What has occurred up north is no occasion for excitement. As you know, alarm spreads very quickly in a military command. You must be extremely careful in a critical situation such as this not to give rise to any undue concern among the troops. Our plans have been changed. We're going to fight, but in a different place. Also, we are going to have to move very fast. We pride ourselves on our ability to move quickly. But we're going to have to do it faster now than we're ever done before. I have no doubt that we will meet all demands made on us. You always have, and I know you will do so again this time. And whatever happens, we will keep on doing as we have always done: killing Germans wherever we find the sons of bitches."

An American M4A3 Sherman medium tank has been whitewashed to blend in with its surroundings. Acutely aware of the serious threat posed by the German offensive operation, Middleton sent Combat Command Reserve (CCR) of 9th Armored Division to the Belgian road-junction town of Bastogne on December 16. The unit arrived the next day. *National Archives*

American medics load a wounded soldier onto a Jeep for a trip to an aid station.
National Archives

At the Verdun meeting, Eisenhower calmly announced, "The present situation is to be regarded as one of opportunity for us and not of disaster. There will be only cheerful faces at this conference table."

Patton, who had often criticized his boss for being too cautious in the past, was very pleased with Eisenhower's comments. To Patton, it meant Eisenhower had grasped that this was a golden opportunity to destroy the last major reserve of German forces in the west, now that they had ventured forth from behind the protection of the Siegfried Line. Not able to contain his excitement, Patton blurted out, "Hell, let's have the guts to let the sons of bitches go all the way to Paris, then we'll really cut 'em off and chew 'em up!"

To the other senior American commanders present at the meeting, Patton's comment seemed to be out of place. Eisenhower responded, "George, that's fine. But the enemy must never be allowed to cross the Meuse [River]."

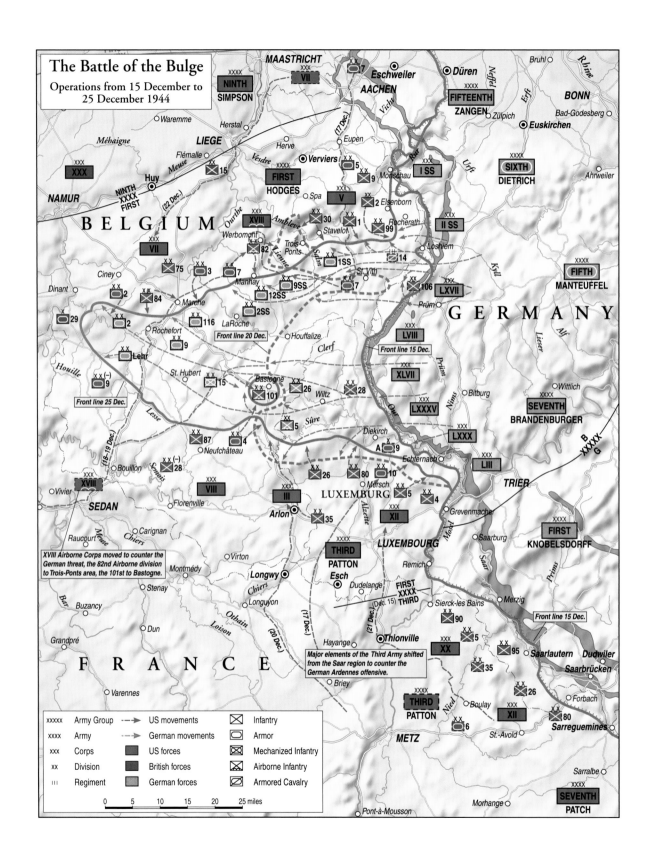

The Battle of the Bulge

Operations from 15 December to 25 December 1944

MAASTRICHT

NINTH SIMPSON

VII

Eschweiler · Düren ·

AACHEN

FIFTEENTH ZANGEN

BONN

Bruhl

Bad-Godesberg ·

Zülpich

· Euskirchen

Ahrweiler ·

Waremme ·

Herstal

Méhaigne

LIEGE

Herve

Eupen ·

Verviers ·

Flémalle ·

Huy ·

Meuse

Vesdre

5

I SS

SIXTH DIETRICH

NINTH
XXXX
FIRST

(22 Dec.)

(17 Dec.)

NAMUR

FIRST HODGES

Spa ·

V

9

Monschau ·

2 Elsenborn

99

Rocherath

II SS

FIFTH MANTEUFFEL

Vichy

Ruor

Urft

Neffel

Erft

Rhine

BELGIUM

XXX

15

XXX XXX

XXX

Ourthe

XVIII

Werbomont ·

82

Amblève

30

1

Stavelot ·

Trois-Ponts

Salm

Lienne

Loshiem ·

14

GERMANY

Kyll

Lieser

Alf

VII

75

3

7

Manhay ·

9SS

12SS

2SS

1SS

St.Vith ·

7

106

LXVII

LXVIII

Prüm ·

Wittlich ·

Ciney ·

Dinant ·

2

84 · Marche

116

LaRoche

Houffalize ·

Clerf

LVIII

XLVII

Bitburg ·

Nims

Chur

SEVENTH BRANDENBURGER

29

2

Rochefort ·

9

Front line 20 Dec.

St. Hubert ·

15

Front line 25 Dec.

Lehr

9

Lesse

Bastogne

101

26

Wiltz ·

28

LXXXV

LXXX

Prüm

Houille

(18–19 Dec.)

87

4

5

Sûre

Neufchâteau ·

Diekirch ·

A

9

Echternach ·

LIII

B
XXXXX
G

TRIER

Bouillon ·

28

VIII

26

80

10

Mersch ·

Grevenmacher ·

FIRST KNOBELSDORFF

Vivier ·

Senois

XVIII

SEDAN

Florenville ·

III

LUXEMBURG

5

4

Saarburg ·

Mosel

Alzette

Arlon ·

35

XII

LUXEMBOURG

Remich ·

Saar

Prims

XVIII Airborne Corps moved to counter the German threat, the 82nd Airborne division to Trois-Ponts area, the 101st to Bastogne.

Raucourt ·

Carignan ·

Montmédy ·

Virton ·

Longwy ·

THIRD PATTON

Esch ·

Dudelange ·

FIRST
XXXX
THIRD

(Dec. 15)

Sierck-les-Bains ·

Merzig ·

Saarburg ·

Mosel

Chiers

Stenay ·

Chiers

Longuyon ·

(17 Dec.)

(21 Dec.)

90

XX

5

Saarlautern · Dudwiler ·

Bar

Meuse

Dun ·

Loison

Orbain

Loison

(20 Dec.)

Hayange ·

Thionville ·

95

35

Saarbrücken ·

Grandpré ·

Major elements of the Third Army shifted from the Saar region to counter the German Ardennes offensive.

Briey ·

26

Forbach ·

Varennes ·

FRANCE

Nied

THIRD PATTON

Boulay ·

XII

80

Sarreguemines ·

6

St.-Avold ·

METZ

Pont-à-Mousson ·

Morhange ·

Sarralbe ·

SEVENTH PATCH

xxxxx	Army Group	- - -→	US movements	⊠	Infantry
xxxx	Army	- - -→	German movements	▢	Armor
xxx	Corps		US forces	⊠	Mechanized Infantry
xx	Division		British forces	⊠	Airborne Infantry
|||	Regiment		German forces	▱	Armored Cavalry

0   5   10   15   20   25 miles

Eisenhower then asked Patton how long before Third Army could launch a counterattack into the south of the German penetration. Patton joyfully announced that his army could attack "on December 22 with three divisions!" Not realizing that Patton had been preparing for this change in direction for several days, the others in the room expressed stunned disbelief that a corps-size operation could be mounted in winter conditions in less than seventy-two hours. Colonel Charles R. Cadman, Patton's aide, described the reaction:

Most of the senior commanders in the room considered it impossible for Patton to shift his forces 90 degrees from a major eastern offensive to one toward the north in such a short time. Eisenhower concluded from Patton's statement that he was underestimating the actual strength of the German attack. Eisenhower also believed that three divisions would not have enough combat power to successfully carry out the kind of attack he knew would be necessary to cut off the advancing German armies. After Patton explained that he would follow up his initial three-division attack with one of three more soon after, Eisenhower approved the plan.

An American soldier with an M1 81mm mortar listens for fire direction on a field phone. It became apparent early on the first day of the German Ardennes offensive that additional forces would be required to stiffen 28th and 106th Infantry Divisions, as well as 14th Cavalry Group. *National Archives*

Returning the favor: a wounded American medic is helped to an aid station. *National Archives*

On December 19, Eisenhower also decided to turn over temporary control of American forces north of the Ardennes (most of Hodges's First Army and all of Simpson's Ninth Army) to Montgomery and his 21st Army Group. Bradley's only remaining First Army Corps, Middleton's VIII Corps, was attached to Patton's Third Army for the upcoming operation. Bradley saw the rearrangement as demonstrating a lack of confidence in his leadership abilities.

Eisenhower had high hopes that by giving Montgomery the bulk of Bradley's 12th Army Group, Montgomery would summon up the courage to commit his reserve forces, arrayed on the northern edge of the Ardennes, to counterattacking the northern flank of the German penetration. The strategy preferred by Eisenhower would involve Montgomery and Patton counterattacking the German penetration at the same time, thus preventing the Germans from concentrating their resources on just one threat at a time. If both Montgomery's and Patton's counterattacks were successful, there was a good chance the German advance could be cut off at its base, thus trapping the bulk of enemy forces within the Ardennes. However, true to form, Montgomery delayed his first counterattack to early January 1945.

Despite the lack of timely help from Montgomery's forces, Patton, with the full support of Eisenhower and Bradley, quickly set out to counterattack the southern flank of the German penetration. There was little time to waste, since the XLVII Panzer Corps of Hasso von Manteuffel's Fifth Panzer Army had already cut off and surrounded the American units in Bastogne.

Almost appearing to simply be ducking for cover, a German machine gunner lies dead in the snow, killed in combat. *National Archives*

An American M2A1 105mm howitzer and crew. The weapon can deliver high-angle plunging or direct fire if the need arises. *National Archives*

American soldiers inspect a captured German Sd.Kfz. 250 half-track with U.S. Army markings painted on it. *National Archives*

PATTON'S THOUGHTS ON FIGHTING IN WOODS

THE BEST WAY for infantry to go through woods in the daytime is to advance in a skirmish line on a distant direct point, if such is available, or, more probably, on a compass bearing. The skirmish line should be at reduced interval, and should move straight forward through the wood, using marching fire. If this is done, it will be surprising how little resistance will be encountered, because, if the enemy attempts to fire through the woods, his rifles, which are always less effective than ours, will not penetrate through the trees, while ours will penetrate and so get him.

In fighting through European woods, which are intersected at right angles every thousand meters by lanes, do not walk down the lanes, and be careful how you cross them, cross them fast, because the enemy usually has them swept with machine guns.

—*War As I Knew It,*
"Reflections and Suggestions"

A line of cold and weary American soldiers line up for a meal during the fighting in the Ardennes. While food was always important to those in the front lines, the monotony of eating the same thing for weeks on end often led some to lose interest in food, which would in turn lower their combat effectiveness. *National Archives*

An American 75mm M1A1 field howitzer could fire six rounds per minute. In response to the growing crisis with Middleton's VIII Corps, Eisenhower sent in his last uncommitted reserves, the 82nd and 101st Airborne Divisions belonging to XVIII Airborne Corps. These divisions moved into the Ardennes front on December 19, 1944. The 82nd went to the Belgium town of Werbomont to help seal off the Losheim Gap. *National Archives*

THE FIGHT FOR BASTOGNE

Though surrounded, the 101st Airborne Division and the other units inside Bastogne, including Task Force SNAFU—a mixture of stragglers who made their way into Bastogne—were not cut off. They still had radio communication with Middleton's VIII Corps and knew a relief column from Patton's Third Army would soon be pushing toward them.

On the evening of December 21, the German commander of the Seventh Army composed the now-famous ultimatum addressed to the American defenders of Bastogne. It demanded "the honorable surrender of the encircled town" in two hours on threat of "annihilation" by the massed fire of German artillery. This was a bluff by the German commander, since the Americans inside Bastogne outnumbered him in both troops and firepower. The acting-commander of the American forces defending Bastogne, Brig. Gen. Anthony C. McAuliffe, expressed his contempt for the German offer of surrender with his famous reply, "Nuts," delivered to the Germans the next day. When the Germans proved puzzled by the term, another American officer was kind enough to explain to the Germans that it meant "Go to hell!"

"Hold Bastogne." Before leaving the town on December 19, 1944, Middleton, the VIII Corps commander, gave that one standing order to Brig. Gen. Anthony McAuliffe (shown here), acting commander of 101st Airborne Division. *National Archives*

A U.S. Army L4 light observation plane has crashed upon landing. *National Archives*

The gun crew of an American 105mm Howitzer Motor Carriage M7 in action. The American generals tasked with defending Bastogne knew that the Germans would need to capture the town to access the road network west of it and thus have any chance of continuing their planned advance to Antwerp. *National Archives*

American soldiers stand over the corpse of a German soldier killed in battle. The initial American defense preparations in and around Bastogne were influenced by the fact that those in command were not really aware of the German forces bearing down on them. *National Archives*

After receiving the rejected surrender offer, the Germans launched more probing attacks along the entire Bastogne defensive perimeter. All were repulsed. On December 23 the enemy probes continued, but for the first time in a week, the weather cleared, and American airpower began to take its toll on the German forces surrounding Bastogne. The clear skies also meant that an aerial resupply system could bring badly needed supplies to the 101st Airborne, sending American morale soaring. There was still hard fighting to come, and few on either side realized the break in the weather sounded the death knell to the last great German offensive.

The Germans were becoming increasingly anxious about the situation at Bastogne. The Fifth Panzer Army was now on the defensive almost everywhere, and the possibility of advancing to the Meuse River and the port city of Antwerp had evaporated. Despite strong reinforcements, numerous uncoordinated attacks launched by the German Seventh Army Corps on Bastogne on December 24 and 25 all failed.

On the evening of December 25, the German Seventh Army commander became highly concerned about the probability of a relief column from Patton's Third Army breaking through to Bastogne. He asked Fifth Panzer headquarters staff for either additional reinforcements or permission to call off his attacks on Bastogne. Both his requests were denied.

An American soldier poses with his M1 Garand rifle. *National Archives*

An American M36 tank destroyer has just fired off a main-gun round during a nighttime firing mission. Despite being surrounded by German forces and suffering countless attacks, Bastogne never fell into German hands during their Ardennes offensive. *National Archives*

An American soldier shows a buddy where a bullet penetrated his helmet. To relieve the besieged Bastogne and the American forces trapped within, Eisenhower decided to use elements of Patton's Third Army to make a narrow thrust into the town. *National Archives*

7

THE ROAD TO BASTOGNE

ON DECEMBER 20, Eisenhower was informed by his intelligence chief that Hitler had committed everything he had to the Ardennes offensive. It was good news. With no uncommitted German reserves remaining, the Allies could counterattack in the Ardennes sector with little risk. Although poor weather conditions grounded Allied reconnaissance planes, it also grounded the remnants of the Luftwaffe, so the Allies were able to regroup for a surprise counterattack along both flanks of the German penetration. The counterattacks were to begin when Patton's Third Army in the south and Montgomery's 21st Army Group in the north were strong enough.

The immediate goal of the planned counterattack against the south flank of the German penetration was to reach Bastogne. Once they made contact with the American defenders, Patton's troops were to restore and maintain a permanent corridor into the town. Additionally, they were to push the German units surrounding Bastogne away from the town's road network so Third Army could use the network for further operations to the north and northeast.

Patton chose the newly arrived III Corps (under command of Maj. Gen. John Millikin) to lead the advance toward Bastogne. The III Corps attack was to begin on December 22, from an assembly area in Belgium near the town of Arlon, only twenty miles south of Bastogne.

An American M36 tank destroyer rolls down a frozen dirt road with infantry passengers. A few days had to pass before Eisenhower could launch the first American counterattacks in the Ardennes and regain the initiative. To gain time and save lives, Eisenhower was willing to let his forces fall back as far as the Meuse River, but no farther. *National Archives*

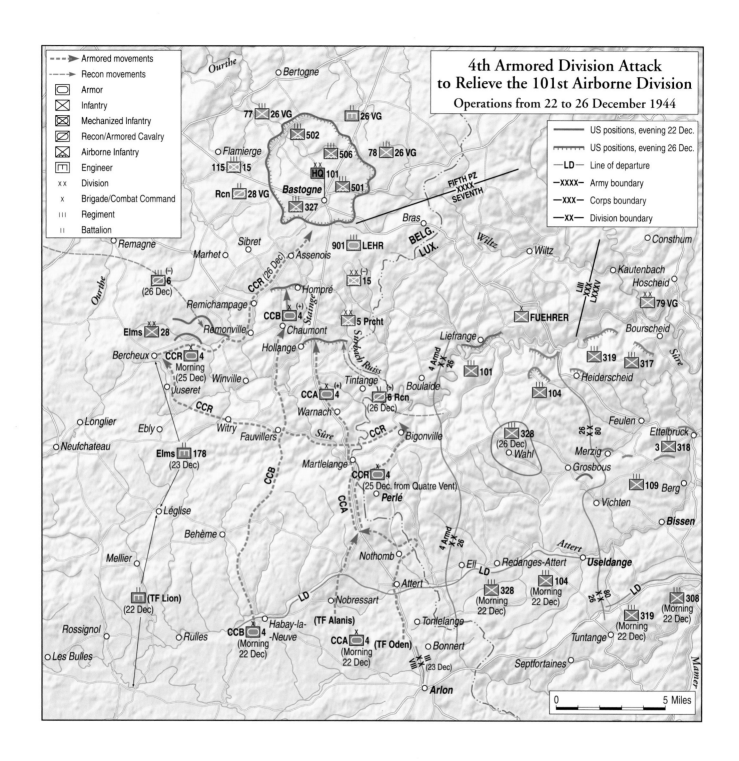

Legend

- ‑‑‑▶ Armored movements
- ‑‑‑‑ Recon movements
- Armor
- Infantry
- Mechanized Infantry
- Recon/Armored Cavalry
- Airborne Infantry
- Engineer
- XX Division
- X Brigade/Combat Command
- III Regiment
- II Battalion

4th Armored Division Attack to Relieve the 101st Airborne Division
Operations from 22 to 26 December 1944

- ——— US positions, evening 22 Dec.
- ‖‖‖ US positions, evening 26 Dec.
- LD— Line of departure
- —XXXX— Army boundary
- —XXX— Corps boundary
- —XX— Division boundary

0 _____ 5 Miles

Bastogne could be reached by the Arlon-Bastogne road, or by the Neufchâteau-Bastogne road, about twenty miles west of Arlon. Millikin and his III Corps staff preferred the Arlon route, where 4th Armored Division was already in position to attack. Major General Troy H. Middleton, the VIII Corps commander, favored a broad thrust using both routes, with the main thrust along the Neufchâteau-Bastogne road. After some discussion, the Arlon-Bastogne road was chosen for its direct line to Bastogne. If they could seize the Arlon approach, it would also stop the reinforcement of the German troops already south of Bastogne (the 5th Parachute Division and the 325th Volksgrenadier Division).

The sector chosen for III Corps' advance lay within the eastern part of Luxembourg and the western part of Belgium. It contained some of the most rugged terrain in all of the Ardennes. The large Sûre and Wiltz rivers ran through the area and presented tough obstacles for the advance of any mechanized or motorized formations from the south. Numerous other smaller rivers and streams of varying width and depth also crisscrossed the entire region.

Eisenhower (left) and Patton. On December 19, 1944, Eisenhower called a meeting at Verdun, France, in response to the German Ardennes attack. The meeting was attended by all of Eisenhower's top generals. It set in motion a series of actions that would regain the initiative lost by the Allies during the early stages of the German advance. *Patton Museum*

American soldiers fire upon a German tank with a 2.36-inch M9A1 bazooka. Eisenhower was well aware of Patton's desire to immediately counterattack the German Ardennes offensive with whatever forces were available to him. Such an attack was not how the more cautious Eisenhower liked to conduct military operations. On the other hand, he knew that he had to relieve Bastogne to regain the initiative. *National Archives*

American soldiers take a break during the Ardennes fighting. Bastogne, an unremarkable Belgian market town of about four thousand people, became a central component of the Battle of the Bulge because of the seven paved roads that radiated from it. *National Archives*

American soldiers man a Browning M2 .50-caliber air-cooled machine gun. Hitler's original plans for his Ardennes offensive called for the seizure of Bastogne by a quick thrust if his troops found the town lightly defended. If they did not, his Panzer divisions were to bypass Bastogne and keep moving westward. The 26th Volksgrenadier Division would then be tasked with the capture of Bastogne. *National Archives*

The forces assigned to III Corps were the 26th and 80th Infantry Divisions, as well as 4th Armored Division. Millikin's orders called for him to advance north with all three divisions in a line-abreast formation. The 80th Infantry Division would be on the right and, during its advance, would maintain contact with the left wing of Patton's XII Corps. The 26th Infantry Division would form the center, and 4th Armored Division would advance on the left, with Bastogne as its goal.

From the first moment of planning, there was no doubt that Patton's main focus would be the progress of 4th Armored Division. It was the most mobile of the three divisions, and its tanks and tank destroyers were the best suited for any engagements along the route of advance. Further, Patton promised Bradley that he would be inside the town by Christmas Day. The 26th and 80th Infantry Divisions were primarily seen as guarding the flanks of the 4th Armored Division. These were conventional, textbook employments. Patton hadn't thrown the book away; he was just writing in it faster than the Germans could read.

American soldiers man an M5 three-inch antitank gun. *National Archives*

The 4th Armored Division sped off in the direction of the Ardennes under Maj. Gen. Hugh J. Gaffey, Patton's former chief of staff. Gaffey, under Patton's direction, sent Combat Commands A and B (CCA and CCB) of his division into the attack in a line-abreast formation. The advance was scheduled to begin in the early morning hours of December 22. CCA would advance along the main Arlon-Bastogne road, while CCB pushed forward on secondary roads to the west. Information available to Gaffey and Patton indicated that the bridges across the Sûre River, at the town of Martelange, had been destroyed. If CCA were delayed at the Sûre River crossings, CCB was to move eastward and take the lead ahead of CCA on the main Arlon-Bastogne road. But even if CCA weren't delayed, CCB, under the command of Brig. Gen. Holmes Dager, was designated to lead the 4th Armored Division into Bastogne. The maneuver was complicated, but American commanders were, by now, seasoned masters of mobile warfare, and the plan was well within their capability.

Even as Eisenhower gave permission to Patton (right) to launch an attack toward Bastogne with elements of his Third Army, he made it clear to Bradley (left) that he had to restrain his subordinate from undertaking any more ambitious plans. *Patton Museum*

American paratroopers within Bastogne recover some air-dropped supplies. During the ten days that the roughly eighteen thousand men inside Bastogne were isolated by German forces, airdrops proved to be the only way in which supplies could be delivered. *National Archives*

HUGH JOESPH GAFFEY

HUGO J. GAFFEY BEGAN his military career as a second lieutenant in the U.S. Army Field Artillery in 1917. He went to Europe to fight the German Imperial Army in 1918. During the years between the end of World War I and the beginning of World War II, he served in a variety of positions in both the artillery and the cavalry.

From 1940 to early 1942, Gaffey served with the plans-and-training section of the newly formed I Armored Corps. He then went on to serve with the 2nd Armored Division from 1942 until 1943, in a variety of staff positions. Gaffey was promoted to the rank of major general in 1943.

Gaffey served as the commanding general of the 2nd Armored Division from May 1943 until being assigned to be the Third Army chief of staff in April 1944. In December 1944, Patton appointed him the commanding general of the 4th Armored Division, which Gaffey commanded until the end of the war in Europe.

National Archives

On December 22, as CCA advanced along the snow-covered Arlon-Bastogne road, it ran into its first delay near the town of Martelange, twelve miles south of Bastogne, where it had to bridge a large crater. CCA also entered into a firefight with elements of the 5th Parachute Division, and it was the next morning before it overcame German resistance.

Meanwhile, CCB, advancing on the west of CCA along a series of secondary roads, was making good progress. By noon on December 22, CCB was close to the small village of Burnon, only seven miles from Bastogne. Encouraged by a lack of enemy resistance, Patton ordered that CCB continue its advance through the night to reach Bastogne. Elements of CCB cleared Burnon by midnight, December 23. As the advance guard of CCB carefully made its way through the darkness toward Chaumont, the next village on the road to Bastogne, it encountered only occasional small-arms fire. When CCB reached the outskirts of Chaumont, however, the level of German resistance increased, forcing the advance guard of CCB to withdraw.

Later that morning, the full force of CCB was brought to bear on the 26th Volksgrenadier Division, the German defenders of Chaumont. American fighter-bombers from the XIX TAC also attacked the village. But the Germans would not give up. At one point in the battle, the Germans counterattacked with a force of fifteen self-propelled tank destroyers. Caught by surprise, CCB was thrown back with the loss of eleven tanks and sixty-five men. By the time the battle was over on December 24, Chaumont had fallen into American hands, and CCB had inflicted heavy losses on the 5th Parachute Division. But CCB was no closer to Bastogne than it had been the day before, and it had only ten Sherman medium tanks remaining.

Montgomery looks over a map with his subordinates. On December 20, 1944, Eisenhower reassigned Hodges's First Army and Simpson's Ninth Army (a total of six corps) to Montgomery's 21st Army Group so Montgomery could counterattack the northern flank of the bulge that the Germans had punched into the American lines. *National Archives*

An American soldier takes a break to eat a food ration. The painted German slogan behind him says: "One people, one empire, one leader." *National Archives*

An American soldier mans a water-cooled, .50-caliber M2 Browning machine gun nicknamed Cognac. On December 22, 1944, Patton launched his rescue of Bastogne from the town of Arlon, located twenty miles south of Bastogne, with Maj. Gen. John Millikin's III Corps, which besides 4th Armored Division included 26th and 80th Infantry Divisions. *National Archives*

Meanwhile, CCA had finally crossed the Sûre River on the afternoon of December 23, moving over a repaired bridge at the town of Martelange. Knowing it would take time for all of its elements to push across the narrow bridge, CCA rushed a small task force forward in an attempt to reach Bastogne as quickly as possible. Pushing aside scattered German resistance, the CCA task force made good progress until it reached the small village of Warnach early in the evening. The German 5th Parachute Division and a battery of self-propelled tank destroyers quickly knocked out the two leading American half-tracks. Since the village could not be bypassed at night, the American task-force commander ordered five light tanks and forty armored infantrymen to take the village. This attempt failed, as did a second and larger attack launched at midnight.

The morning of December 24, the Americans renewed their attacks on Warnach. After fierce house-to-house fighting, the German defender finally surrendered to the task force from CCA at about noon. The Germans lost 135 men, and an equal number were taken prisoner. American casualties numbered 68.

American soldiers whitewash a Jeep. *National Archives*

A very tired and dirty American tanker knows that there's still a long fight ahead. When he sent Millikin's III Corps to relieve Bastogne, Patton's orders were simple. The corps would advance north to St. Vith. The 80th Infantry Division would form the right flank and 26th Infantry Division would be in the center, with 4th Armored Division on the left flank. *National Archives*

PATTON'S THOUGHTS ON SUPPORTING FIRES

SUPPORTING FIRES must be arranged first to attack the enemy after our infantry has been discovered, and second to destroy counterattacks at dawn. Assaulting columns are preceded by a security detachment, which in turn is preceded by a patrol. The security detachment and patrol are absorbed when contact is made. In addition to the assaulting columns, a reserve should be available for exploitation after daylight. Countersign and challenge and identification marks on helmets or sleeve are necessary. Landmarks and compass bearings to the objective are necessary. Offensive grenades should be used. When discovered, open rapid fire and make as much noise as possible, while rushing in to use the bayonet.

—*War As I Knew It,*
"Letter of Instruction No. 2"

The two combat commands of the 4th Armored Division relentlessly advanced in a race against time to reach Bastogne. The men of the 101st Airborne and other units trapped inside the town were fighting and waiting for relief. Radio messages sent from Bastogne not so subtly hinted that the 4th Armored Division could move a little faster. On the night of December 23, the commander of the American forces inside Bastogne sent the message "Sorry I did not get to shake hands today. I was disappointed." Another December 23 message from inside Bastogne, addressed to the 4th Armored Division, said, "There is only one more shopping day before Christmas." If Bastogne fell to the Germans, the 4th Armored Division would have to fight to retake the town instead of relieving the American forces already there.

Patton was not pleased by the unexpectedly slow progress of CCA and CCB toward Bastogne. He called III Corps headquarters and said, "There is too much piddling around. Bypass these towns and clear them up later. Tanks can operate on this ground now." Even as Patton complained to III Corps about the various delays at Chaumont and Warnach, a third delay developed at Bigonville, a village two and a half miles east of the Bastogne highway and close to the boundary between 4th Armored Division and 26th Infantry Division. The gap between these two divisions suddenly became a matter of serious concern when, on the night of December 22, there were reports that a large formation of German armor was moving into the area. To protect the CCs' open right flank, Gaffey ordered Col. Wendell Blanchard to form the division's reserve combat command (CCR) into a balanced task force (using the 53rd Armored Infantry Battalion and the 37th Tank Battalion) and move quickly toward Bigonville.

The American crew of a M1919A4 .30-caliber, air-cooled light machine gun stand guard in their foxhole. *National Archives*

Beginning on December 23, there was a five-day break in the weather over the Ardennes. This clearing allowed American airpower to weaken the German forces surrounding the town and eased the later entrance of the 4th Armored Division into Bastogne.

Early on December 23, 4th Armored Division's CCR left the village of Quatre-Vents, north of Arlon, followed the Arlon-Bastogne road to Martelange, and then turned right onto a secondary road, which angled northeast. This ice covering the road delayed CCR, and a great deal of time was spent moving the column slowly forward. At about noon, the advance guard of CCR came under fire from a small wooded area near a crossroads where the unit would turn north to reach Bigonville, and CCR could not make any progress for the rest of the day. Only after elements from the German 5th Parachute Division withdrew that night could CCR continue its advance to Bigonville. The next morning, CCR launched its attack on the town and cleared it before noon, taking over four hundred German prisoners.

An American soldier stands guard over a German prisoner wearing a snow-camouflage overall. As with all of Millikin's III Corps divisions, 80th Infantry Division eventually ran into stiff German opposition as it made its way toward Bastogne. By December 24, 1944, 80th had advanced far enough northward to hinder German Seventh Army's reinforcements heading to the Bastogne battleground. *National Archives*

An American talks on his AM SCR-536 "Handie Talkie" portable radio. *National Archives*

A long line of American soldiers trudge down a muddy road through a small Belgian town, passing a destroyed and burned-out American Jeep. They might wonder what happened to those who drove the vehicle, or they might be much more worried about what awaits them down the next street at the hands of their opponents. *National Archives*

NEW TACTICS ARE NEEDED

By Christmas Eve, it was clear to both Gaffey and Millikin that leading the advance toward Bastogne with tanks was getting them nowhere. The ice- and snow-covered terrain of the Ardennes forced the American tanks to stay on the narrow, hard-surfaced roads, where they made easy targets for a variety of German antitank weapons. More infantry was brought forward to clear the way for the tanks of 4th Armored Division, slowing the advance even further. Gaffey and Millikin also agreed that the around-the-clock tank attacks ordered by Patton and the night attacks by the infantry divisions of the III Corps failed to achieve any significant gains. Millikin, therefore, ordered that all three of his divisions hold in position on Christmas Eve, in preparation for attack early on Christmas morning.

With the destruction of all the bridges along the Arlon-Bastogne road beyond Martelange, Gaffey saw little chance for the tanks and armored infantry of CCR to reach Bastogne along this path. He therefore had Millikin shift the responsibility for the Bigonville sector to 26th Infantry Division late on Christmas Eve. This freed up CCR for employment on the west flank of the III Corps, along the more easily traversed Neufchâteau-Bastogne road. To reach their new assembly area near the village of Remoiville, CCR and its four hundred vehicles had to travel in a sixteen-mile-long column almost thirty miles at night and with the moon providing the only light. While relocating to the western flank of the 4th Armored Division, CCR passed behind both CCA and CCB.

The attacking infantry regiments of 26th Infantry Division employed armored half-tracks from their supporting antiaircraft units—such as this M15 equipped with a single 37mm automatic cannon and two Browning M2 .50-caliber, air-cooled machine guns—to blast anything in their path that might conceal German soldiers. *National Archives*

An American M1 155mm towed artillery piece, nicknamed the "Long Tom," is being set up. *National Archives*

An American tanker stands on the hull of his vehicle and listens to the intercom system in his helmet. Notice the M1 Garand rifle hanging in a sling off the tank's turret. Additional assistance for the advancing infantry regiments of 26th Infantry Division came from its supporting artillery, tank, and tank-destroyer units, all of which blasted the Germans out of their numerous defensive positions. *National Archives*

As 4th Armored Division prepared itself for the Christmas Day advance toward Bastogne, Gaffey's plans still called for CCB, in the center, to reach Bastogne first. Both CCA and CCR were to act as flank guards during the upcoming attack. To beef up the infantry complement of 4th Armored Division, Gaffey transferred in the 1st and 2nd Battalions of the 318th Infantry Regiment from 80th Infantry Division. The 1st Battalion went to CCA; the 2nd Battalion went to CCB.

The 80th and 26th Infantry Divisions were east of 4th Armored Division. The infantry divisions' main mission was to root out the German forces south of the Sûre River and close in the north along the Our River. This mission was important because it would block any efforts by the German Seventh Army to move its reserve units into the Bastogne area.

A German soldier lies dead in his frozen and snow-covered foxhole. Unlike the hilly and wooded terrain in which 26th and 80th Infantry Divisions were to fight, 4th Armored Division was to attack toward Bastogne through relatively open country. Patton ordered his 4th Armored Division tankers to "drive like hell." *National Archives*

Belgian women sew white bed sheets together to make snow capes for American soldiers. *National Archives*

American soldiers, armed with M3 submachine gun and wearing snow capes, prepare to go out on a patrol. *National Archives*

However, ahead of the 80th Infantry Division, the German Seventh Army was already moving reinforcements into the Bastogne area on the morning of December 24. Reinforcements included the Fuehrer Grenadier Brigade and the 79th Volksgrenadier Division. Prior to this, the LXXXV Corps of the German Seventh Army had faced Millikin's III Corps with only two units, the 5th Parachute Division and the 352nd Volksgrenadier Division. Despite fears that the two German divisions in front of the American advance from the south might not hold for long, Hitler and his senior staff were very reluctant to commit Seventh Army reinforcements until it was almost too late. It was only when the threat to the German southern flank dramatically increased, as Millikin's III Corps closed in on Bastogne, that reinforcements were sent to the Seventh Army.

Patton was also intent on reinforcing the three-division advance of his III Corps. Patton quickly pushed 35th Infantry Division, under command of Maj. Gen. Paul W. Baade, into the fray. On December 26, as Baade's division came on line with III Corps, 80th Infantry Division was transferred from III Corps to XII Corps without moving from its position. Patton was reluctant to assign XII Corps the mission of attacking northward across the cold and swollen Sûre and Our rivers. At almost the same time, the German Seventh Army commander was considering plans to launch a spoiling attack against the eastern flank of the American forces congregated around Bastogne. Fortunately for the American III Corps, he was unable to muster the men or equipment to implement his plan.

American medics carry wounded recovered from the front lines to an aid station. Almost 47,500 American soldiers were wounded during the Battle of the Bulge. Many owed their lives to medics who pulled them to safety while under hostile fire. *National Archives*

American soldiers man a camouflaged Browning MI917A1 water-cooled .30-caliber machine gun. The terrain 4th Armored Division would have to traverse to reach Bastogne was the most favorable of that faced by the three III Corps divisions. The 4th Armored faced the toughest unit in the German Seventh Army, the crack 5th Parachute Division. *National Archives*

One of the greatest morale builders for American troops during World War II was the delivery of mail from home. The U.S. Army always did its best to move the mail up to the front lines in the most expedient manner possible. *National Archives*

An American M32 tank-recovery vehicle with an attached T1E1 mine exploder makes sure the road is clear. *National Archives*

THE LAST FEW MILES TO BASTOGNE

On Christmas Day 1944, all three combat commands of 4th Armored Division were slowly grinding their way toward Bastogne from the south. That same morning, the German Fifth Panzer Army launched a strong attack against the northwest sector of the 101st Airborne's defensive perimeter around Bastogne. After some hard fighting, the German attackers were defeated.

During the heavy fighting at Warnach on December 23, a few tanks from CCA had tried to drive on to Tintange, the next village on the road to Bastogne, but were quickly bogged down. Gaffey had provided reinforcements from 80th Infantry Division to take Tintange on the way to Bastogne. After a freezing night in the snow, Maj. George W. Connaughton's 1st Battalion, 318th Infantry (attached to CCA), had marched off to the small creek south of the village that was their planned line of departure on Christmas Day. After suffering heavy casualties from a German assault gun, the remaining American soldiers had charged the town of Tintange rather than make themselves ready targets for the Germans. Supported at the last minute by a formation of eight American fighter-bombers, which had blasted the village with bombs and rockets, the American infantrymen had managed to capture Tintange, the assault gun, and the 161 German soldiers who defended the village.

Two weary-looking American soldiers take a break from the fighting. Their faces reflect the overwhelming physical fatigue common to many of those on the front lines. The psychological toll of combat accounted for between 10 and 15 percent of American battle casualties in World War II. *National Archives*

Meanwhile, 2nd Battalion, 318th Infantry, under the command of Lt. Col. Glenn H. Gardner, was fighting on Christmas Day alongside the armored infantry and tanks of CCB. By the end of the day, 2nd Battalion had reached the woods near the village of Hompre, some four thousand yards from the Bastogne perimeter. A lieutenant and a four-man patrol from the battalion managed to sneak through German lines to reach a Bastogne outpost in the early morning darkness of December 26. They learned that CCR, on the left flank of CCB, was already in Bastogne.

CCR moved from the eastern flank of CCA to the western flank of CCB. Its commander selected his own route, to avoid destroyed bridges. An assembly area was established southwest of the village of Bercheux on the Neufchâteau-Bastogne road. It was here that the men and equipment of CCR would gather before heading toward Bastogne at dawn on Christmas Day. A big concern was the lack of information on German strength or dispositions along the sixteen-mile stretch of road that lay ahead of CCR.

Leading the advance toward Bastogne was 37th Tank Battalion, commanded by Lt. Col. Creighton W. Abrams, and 53rd Armored Infantry Battalion, commanded by Lt. Col. George Jaques, nicknamed "Jigger Jakes" by his men. Support for these two leading units came from the self-propelled 105mm howitzers of 94th Armored Field Artillery Battalion and a battery of self-propelled 155mm howitzers from 177th Field Artillery Battalion.

PATTON'S THOUGHTS ON THE BAYONET

FEW MEN ARE killed by the bayonet; many are scared of it. Bayonets should be fixed when the firefight starts. Bayonets must be sharpened by the individual soldier. The German hates the bayonet and is inferior to our men with it. Our men should know this.

—*War As I Knew It,* "*Letter of Instruction No. 2*"

American soldiers take aim with their M1 Garand rifles at possible advancing enemy troops. The 4th Armored Division had to do more than just punch a hole through enemy lines to reach Bastogne. It had to restore and maintain a permanent corridor into Bastogne and clear away the German force surrounding it. *National Archives*

A group of young Red Cross women pose in front of their clubmobiles, which dispensed hot coffee and donuts free to all American soldiers. Clubmobile detachments traveled with the rear echelon of each American army corps in Western Europe during World War II and were a welcome sight to all. *National Archives*

A mile and a half up the road from Bercheux stood the village of Vaux-lez Rosières. Beyond Vaux-lez Rosières was the German-occupied village of Remoiville. After some hard fighting, Remoiville fell to CCR. The light tanks in the advance guard of CCR moved on, but had advanced only a few hundred yards by the end of Christmas Day. At Remoiville, CCR came abreast of CCB. Gaffey was still expecting CCB to make the breakthrough to Bastogne, now that CCR was guarding its west flank.

On Christmas night, Colonel Blanchard and the other officers of CCR gathered over a map that just arrived by air courier. The map showed the disposition of the 101st Airborne within the Bastogne perimeter and a rough estimate of the German order of battle as it faced in toward Bastogne and out toward 4th Armored Division. Blanchard gave his plan for attack the next day. The plan called for an advance through Remichampagne (one and a half miles from Remoiville), and a contingent objective was the village of Clochimont.

At Clochimont, CCR was expected to either run into the German main line of defenses or face a serious counterattack. So when CCR advance elements reached the outskirts of Clochirnont, they began to move with great caution. Tanks and infantry moved out on either side of the main column to provide flank protection in case of a German counterattack. Abrams sent one tank company northward, hoping to draw fire from and uncover the next enemy position. A second objective was to uncover enemy positions in the village of Assenois, straight to his front, or Sibret, the objective assigned by Blanchard, on the Bastogne highway.

A group of American artillerymen pose for a Signal Corps photographer with a 105mm round. They have written "Gateway to Hell" in chalk on the cartridge case and "1,000" upon the projectile. "1,000" probably refers to the number of rounds fired from a particular howitzer. *National Archives*

A dead German soldier lies sprawled in front of an American-defended building. *National Archives*

PATTON'S THOUGHTS ON GERMAN ANTITANK GUNS

WHENEVER GERMAN antitank guns have gotten our tanks, it has almost always been our fault. In spite of years of instruction, tanks will go up obvious tank lanes such as cart tracks, open river bottoms, small roads or paths, or along hedges; all of which any intelligent antitank gunner will have arranged to cover. Furthermore, tanks will insist, as I have already said, insist crossing skylines or emerging from cover without looking, in spite of the fact that it is well known that German antitank guns are generally on reverse slopes or in positions to fire at right angles to the axis of advance. Again, due to maneuver experience, tanks seek visual cover afforded by bushes, failing to remember that these do not stop bullets. The only cover behind which a tank has any security is that afforded by earth defilade.

—*The Unknown Patton,*
"Letter of Instruction No. 3"

American soldiers wearing snow capes await the enemy. On noon of December 22, 1944, CCB of 4th Armored Division was in sight of the village of Burnon, only seven miles from Bastogne. However, a blown bridge and an enemy rearguard unit kept CCB from taking Burnon until the next morning. *National Archives*

Two American soldiers are ready to repel any enemy attack with a Browning MI9I9A4 .30-caliber, air-cooled machine gun. The next sizeable village approached by CCB of 4th Armored Division on December 23, 1944, was Chaumont. Unlike Martelange, Chaumont was defended by numerous antitank guns, which had to be knocked out before the advance to Bastogne could continue. *National Archives*

Orders from the commanding officer of CCR specified that the unit take the village of Sibret before moving on to Assenois. Abrams had information indicating that Sibret was heavily defended. Having no more than twenty M4 Sherman medium tanks left within his battalion, Abrams was reluctant to risk losing them in an attempt to take Sibret and then have nothing left for the continued advance to Bastogne. The 53rd Armored Infantry Battalion, already weakened by previous conflicts, was, like Abrams's 37th Tank Battalion, short of men. Abrams and Jaques, the battalion commanders, decided to modify Blanchard's orders and dash through the village of Assenois and straight on to Bastogne. They contacted Patton by radio to request his permission to change plans; Patton readily gave his permission and urged them on. It was a gutsy move on the part of the two lieutenant colonels. By contacting Patton directly, they not only went over the head of their immediate superior, but over the heads of their division and corps commanders as well. Abrams quickly began to pull together the resources of CCR, with artillery support from CCB on its right flank, for an attack on Assenois. As the tanks and armored infantry of CCR began their advance, thirteen batteries of artillery opened fire on the German defenders of the village.

A German Sd.Kfz. 251 half-track is pressed into American military service. As CCB fought hard to take Claumont, CCA continued its advance to Bastogne. It approached the village Warnach on the night of December 23, 1944, and ran into heavy German resistance. The fighting would continue until the next day. *National Archives*

American soldiers walk alongside and ride on an M4A3(75)W Sherman medium tank. On the night of December 22, 1944, enemy tanks were reported heading toward the village of Bigonville, located two and half miles east of the Arlon-Bastogne road in an unguarded gap between 4th Armored Division and 28th Infantry Division. *National Archives*

The tankers and armored infantrymen of CCR tried to race through Assenois using the artillery barrage as cover. However, the intensity of the barrage forced the armored infantrymen to disembark from their open-topped, armored half-tracks and seek cover in the nearest building doorways or along walls. In the smoke and confusion, the German defenders poured out of the buildings' cellars, where they had sought cover from the American artillery barrage, to challenge the American infantrymen in a close-range melee. The tanks and a few armored half-tracks of CCR continued on to Bastogne without the armored infantrymen, who were unable to disengage from this fight.

Leading the armored fighting vehicles of CCR the last few miles to Bastogne was 1st Lt. Charles Boggess Jr. A colorful and vivid description of his final advance to Bastogne can be found in the 4th Armored Division official history. It starts:

The four lead tanks in Boggess' column drew ahead as the half-tracks were slowed by German shells and debris. The tankers rolled along, sweeping the wooded ridge with machine gun fire. Finally, they burst through the German defenses and into the 101st Airborne perimeter.

Lieutenant Boggess ordered the roaring Sherman tank down to a canter. In the open fields beyond the pines he saw red, yellow, and blue supply parachutes spilled over the snow like confetti. Some of the colored chutes, caught in the tall pines, indicated where ammunition, food, and medicine had been dropped to the besieged troops. The column halted.

Standing up in his turret, Lieutenant Boggess shouted, "Come here; come on out," to khaki-clad figures in foxholes. "This is the 4th Armored." There was no answer. Helmeted heads peered suspiciously over carbine sights. The lieutenant shouted again. A lone figure strode forward. Lieutenant Boggess watched him carefully.

"I'm Lieutenant Webster of the 326th Engineers, 101st Airborne Division," the approaching figure called. "Glad to see you." The time was 4:45pm, December 26. The gap behind the four front-running tanks had, however, given the Germans a chance to lob mines onto the road. One half-track struck a mine and was destroyed. Infantrymen ran forward against bazooka and machine gun fire to clear the mines, but three more half-tracks exploded. Fighting mostly on foot, the rest of the column reached the trapped troops.

A German soldier lies frozen in position where he fell in action. Despite help from the fighter-bombers of Weylands XIX TAC, the Germans would not give up the village of Chaumont to CCB (4th Armored Division) without a stiff fight, which caused heavy losses on both sides. At one point, the Germans brought up a dozen or more armored assault guns that knocked out eleven American tanks. *National Archives*

An American M4A3(76)W Sherman medium tank is armed with a 76mm main gun. To protect his open right flank, Gaffey ordered CCR (combat command reserve) to take Bigonville, which it did on December 24, 1944. While the stiff fighting at Claumont, Warnach, and Bigonville took a toll on the German defenders, Bastogne was still out of reach of the 4th Armored Division. *National Archives*

Shortly after CCR of 4th Armored Division managed to link up with the defenders inside Bastogne, Patton wrote to Gaffey: "The outstanding celerity of your movement and the unremitting, vicious, and skillful manner in which you pushed the attack terminating at the end of four days and four nights of incessant battle in the relief of Bastogne constitute one of the finest chapters in the glorious history of the United States Army." Patton also wrote to his wife that "[t]he relief of Bastogne is the most brilliant operation we have thus far performed and is in my opinion the outstanding achievement of this war."

A German soldier lies sprawled dead next to a destroyed American Jeep. *National Archives*

An American soldier lies dead in an Ardennes forest. *National Archives*

An up-armored type of M4A3E2 Sherman medium tank, known as the Jumbo, was employed by CCR to break into Bastogne. On December 26, 1944, CCR of 4th Armored Division began its advance. With the support of Weyland's XIX TAC and artillery, CCR broke through the German positions surrounding Bastogne late that afternoon. *National Archives*

The road network in the Ardennes was not designed and built to support the large number of wheeled and tracked vehicles that the opposing sides threw into the Battle of the Bulge. The narrowness of the roads is clearly illustrated in this picture of two-way American traffic trying to move to its assigned destinations. *National Archives*

An American M10 tank destroyer lights up the night during a firing mission. Even as relief convoys entered Bastogne through the narrow corridor punched through the German lines by CCR of 4th Armored Division, the two main roads east and west of the American corridor were still barred by the defending German Seventh Army.
National Archives

8

CLOSING THE BASTOGNE AREA

WHEN CCR REACHED the American defensive perimeter around Bastogne on December 26, the contact between the l0lst Airborne and Millikin's III Corps was tentative at best. The road between Assenois and Bastogne was still subject to enemy harassing fire. The two main highways east and west of the Assenois-Bastogne corridor were still held by the German Seventh Army, under the command of Gen. Erich Brandenberger. Millikin's III Corps would have gain access to Bastogne by first widening the breach that CCR had punched through German lines and then securing the Arlon-Bastogne highway. The segment of the main road between Neufchâteau and Assenois would also have to be cleared to prevent the Germans from rushing in with armored units.

The bulk of Gaffey's 4th Armored Division still lay east of Assenois, along the Arlon-Bastogne road. Patton assigned 9th Armored Division's CCA to Gaffey on the morning of December 26 for an attack along the left flank of 4th Armored Division's CCR to clear the villages along the Neufchâteau-Bastogne highway.

All soft-skinned vehicles traveling in and out of Bastogne on December 26 required escort, and CCR provided convoy protection. CCA and CCB of 4th Armored Division continued to push slowly toward Bastogne. On the morning of December 26, CCB attacked the German-defended village of Hompre (five miles south of Bastogne).

An American M4A1(76)W Sherman medium tank advances across a snow-covered landscape. Everybody on the Allied side knew that the narrow corridor that linked the defenders of Bastogne with Patton's Third Army would have to be quickly widened to maintain the breach in the German lines. *National Archives*

A German soldier carrying an MG34 machine gun and ammo box has fallen to American firepower. On December 27, CCB of 4th Armored Division launched an attack from west of the village of Hompre against troops of 15th Panzer Grenadier Division. By that same night, its patrols reached 101st Airborne Division's defensive perimeter around Bastogne. *National Archives*

By nightfall, patrols from CCB reached the 101st Airborne's defensive perimeter. But CCA had a much harder time getting near Bastogne. Ten miles south of Bastogne, the Americans had to destroy the village of Sainlez in order to flush the Germans out of hiding. When the German defenders of Sainlez fled, they moved east and struck 1st Battalion, 318th Infantry Regiment (attached to CCA), which had just cleared the nearby village of Livarchamps. The fighting in Livarchamps continued through the night and resulted in heavy American casualties. Frostbite cases among the infantrymen of CCA soon equaled the unit's battle losses.

As CCA and CCB and their attached formations continued to push forward to Bastogne, the American defensive perimeter around the town remained unusually quiet. Major General Maxwell Taylor, commander of the 101st Airborne, entered the town on December 27 to reassume his command after returning from a staff conference back in the States. He also took the time to congratulate his subordinate, Brig. Gen. Anthony McAuliffe, on doing such an outstanding job in his absence. A large number of supply trucks and replacement troops for the 101st Airborne followed Taylor into Bastogne, and a medical collecting company arrived to move the casualties back to hospitals. By noon on December 28, the last ambulance left the town.

December 27 also marked the return of winter's full fury and the end of five days of clear weather over the Ardennes. After that day, the poor weather allowed the XIX TAC to put aircraft into the air only sporadically. These brief periods of flying time still proved very important to Third Army operations. The Germans saw the return of bad weather as an opportunity to even the odds and began bringing in additional units for a new Bastogne offensive.

The barrel on this 155mm Gun M1 is in full recoil. To truly secure the relief of Bastogne, Millikin's III Corps would have to clear additional roads leading into the town. *National Archives*

American soldiers clean a Browning M2HB air-cooled .50-caliber machine gun.
National Archives

While the idealized goal of the U.S. Army in World War II was to provide hot food for all its soldiers on a regular basis, those who needed it the most (troops in the front lines) seldom saw it for long periods. They often made do with cold rations consisting of canned or dehydrated meat and vegetable dishes.
National Archives

An American soldier smokes a pipe while standing guard with a Browning M1917A1 .30-caliber, water-cooled machine gun, grenades at the ready. *National Archives*

An American M4A3(75)W Sherman medium tank awaits recovery and repair. CCA of 4th Armored Division entered Bastogne on the night of December 30, 1944. It quickly took up positions within the defense set up by l0lst Airborne Division and its supporting units. *Patton Museum*

By the morning of December 28, Millikin's III Corps noticed that the German units in their path were putting up more of a fight. Anticipating Eisenhower's impatience with the slow progress of Third Army's drive to clear the area around Bastogne, Patton twice called his boss to apologize. In addition, Patton had already ordered his staff to work on plans for a prompt redirection of Third Army's attack. The impetus for this redirection of forces came from a set of three plans presented on December 27 by Lt. Gen. Joseph Lawton Collins, commander of the VII Corps of the First Army. Two of Collins's plans called for merging with Patton in the Bastogne area; the third plan specified that the Belgian village of St. Vith, about twenty-five miles northeast of Bastogne, was the objective.

HOBART R. GAY

A NON–WEST POINTER, Hobart R. Gay graduated from a civilian college with a reserve-army commission as a second lieutenant in 1917. Gay did not see combat in World War I. He started out in the cavalry, but left that branch to join the Quartermaster Corps in 1934. By 1940, Gay had made the rank of lieutenant colonel, and a few weeks after the Japanese attack on Pearl Harbor, he rose to the rank of colonel.

Like Dwight D. Eisenhower and Omar Bradley, Gay played an important role in the American invasion of French North Africa, code-named Operation Torch, in November 1942. He was picked to be the chief of staff of the I Armored Corps and was awarded a Silver Star for his actions during the invasion. Gay was promoted to a one-star brigadier general in June 1942 and served as Patton's chief of staff of the Seventh Army during the invasion of Sicily.

From author Martin Blumenson's book on Patton, titled *Patton: The Man Behind the Legend 1885–1945*, comes this description of Gay: "[He was] a splendid companion [for Patton] who liked to ride and hunt, a superb staff officer who ran the military details of the [Patton] headquarters with exceptional efficiency."

Gay would be chief of staff of Patton's Third Army from December 1944 until the end of the war in Europe.

By March 1945, Gay had acquired the two stars of a major general. He remained on Patton's staff after the war had concluded in Europe and went with him when Patton took command of the Fifteenth Army. Upon Patton's death in December 1945, he took command of the Fifteenth Army. He saw combat again as the commander of the 1st Cavalry Division during the Korean War.

National Archives

Collins's proposed plans brought home an important issue for the American commanders regarding German penetration in the Ardennes. The two best options were to cut off the German penetration close to its shoulders or at its base. Patton argued that it should be cut off at its base by Allied attacks from both the northern and southern flanks. If this plan of action were adopted, Patton would move Third Army northeast from Luxembourg City toward the vicinity of Prum, a little over ten miles inside Germany. At Prum, it could link up with the American First Army under Hodges, which was coming from the north. By joining together at Prum, the two American armies would effectively prevent the German forces in the Ardennes from pulling back behind the safety of the West Wall. Hodges agreed with Patton's approach in principle, but felt that the roads in the area could not support the large armored force needed to successfully achieve this objective.

Bradley, the 12th Army Group commander, believed that the combination of inhospitable terrain and weather would doom Patton's plan to certain failure. He was also concerned about the lack of reserves that Patton's plan would create for the Supreme Headquarters Allied Expeditionary Force (SHAEF). The 6th Army Group had already dangerously thinned its lines to help release the bulk of Patton's Third Army for battles in the Ardennes. On December 27, Bradley suggested to Eisenhower that the Third Army attack start from the Bastogne area and continue northeast toward St. Vith. Bradley took great pains to inform Eisenhower that this plan was not Patton's concept of an advance against the base of the German penetration. Instead, it was clearly aimed at the shoulders of the German formation. Eisenhower accepted Bradley's suggestion, much to Patton's dismay. Montgomery, commander of 21st Army Group, had thus far not directly participated in the battle, but nonetheless maintained a keen interest in the Allied war effort conducted by the other two army groups. Montgomery also favored a two-pronged attack at the shoulders of the German penetration. He wanted to see Hodges's First Army, then under his command, link up with Patton's Third Army at Houffalize, Belgium, nine miles northeast of Bastogne. Despite these rebuffs, Patton still had plans to launch his XII Corps in the direction of Prum, Germany, if the opportunity arose. (The XII Corps, commanded by Maj. Gen. Manton S. Eddy, was located on the south flank of III Corps.)

An American M29 Weasel has been pressed into the role of an off-road ambulance. As Hitler was ordering Bastogne to be taken at all costs, Eisenhower was rushing in reinforcements to launch his own attack to clear the entire area around Bastogne of German forces. A very large and bloody collision between the two attacking forces was about to take place. *National Archives*

An American soldier looks over a captured German 8.8cm (88mm) PaK 43 (antitank gun). *National Archives*

On December 28, Eisenhower added the 11th Armored Division and the 87th Infantry Division to Bradley's depleted 12th Army Group. Both divisions came from the reformed SHAEF reserves. Bradley, in turn, informed Patton that the only reinforcements he could use were his VIII Corps, which was advancing from the center of the Ardennes toward Bastogne. (After the initial German attack on December 16, and prior to December 28, the VIII Corps had under its control only the units within Bastogne, remnants of the 28th Infantry Division, and an assortment of other smaller units.)

On the night of December 28, Patton met with the VIII and III Corps commanders to lay out the plans for the new Third Army attack. Middleton's VIII Corps would attack from west of Bastogne on the morning of December 30. Its assigned objective was the high ground and road network just south of Houffalize. The next day, Millikin's III Corps, moving up from the south, would begin advancing in a northeast direction toward St. Vith. (St. Vith had passed into German hands on December 21, while Houffalize had fallen to the Germans on December 22.)

An M4A3(75)W Sherman medium tank equipped with an M1 bulldozer blade. In the Ardennes, hedgerows had been replaced by winter roads as obstacles for the Allies. *National Archives*

American soldiers discover German dead during the fighting in the Ardennes.

The frozen bodies of the dead are loaded into a small trailer attached to a Jeep.
National Archives

WIDENING THE PATH TO BASTOGNE

The 9th Armored Division's CCA received its orders on December 26. CCA was to push forward on the left flank of CCR of the 4th Armored Division and attack in the direction of Sibret. There was more at stake than defending the corridor opened by CCR into Bastogne; Middleton had already begun making plans for his VIII Corps to join the Third Army attack beyond the area. The one thing that the VIII Corps commander wanted to avoid was pushing his divisions through Bastogne's narrow streets. He therefore convinced Bradley and Patton that VIII Corps should start its advance from a line of departure west of Bastogne. This tactic required opening the entire Neufchâteau-Bastogne road and driving the enemy back to the northwest.

When CCA started down the Neufchâteau road to Sibret on the morning of December 26, it had little or no information on enemy units in its path. (Lack of information on the opposing force was a serious problem for both sides throughout the campaign.) The CCA commander, Col. Thomas L. Harrold, therefore, divided his command into two task forces, called Collins and Karsteter. Task Force Collins was to take Sibret, and Task Force Karsteter was to take the nearby village of Villeroux. Both villages were key defensive positions for the Germans, since they overlooked the Neufchâteau-Bastogne road. Task Force Collins rushed into Sibret with all guns blazing on the morning of December 27. The village fell that night after heavy fighting. In a futile effort to retake Sibret, the Germans launched counterattacks on the mornings of December 28 and 29. On the morning of December 29, Task Force Collins pushed on to the nearby village of Chenogne, reaching it late that afternoon. Shortly after the task force arrived, German tanks destroyed four American tanks. American tank gunners were unable to spot the enemy tanks in the twilight, and the Americans decided to wait for morning to mount an attack on the village. That night, the VIII Corps artillery blew Chenogne apart to open a path for the attack. When the artillery barrage hit Chenogne, German tanks within the village withdrew to a safe area, but rushed back in to defend it when the American artillery barrage concluded.

Task Force Collins was not the only American force in Chenogne on December 29. In the confusion of battle, a small unit from the American 11th Armored CCB (known as Task Force Pat) had also made Chenogne its objective. On the way to the village, Task Force Pat had the misfortune of running into elements of the Fuehrer Escort Brigade, and it withdrew after suffering heavy losses in men and equipment.

German soldiers are marched into captivity.
National Archives

PATTON'S THOUGHTS ON TANKS IN VILLAGES

TANKS SHOULD never enter villages, and under those exceptional circumstances where such an entry is demanded, they should take the place from the rear. In passing villages they should move around them at a range in excess of the effective range of the antitank guns which are apt to be concealed in the villages. Personally, I have seldom seen a tank stuck on the front silhouette by an antitank gun because the Germans generally put their antitank guns on reverse slopes or in places where they can get flanking fire. This being known, we should act accordingly and not rush in where the angels fear to tread.

—*The Unknown Patton,*
"Letter of Instruction No. 3"

Task Force Karsteter, consisting of two M4 Sherman medium-tank companies, managed to reach the village of Villeroux on the evening of December 27. There it waited while American artillery and fighter-bombers laid waste to the village and its defenders. The tanks of Task Force Karsteter were then sent in to Villeroux to finish off any survivors. The American task force then moved northward toward the nearby village of Senonchamps, the scene of hard fighting in previous days and an entrance onto the main road running west from Bastogne to Marche.

As it left Villeroux, Task Force Karsteter came under heavy fire from the woods near the village of Bois de Fragotte. The Americans encountered the main body of the 3rd Panzer Grenadier Division. Four of the tanks from the task force ran the gauntlet of fire from the woods and entered Senonchamps, but the armored infantry was unable to follow. The losses sustained by the 9th Armored Division CCA in the three-day operation left it with a company and a half of infantry and only thirty-eight light and medium tanks.

American soldiers use a blow torch to heat up their coffee. Hot coffee and cigarettes did much to keep up the morale of American soldiers during the long slog that was the Battle of the Bulge. *National Archives*

Poker, another task force of 11th Armored Division's CCB, was aiming for the village of Lavaselle, about one and a half miles west of Chenogne. The surrounding terrain made Lavaselle inhospitable for tanks, so the task-force commander decided to move on to the villages of Brul and Houmont, which were on high ground just to the north. The task force needed to cross a creek with a single rickety bridge, but the tanks made it. Only a few German infantrymen defended the twin hamlets, and the villages fell easily. As soon as the Germans realized what had happened, they bombarded the Americans with intense rocket and mortar fire from Lavaselle. Task Force Poker was on its own, well in front of the rest of 11th Armored Division, waiting for the division's other task forces to pull abreast of its position at Chenogne.

The 11th Armored Division would continue its advance as part of Middleton's VIII Corps for three more bloody days of combat until it was replaced by 17th Airborne Division on January 3. Once relieved, 11th Armored Division was returned to SHAEF reserve.

An American 155mm M1 howitzer at the moment of firing. Middleton's VIII Corps, part of Patton's Third Army, was scheduled to provide the American spearhead on the left wing of the attack. The untested 11th Armored Division and 87th Infantry Division would provide the fighting tip of the VIII Corps. *National Archives*

An American soldier (in the foreground) turns a captured German M42 machine gun back on its former owners. *National Archives*

THE TWO ATTACKS COLLIDE

December 30 would be an incredibly confusing day for both American and German soldiers fighting in the snow and ice around Bastogne. Both sides began a major offensive aimed at Bastogne and the open corridor that connected it to Third Army at the same time. Almost every American advance ran into a German advance coming from the opposite direction.

Middleton's VIII Corps was assigned to lead the American attack toward Bastogne. This move was to be the American curtain-raiser thrust of the left wing of Patton's Third Army. At Bastogne, the corps was to swing northeast to establish contact with First Army's VII Corps at Houffalize. Successful implementation of this strategy would effectively block the German lines of communication west of Bastogne.

On the evening of December 29, VIII Corps took control of 101st Airborne Division and 9th Armored Division. Although Gen. Maxwell Taylor's 101st Airborne paratroopers and glider infantry would play no offensive role in the first stages of the Third Army operation, they were ordered to hold the pivot position at Bastogne throughout the entire American offensive. Of the 9th Armored's combat commands, only CCA was already committed at the beginning of the VIII Corps advance toward Houffalize. On the morning of December 30, the corps' east-to-west order of battle would be the 101st Airborne Division, CCA of the 9th Armored Division, 11th Armored Division, and 87th Infantry Division.

American soldiers take a moment from their duties to pet a stray cat. No doubt something like this would remind them of their life back home and offer a moment of distraction from the often deadening routine of their everyday military jobs. *National Archives*

An American M7 "Priest," armed with a 105mm howitzer, is ready to be fired. *National Archives*

Meanwhile, in the afternoon of December 29, Manteuffel, the German Fifth Panzer Army commander, met with his corps and divisional commanders to inform them of the major attack to begin the next morning. On December 26, at Manteuffel's request, a single commander was placed in charge of all German forces around Bastogne. Chosen for the job was Gen. Freiherr V. Luettwitz, formerly in charge of XLVII Panzer Corps of Manteuffel's Fifth Panzer Army. Army Group Luettwitz, as it was now named, would conduct the fight to restore the German positions around Bastogne, using the XXXIX and XLVII Panzer Corps to attack east to west and then make a second strike west to east.

Since a number of German divisions en route to Bastogne for the attack had not yet arrived, the attack would be neither as strong nor as coordinated as Manteuffel had originally hoped. Because Hitler was pressuring him to immediately launch the attack, Manteuffel was forced to take more risks. The eastern assault force would consist of the 1st SS Panzer and the 167th Volksgrenadier divisions; its drive was to be made via Lutrebois toward Assenois. From the west of Bastogne, the German forces led by the Fuehrer Escort Brigade would aim for the village of Sibret. If the German formations approaching Bastogne from two directions could successfully link up south of the town, they would close the corridor that had been opened by CCR of the 4th Armored Division on December 26.

American soldiers man a dugout with a Browning M1919A6 .30-caliber, air-cooled machine gun. The German Fifth Army's plans for a December 30, 1944, attack on Bastogne called for two armored divisions to attack the narrow American corridors into the town from both the western and eastern side at the same time. *National Archives*

The German attack launched by Fifth Panzer Army from the eastern side of Bastogne made limited progress, but was stopped by elements of Millikin's III Corps. It was tired, cold, and hungry American soldiers, like the one pictured here, who blunted and eventually stopped Hitler's Ardennes offensive. *National Archives*

An American soldier holds a Belgian child during the Battle of the Bulge. Despite the terrible damage inflicted on the homes and businesses of Belgian civilians by American firepower, most felt it was better than having the Germans back. *National Archives*

The 3rd Panzer Grenadier Division was to advance on the left of the Fuehrer Escort Brigade, while the battle-scarred remnants of 26th Volksgrenadier Division and 15th Panzer Grenadier Division advanced to the west and north of Bastogne. The timing for the arrival of the reinforcements, from the 12th SS Panzer, 9th SS Panzer, and 340th Volksgrenadier divisions, was unknown.

The eastern attack forces of Army Group Luettwitz managed to capture the village of Lutrebois (only 1,200 yards from the main Arlon-Bastogne highway) and cut out a salient four miles deep and four miles wide into the lines of Third Army's III Corps. The artillery of 4th Armored Division poured an unprecedented concentration of rounds into this small area.

The Germans clung to the Lutrebois pocket for a week, but it cost them dearly. In one day (December 30), they lost fifty-five tanks to the 4th Armored Division and 35th Infantry Division, as air support from P-47 Thunderbolts braved a low cloud ceiling.

In contrast to the limited success of the German eastern attack force, the western attack forces had barely set out toward Sibret before being repelled. By noon of December 31, *Generalfeldmarschall* Karl Rudolf Gerd von Rundstedt's headquarters agreed that any further attempt to break through the Bastogne corridor via Sibret would depend on the success of the eastern counterattack force—success that never materialized.

Despite recent events, Patton insisted that the III Corps continue its attack toward St. Vith, with 6th Armored Division leading the charge.

The 6th Armored Division's December 31 attack would involve the division's two CCs advancing abreast. CCA, attacking on the right, would use the Arlon-Bastogne highway, while CCB, picked for the left wing, would pass through the VIII Corps area by way of the Neufchâteau-Bastogne road. By daylight of December 31, CCA was in a forward assembly position behind the 101st Airborne Division line southeast of Bastogne. However, due to a series of misunderstandings and mistakes, CCB failed to make its appearance as scheduled.

Colonel John L. Hines, Jr., commander of CCA, wanted to postpone his attack until CCB could reach its jumping off location. However, due to a lack of cover combined with heavy enemy fire, Hines and Grow decided to launch a limited objective attack in which the CCA's Task Force Kennedy and Task Force Brown would start from a location near the Bastogne-Bras road and thrust northeast. Task Force Kennedy was to capture the town of Neffe and to clear the enemy from the woods to the east. Task Force Brown was to move alongside Task Force Kennedy, scour the woods south of Neffe, and seize the high ground around the village of Wardin on the northeast. The attack, begun shortly after noon, rolled through Neffe with little German opposition. However, a combination of heavy snow squalls and a lack of air support soon slowed CCA's advance to a crawl.

Another problem developed for CCA when 35th Infantry Division (on its right flank) started to lag behind because of the weather and occasional enemy fire. Just before dark, small German units struck at Hines's exposed flanks, and CCA was forced to stop its advance. The artillery maintained a protective barrage around CCA throughout the night.

PATTON'S THOUGHTS ON TANK CONDUCT IN BATTLE

WHEN TANKS ARE advancing, they must use their guns for what is known as reconnaissance by fire; that is, they must shoot at any terrestrial objective behind which an antitank gun might be concealed and take these under fire at a range greater than that which an antitank gun is effective; in other words, at a range greater than 2,000 yards. They should fire at these targets with high explosive or with white phosphorus, because if the enemy receives such fire, he will consider himself discovered and reply at a range so great as to render him ineffective.

—*The Unknown Patton*, *"Letter of Instruction No. 3"*

Two American M8 armored cars on patrol. The failure of the German armored divisions to close the corridors opened by Millikin's III Corps into Bastogne convinced the senior commander of Fifth Panzer Army that German forces in the Ardennes must relinquish all thought of continuing the offensive. *National Archives*

American soldiers man a towed 57mm M1 antitank gun. Despite the large German offensive operation of December 30, 1944, there was no thought in Patton's mind that Millikin's III Corps would delay its attack in a northeastern direction past Bastogne toward the road center of St. Vith. *National Archives*

American soldiers huddle around a fire during a break in the action. *National Archives*

THE FIGHTING CONTINUES INTO THE NEW YEAR

On the morning of New Year's Day, 1945, the 6th Armored Division's CCB was finally in place on the left of CCA. While CCA was to try again to clear the woods and ridges beyond the village of Neffe, CCB was to cut through the German supply routes feeding into and across the Longvilly road, to permit north-south movement along the eastern face of the Bastogne pocket. This was the same path the Germans were using to assemble their forces near Lutrebois. CCB divided itself into two task forces to attack Bourcy and Arloncourt, aiming to capture the high ground and thus dominate the German road net.

The commander of CCB counted on 101st Airborne troops on his left flank to push the Germans out of the Bois Jacques area, north of Bizory. The previous afternoon, Middleton, the VIII Corps commander, had ordered Gen. Maxwell Taylor, commander of the 101st Airborne, to use the reserve battalion of the 506th Parachute Infantry Regiment for this purpose. He had then countermanded this order. Unfortunately, 6th Armored Division was unaware of the change in plans until the last minute. Suddenly lacking 101st Airborne Division's support and faced with a front normally considered too wide for a linear advance by armor, Grow put five of its six task forces into the attack on January 2. German resistance to the division's advance was extreme and even included attacks by the German air force. Despite heavy losses, 6th Armored Division gained a great deal of ground by January 2. It would be another eight days before it would achieve similar gains.

By January 2, the 6th Armored was the only division in Patton's III Corps that made any progress in the offensive that began on December 30. The 35th Infantry Division, on the right flank of 6th Armored Division, ran headlong into the German units battling for Lutrebois and failed to reach its objectives. Even though the German effort to open a path through the left wing of 35th Infantry Division failed, it managed to put the division out of action. Before the division could regain its place in Patton's offensive operations, it would have to eliminate German opposition at three locations: Lutrebois, Villers-la-Bonne-Eau, and Harlange.

A medic takes notes prior to a burial detail of American dead. *National Archives*

An M4A3(76)W Sherman medium tank drives by a destroyed Panther Ausf. G medium tank pushed to the side of the road. German resistance to Millikin's III Corps advance toward St. Vith was determined and tough. American casualties soared. Despite the heavy losses, 6th Armored Division did make some gains by January 2, 1945. *National Archives*

ARMORED BATTLES

against infantry and antitank guns are short and violent. They take great strength of mind and both physical and moral courage because of this violence and the speed with which they are terminated. When once launched, tanks must close at their best speed just the same as infantry, and also just the same as infantry, they must fire while closing. The true objective of armor is enemy infantry and artillery, and above all his supply installations and command centers.

—*The Unknown Patton,*
"Letter of Instruction No. 3"

Meanwhile, on December 27, the 26th Infantry Division, on the right flank of 35th Infantry Division, had managed to put its leading battalions across the Sûre River. Its far-term objective was the village of Wiltz, about four miles to the north of the river. Its near-term objective was the Wiltz-Bastogne highway, then being used by the German Seventh Army to support the buildup of forces east of Bastogne.

At the same time, 80th Infantry Division of the XII Corps was pushing due north, and 26th Infantry Division was pushing northwest. Beset by its own problems, 35th Infantry Division was unable to provide 26th Infantry Division with protection on its left or right flanks. Therefore, the commander of 26th Infantry Division was faced with leading the III Corps attack while simultaneously watching both of his exposed flanks.

Four American soldiers lie dead along a Belgian road during the Battle of the Bulge. The U.S. Army infantry regiments that fought through January 1945 in the European Theater of Operations commonly sustained a 100 to 200 percent casualty rate. *National Archives*

THE GERMAN VIEW

Brandenberger's Seventh Army became greatly alarmed as the leading battalion of the American's 26th Infantry Division pushed forward toward Wiltz. Brandenberger saw that the American attacks around Marvie and Harlange could suddenly break through and trap 5th Parachute Division in what the Germans now were calling the Harlange pocket. The renewal of 26th Infantry Division's attack on January 2 and the threat to the Bastogne-Wiltz road increased the overall threat to 5th Parachute Division and the link it provided between Seventh and Fifth Panzer Armies.

Brandenberger asked Model's permission to pull his troops back from Villers-la-Bonne-Eau and Harlange. Manteuffel also asked permission to withdraw. Model refused both requests, reminding them that Germany now was in a battle of attrition, by which the Allies would become enmeshed and ground down. Such thinking ignored the material disparity that existed between the two opposing sides by this stage of the war—a disparity that overwhelmingly favored the Allies. Attrition was the last thing the Germans could afford. Practically speaking, Model's refusal had no effect, since he had no authority to order a withdrawal anyway. Hitler demanded that the German army give no ground. It was Fifth Panzer Army's failure to close the gap around Bastogne that convinced Manteuffel that offensive operations in the Ardennes should be replaced by a withdrawal. Adding to Manteuffel's concern was the capture of the village of Mande-Saint-Etienne on January 2 by VIII Corps. With Mande-Saint-Etienne under Allied control, the three weak German divisions at the tip of the German penetration, in the Rochefort area of the Ardennes, were in grave danger of being cut off. With permission to withdraw denied, the staff at the German Army Group B continued to prepare plans for a January 4 offensive to take Bastogne. On January 3, before these desperate plans could be put into effect, the Allies launched another large counteroffensive. Montgomery now felt of a proper mood to get into the game, and this new attack consisted of Patton's Third Army advancing from the south and Hodges's First Army advancing from 21st Army Group's sector in the north.

A wounded German soldier rides into captivity on the hood of an American Jeep. *National Archives*

American soldiers ride into combat on the rear engine deck of an M4A3(75)W Sherman medium tank. The right wing of Millikin's III Corps consisted of 26th Infantry Division, which had been brought into the line on December 27, 1944, when it put its leading battalions across the Sûre River. *National Archives*

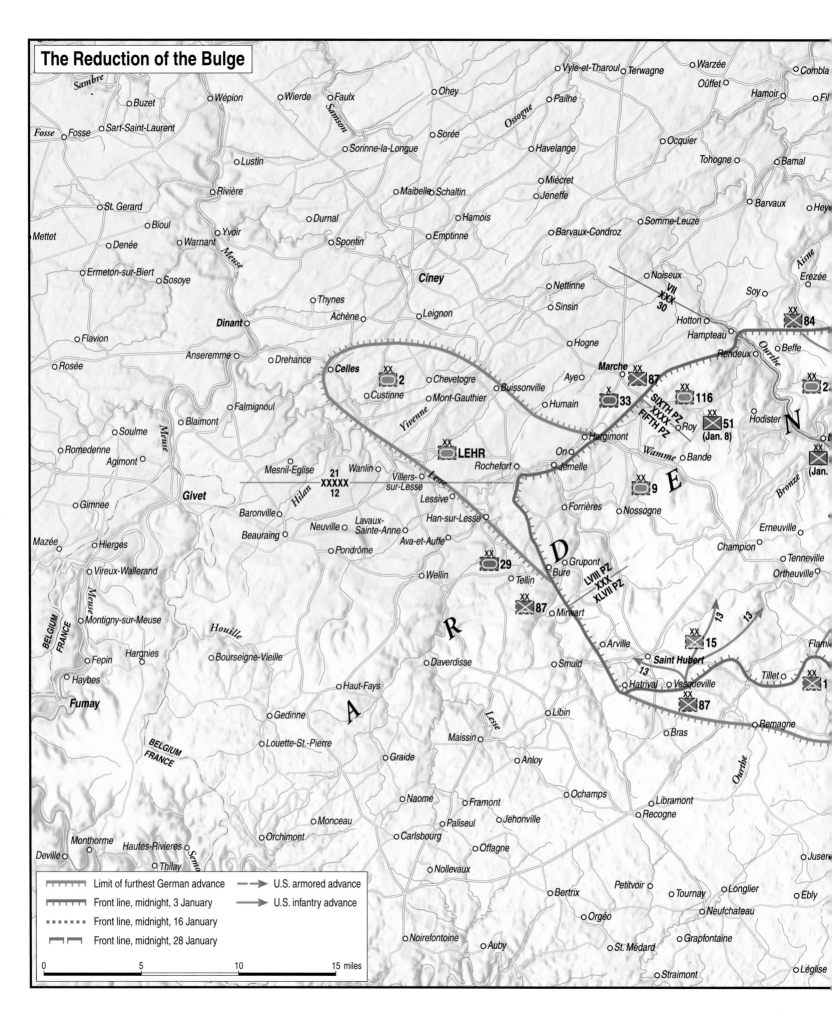

The Reduction of the Bulge

Sambre
Fosse • Fosse
Buzet •
Wépion •
Wierde •
Faulx •
Ohey •
Vyle-et-Tharoul • Terwagne
Warzée •
Oûffet •
Combla
Hamoir •
Fil

Sart-Saint-Laurent •
Samson
Pailhe •
Ossogne
Ocquier •
Tohogne •
Bamal •

Mettet •
Lustin •
Sorée •
Havelange •
Somme-Leuze •
Barvaux •
Heye

St. Gerard •
Rivière •
Sorinne-la-Longue •
Miécret •
Jeneffe •
Barvaux-Condroz •

Bioul •
Yvoir •
Durnal •
Maibelle • Schaltin
Hamois •
Noiseux •
VII
XXX
30
Soy •
Erezée •

Denée •
Warnant •
Spontin •
Emptinne •
Nettinne •
Sinsin •
Hotton •
Hampteau •
84

Ermeton-sur-Biert •
Meuse
Cíney
Barvaux-Condroz •
Ourthe
Beffe

Sosoye •
Thynes •
Achène •
Leignon •
Hogne •
Marche
87
Rendeux •
2

Flavion •
Dinant •
Anseremme •
Drehance •
Celles
2
Chevetogre •
Buissonville •
Aye •
X
33
116
Hodister •
N

Rosée •
Falmignoul •
Custinne •
Mont-Gauthier •
Humain •
Hargimont •
SIXTH PZ
XXX
FIFTH PZ
Roy •
51
(Jan. 8)

Soulme •
Blaimont •
Yvenne
On •
Wamme
Bande •
(Jan.

Romedenne •
Meuse
LEHR
Rochefort •
Jemelle •
9
E

Agimont •
Mesnil-Eglise •
Wanlin •
21
XXXXX
12
Villers-
sur-Lesse
Lesse
Forrières •
Nossogne •

Gimnee •
Givet •
Hilan
Baronville •
Lessive •
Bronze

Mazée •
Hierges •
Neuville •
Lavaux-
Sainte-Anne •
Han-sur-Lesse •
Grupont •
Erneuville •

Vireux-Wallerand •
Beauraing •
Ava-et-Auffe •
D
Bure •
LVIII PZ
XXX
XLVII PZ
Champion •
Tenneville •

Meuse
Pondrôme •
29
Wellin •
Tellin •
Mirwart •
Ortheuville •

Montigny-sur-Meuse •
Houille
Daverdisse •
R
87
Arville •
15
Saint Hubert
Flami

Hargnies •
Bourseigne-Vieille •
Smuid •
13
13
Tillet •
1

Fepin •
Haut-Fays •
A
Libin •
Hatrival •
Vesqueville •
13

Haybes •
Fumay •
Gedinne •
Maissin •
Bras •
87
Remagne

Louette-St.-Pierre •
Naome •
Framont •
Ochamps •
Libramont •
Ourthe

Monthorme •
Hautes-Rivieres •
Orchimont •
Monceau •
Paliseul •
Jehonville •
Recogne •

Deville •
Thilay •
Semo
Carlsbourg •
Offagne •
Longlier •
Ebly •

Bertrix •
Petitvoir •
Tournay •
Neufchateau •
Juser

Nollevaux •
Orgéo •
Grapfontaine •

Noirefontoine •
Auby •
St. Médard •
Léglise

Straimont •

BELGIUM
FRANCE

	Limit of furthest German advance		U.S. armored advance
	Front line, midnight, 3 January		U.S. infantry advance
	Front line, midnight, 16 January		
	Front line, midnight, 28 January		

0   5   10   15 miles

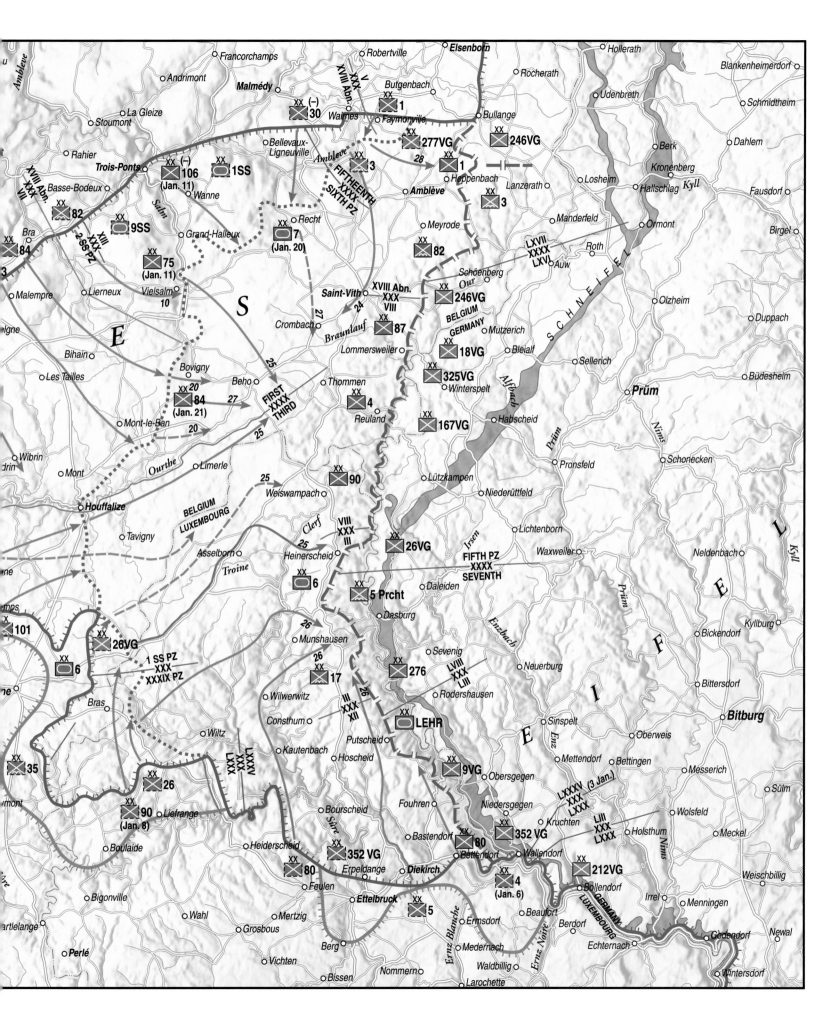

ONE MORE TRY BY BOTH SIDES

The main thrust of the First Army assault was to be led by Collins's VII Corps. It was to advance southeast between the Ourthe and Lienne rivers and seize the area around Houffalize. The XVIII Airborne Corps was to advance on the right flank of the VII Corps. The V Corps would hold in place. Elements of two British divisions (in a token display of British involvement) were to push into the German penetration from the west, aiming at an area just short of Houffalize.

An American 105mm howitzer M2A1 crew performs a fire mission. The 6th Armored Division advance was just getting underway on January 1, 1945, and the 35th Infantry Division's advance was already stalled by strong German resistance. *National Archives*

An abandoned German half-track prime mover, known as the Maultier, and a 10.5cm (105mm) le. F.H. 18 (M) field howitzer. *National Archives*

Even though Hitler had begun to withdraw many of his more elite Waffen SS units from the Ardennes, Patton's troops, fighting in the cold, biting snow in the Bastogne area on January 3, could see little evidence of slackening German resistance. Surveillance patrols around Bastogne found the Germans as full of fight as ever. Every American attempt to move a little farther forward was met by a fierce counterattack, led by one or more German tanks. As it had been with the December 30 offensive by Third Army, it was 6th Armored Division on the left wing of the III Corps that made the most progress. On the first day of the renewed offensive, 6th Armored Division took the battered villages of Oubourcy, Mageret, and Wardin.

On the morning of January 4, the Germans launched their last big offensive aimed at the area around Bastogne. Most of the fighting centered near the Houffalize highway leading to Bastogne. One of the German objectives turned out to be the village of Longchamps, on the western side of the Houffalize highway, which was defended by paratroopers of the 101st Airborne, part of Patton's VIII Corps. By the end of the day on January 4, the German offensive recaptured the villages of Oubourcy, Mageret, and Wardin from 6th Armored Division, although the Germans were unable to make any further progress. The fighting around Bastogne disintegrated into a pattern of frequent attacks and counterattacks by both sides. Patton, who was visiting his front-line units on January 4, glumly noted to himself, "We can still lose the war."

American soldiers dig foxholes in the snow and ice for protection from enemy artillery, which killed the soldier in the foreground. Millikin, commander of III Corps, gave orders on January 2, 1945, for 26th Infantry Division to increase its efforts to cut the Wiltz-Bastogne road. The road was supporting not only the German Seventh Army, but also a portion of the enemy buildup east of Bastogne. *National Archives*

An American M4A3E2 Sherman "Jumbo" medium tank passes through a town on the way to the front. The commander of 26th Infantry Division redoubled his efforts to secure the Wiltz-Bastogne road, but to no avail. However, the German Seventh Army commander was so unnerved by the continued attacks that he asked his superiors for permission to withdraw, which was refused. *National Archives*

By January 6, Patton began to suspect that the Germans might soon withdraw from their Ardennes positions. Only the day before, Bradley had convinced Patton to transfer a newly available division from the XX Corps to the fighting around the southeast of Bastogne (under III Corps' command) rather than to the XII Corps. Patton was not very happy about this turn of events. He had hoped to launch an attack with the XII Corps against the base of the German penetration, and he now worried that the Germans could escape before he could act.

On January 9, the III Corps, having reorganized itself from the blows it suffered from the German offensive launched on January 4, rejoined the general Third Army offensive operations.

It was not until January 11 that Third Army reports reflected firm indications of a German withdrawal in the Ardennes. From January 11 forward, as German resistance continued

A wounded American soldier on a stretcher is being loaded into a captured German Sd.Kfz. 251 half-track ambulance. On January 4, 1945, as Patton's Third Army prepared to renew its efforts to clear the area around Bastogne, it was faced with the largest concentration of German troops (nine divisions) remaining in the Ardennes. Casualties were high. *National Archives*

American soldiers string telephone wire over an abandoned German Tiger B heavy tank. On January 4, 1945, the Germans launched another series of attacks around Bastogne and managed to blunt the planned advance of Patton's Third Army. As the two sides struggled in the fierce Ardennes winter, neither Patton nor his troops could see any end to the bloody fighting. *National Archives*

An American looks over a German Panther tank modified to resemble an American M10 tank destroyer. Unknown to Third Army, the German fervor for taking Bastogne had begun to wane on January 3, 1945, when Montgomery used elements of Hodges's First Army to counterattack the northern flank of the German advance into the Ardennes. *National Archives*

A German staff car ambushed in the Ardennes, its occupants lying by its side. The goal of the First Army divisions involved in the attack on the northern flank of the German advance into the Ardennes was to link up with Patton's Third Army, coming up from the south, at the Belgian town of Houffalize. *National Archives*

An American M4 Sherman medium tank drives through a farmyard. The Fifth Panzer Army around Bastogne knew that it needed complete control of the Bastogne road net to secure its southern flank against Patton's Third Army. This security, in turn, would allow it to help Sixth Panzer Army resist Hodges's First Army divisions, which were coming down from the north. *National Archives*

Two young Waffen SS soldiers, obviously young late-war recruits, surrender to American troops. *National Archives*

to crumble in the face of Third Army's advance, the belief that the Battle of the Bulge was nearing its end raised the morale of Patton's troops.

On January 12, the Soviet army launched its massive winter offensive from the frozen plains of southern Poland, and quickly began to punch holes in the German eastern defensive lines. Hitler quickly began to move more units out of the Ardennes toward the eastern front, which had not received any significant reinforcements since Hitler began preparations for his Ardennes offensive. With the western Allies still undefeated and still in the war, the German gamble failed.

On January 13, a combat command from the 3rd Armored Division managed to cut off the only major escape route available to the German defenders of Houffalize. On the night of January 13, the men of the VII Corps of the First Army could see the lightninglike flashes of artillery pieces supporting Patton's Third Army to the south.

On January 14, Rundstedt appealed to Hitler to authorize a further withdrawal in the Ardennes. The line Hitler earlier picked west of Houffalize was already compromised in the north and was being rolled up in the south. Rundstedt asked approval to pull back farther to anchor a new defensive line on the high ground just east of Houffalize, so that it extended northward behind the Salm River and southward through existing positions east of Bastogne.

Red Army T34/85 medium tanks advance into a captured Eastern European city. The American cause in the Ardennes was aided by a massive Red Army offensive on the eastern front; that offensive began on January 12, 1945.
Patton Museum

PATTON'S THOUGHTS ON STREET FIGHTING

STREET FIGHTING is simply a variation of pillbox fighting. A similar group, but reinforced with more rifleman, is effective. The additional riflemen are split on opposite sides of the street so as to take under fire enemy personnel appearing in the upper stories on the side across from them. When a house offers resistance, the windows are silenced as in the case of pillboxes, and under cover of this immunity a bazooka crew fires one or two rounds at the corner of the house about three feet from the ground. When a hole has been made by this means, phosphorus or high-explosive grenades are thrown into the lower floor and cellar to discourage those operating there. The demolition essential in pillboxes is really not needed in street fighting.

In street fighting, it is very essential to avoid hurrying. One group, as above described, can usually clear a city block in twelve hours. When tanks are available, they replace the bazookas in blowing holes in the walls of the lower floors, and should be further protected by rifleman to keep the enemy from the windows. Self-propelled 155mm guns are extremely useful in cities against moderate masonry construction. One round with delayed fuse will breach all the houses on one side of a city block if fired at a very obtuse angle.

—*War As I Knew It*, *"Reflections and Suggestions"*

On January 15, a patrol from 101st Airborne Division (part of Patton's VIII Corps) entered the village of Noville, five miles south of Houffalize. Early the next morning, 11th Armored, also part of the VIII Corps, secured the high ground immediately south of Houffalize. Shortly afterward, another 11th Armored patrol met a patrol from 2nd Armored Division, belonging to the First Army's VII Corps, outside the town. Patton's notes of January 16 describe the meeting: "At 0905, 41st Cavalry of the 11th Armored Division made contact with 41st Infantry of the 2nd Armored Division in Houffalize, thus terminating the Bastogne operation so far as the Third Army is concerned."

This meeting at the shoulders of the German penetration was somewhat of an empty accomplishment, since the slow pace of the American advance had allowed most of the best German units within the Ardennes to escape to fight another day. Patton had foreseen this situation from the beginning, but had not successfully persuaded his superiors to take measures to prevent it.

Patton's one-of-a-kind Jeep, in Bastogne. By January 23, 1945, the German forces left in the Ardennes were being hard-pressed by both Hodges's First Army and Patton's Third Army. Their once orderly retreat soon turned into a disorganized rout. *National Archives*

American soldiers working in conjunction with an M4A3(75)W Sherman medium tank. Hitler ordered what was left of Sixth Panzer Army out of the Ardennes on January 8, 1945. It took until January 22 for this movement to be completed. This action would significantly relieve the pressure on the advancing American First and Third Armies in the Ardennes. *National Archives*

On January 16, 1945, elements of Middleton's VIII Corps, under Third Army control, linked up with elements of Hodges's First Army at Houffalize. As soon as this connection took place, Bradley took control of Hodges's First Army back from Montgomery. A 41st Cavalry Reconnaissance Squadron armored car crew welcomes 84th Infantry Division troops at the First and Third Armies' linkup. *National Archives*

American soldiers load the frozen corpses of German soldiers who perished during the Battle of the Bulge into the back cargo bay of a two-and-a-half-ton 6x6 truck. It would take the American forces advancing in the Ardennes until January 28 to regain all the territory lost to the Germans during the Battle of the Bulge. *Patton Museum*

Patton now knew that he could not stage a large attack northward across the German frontier to Prum and thus prevent the remaining Germans from retreating behind the West Wall (the Siegfried Line). Eisenhower and Montgomery planned for Third Army to continue attacking northward in the direction of St. Vith. Once it had reached that town, the mop-up of remaining German forces in the eastern half of the Ardennes would begin.

Bradley, who was now in command of Hodges's First Army again, proposed that First Army also move to take St. Vith and once there, Hodges could send a corps to link up with XII Corps of Patton's Third Army and form a shallow envelopment for trapping any German forces still within the Ardennes. This plan was ultimately rejected. Instead, First and Third Armies advanced in a methodical manner in an easterly direction, slowly pushing back the rear guard formations left by the Germans. It would take until the end of January 1945 for the two American armies to reach the German frontier and reestablish the line that existed prior to Hitler's Ardennes counteroffensive.

An American soldier escorts two German prisoners. On March 7, CCB of 4th Armored Division was only three miles from the Rhine River. It had driven forty-four miles in just over two and a half days, and in the process, the division took five thousand prisoners and killed or wounded another seven hundred German troops. *National Archives*

9

FINISHING OFF THE THIRD REICH

HITLER'S ARDENNES OFFENSIVE managed to delay the advance of the Allied armies on the Rhine River, forcing Eisenhower to spend much of December 1944 concerned with the elimination of the German forces in the Ardennes. His staff continued working on plans to clear the area west of the Rhine in preparation for crossing the river and for advancing eastward into Germany. At the end of December, Eisenhower decided that the advance of the American armies' toward Germany must continue only after the Germans in the Ardennes retreated.

On January 18, Eisenhower directed Bradley to continue his offensive, instructing him "to take advantage of the enemy's present unfavorable position in the Ardennes, inflict the maximum losses on him, seize any opportunity of breaching the Siegfried Line [West Wall] and, if successful, advance northeast on the axis Prum-Euskirchen." Eisenhower also informed Bradley that if the attacks of First and Third Armies failed in these objectives, he would order them to go on the defensive at the end of January and pass the attack on to Montgomery's 21st Army Group.

By the end of January, Bradley's forces had pushed the Germans back to the West Wall fortifications in their sector. But Bradley's troops were also beginning to encounter delays, and there appeared little chance of meeting the objectives set by Eisenhower. Bradley showed no surprise when, on

A British Cromwell tank passes through a captured town. Even before the Battle of the Bulge, it was clear to Allied leaders that neither their forces north or south of the Ardennes were strong enough on their own to reach the Rhine River. It was, therefore, decided that the main offensive operation would be north of the Ardennes, with Montgomery's 21st Army Group. *Tank Museum/Bovington*

An American soldier carries a Browning MI9I9A4 .30-caliber, air-cooled machine gun. *National Archives*

February 1, Eisenhower ordered him to go on the defensive, except for an attack by First Army units to clear the area around the Roer River dam. Eisenhower also ordered Bradley to divert divisions from both Hodges's First Army and Patton's Third Army to reinforce Simpson's Ninth Army for its upcoming attack.

On February 2, Bradley asked Patton and Hodges if they could continue their advances until February 10 with their remaining divisions. Both commanders indicated that they would do their best to keep moving forward. Bradley gave tacit permission for Patton to make limited advances in Germany's Eiffel region, north of the Moselle River. The matter was kept quiet so as not to draw objections from Montgomery. On February 23, First Army crossed the Roer River and then advanced to the Erft River by February 28. This operation allowed Hodges's First Army to protect the right flank of Simpson's Ninth Army as it began driving northward.

An American soldier guards a group of German prisoners. *National Archives*

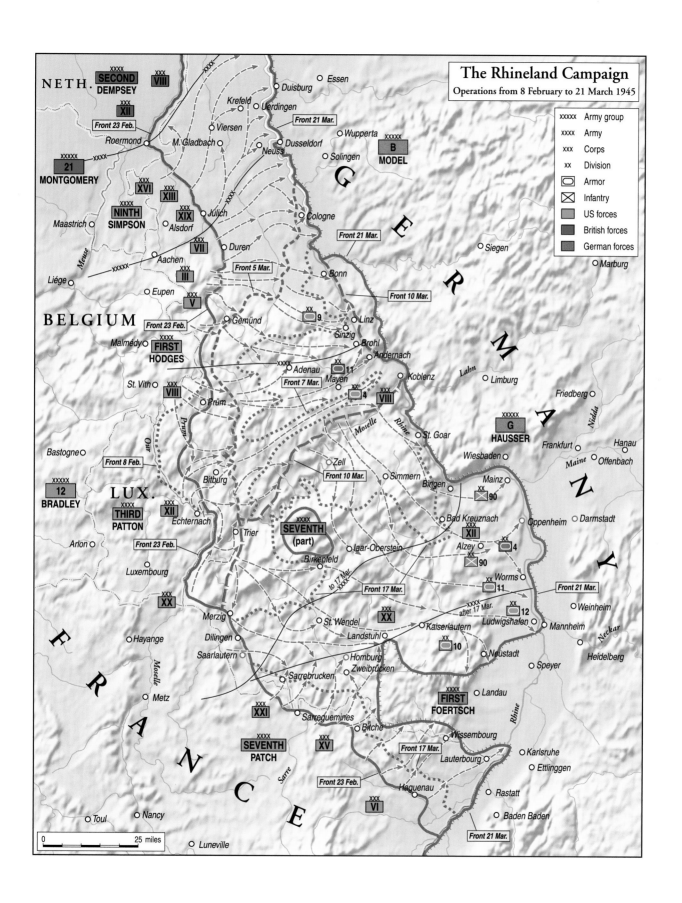

The Rhineland Campaign
Operations from 8 February to 21 March 1945

xxxxx	Army group
xxxx	Army
xxx	Corps
xx	Division
▭	Armor
⊠	Infantry
	US forces
	British forces
	German forces

NETH.

SECOND
DEMPSEY
XXX VIII
Front 23 Feb.
XXX XII
Roermond
M. Gladbach
Viersen

Essen
Duisburg
Krefeld
Uerdingen
Neuss
Dusseldorf
Wupperta
Solingen
B
MODEL

GERMANY

21
MONTGOMERY
XVI
XIII
NINTH
SIMPSON
XIX
Maastrich
Alsdorf
Julich
VII
Duren
Cologne
Front 21 Mar.

Liége
Aachen
III
Eupen
V
Front 5 Mar.
Bonn
Front 10 Mar.
Siegen
Marburg

BELGIUM

Malmédy
FIRST
HODGES
Front 23 Feb.
Gemünd
XX 9
Linz
Sinzig
Brohl
Andernach

St. Vith
VIII
Prüm
Adenau
XX 11
Mayen
Front 7 Mar.
XX 4
VIII
Koblenz
Lahn
Limburg
Friedberg
Nidda

Bastogne
Front 8 Feb.
Bitburg
Oar
Zell
Front 10 Mar.
Simmern
Bingen
Moselle
Rhine
St. Goar
G
HAUSSER
Wiesbaden
Frankfurt
Hanau
Maine
Offenbach

12
BRADLEY
LUX.
THIRD
PATTON
XII
Echternach
Front 23 Feb.
Trier
SEVENTH
(part)
Birkenfeld
Iaar-Oberstein
Bad Kreuznach
XII
Alzey
XX 90
Mainz
XX 4
XX 90
Oppenheim
Darmstadt

Arlon
Luxembourg
Front 17 Mar.
to 17 Mar.
XX Worms
XX 11
Front 21 Mar.
Weinheim

XX
Merzig
St. Wendel
XX
Kaiserlautern
after 17 Mar.
XX 12
Ludwigshafen
Mannheim
Neckar

Hayange
Dilingen
Landstuhl
XX 10
Neustadt
Speyer
Heidelberg

Saarlautern
Homburg
Zweibrücken
Sarrebrucken
FIRST
FOERTSCH
Landau

Metz
XXI
Sarreguemines
Bitche
Wissembourg
Front 17 Mar.
Karlsruhe
Ettlinggen

SEVENTH
PATCH
Sarre
XV
Lauterbourg
Rastatt

FRANCE
Front 23 Feb.
Haguenau
Baden Baden

Toul
Nancy
VI
Front 21 Mar.

0   25 miles

Luneville

American soldiers climb over a German roadblock. The caveat set by Eisenhower on Bradley's late-January offensive was that it had to show almost immediate success. If not, Bradley would have to pass on a number of his divisions to Montgomery's 21st Army Group and go on the defensive with his 12th Army Group. *National Archives*

Living in the field with bombs and bullets whizzing overhead is a dirty, thankless job most of the time. Lice and other vermin are your foxhole companions. A chance to clean up, as this American soldier is doing, is a moment to rejoice. *National Archives*

Emaciated inmates liberated from a concentration camp. Among the most unpleasant things encountered by the Third Army divisions as they plunged deeper into Germany were a number of concentration camps, which clearly illustrated the depravity of Nazi Germany. *National Archives*

A group of German Messerschmitt Bf 109 fighters sit abandoned on a captured airfield. *National Archives*

An American soldier inspects the paperwork of a dead German soldier. *National Archives*

AMERICAN FIELD ARMIES

FIELD ARMIES LIKE the Third Army were administrative organizations. The only parts of the unit that remained permanent were its headquarters and some signal units. The signal units transmitted the orders and directions of the headquarters staff to all the temporary units, such as corps and divisions assigned to the field army for varying periods of time. The Third Army headquarters under Patton's leadership consisted of the regulation 450 officers and 1,000 enlisted men at full strength.

Corps, like divisions, where shifted from one field army to another by army-group commanders, such as General Omar Bradley, who were one level above the field-army commanders, like Patton. Between August 1944, when Patton took command of the Third Army in France, and the German surrender in May 1945, a total of six corps served under Patton's Third Army: the XII, XX, VIII, III, XV, and V Corps. Divided among these six corps were forty-two divisions that spent time as part of Patton's Third Army. Of those forty-two divisions, twenty-six were infantry, fourteen were armored, and two were airborne.

American soldiers board an M5 light tank. *National Archives*

American soldiers pose for a picture on the German West Wall. Bradley's goal of quickly penetrating the German West Wall in the Eifel region was hampered by difficult terrain and poor weather conditions. *National Archives*

To the south of Hodges's First Army, Patton never stopped pushing Third Army slowly forward. By the end of February, Third Army had opened a path up the Prum Valley toward the Rhine River, cleared the Moselle-Saar Triangle, and passed through most of the West Wall defenses in its sector to within three miles of the city of Trier. As Third Army continued to push forward, Patton pleaded with Bradley to give him an additional division so he could mount a large attack in the area of Trier and the Saar. Patton also pointed out that the great majority of American soldiers in Europe were not fighting and warned, "All of us in high position will surely be held accountable for the failure to take offensive action when offensive action is possible."

An American M24 light tank armed with a 75mm main gun. In spite of Eisenhower's decision to end the offensive operations of Bradley's 12th Army Group in early February 1945, Patton had no intention of letting Montgomery's 21st Army Group be the first to the Rhine River. With Bradley's support, the two of them set about circumventing Eisenhower's decision. *National Archives*

A crash-landed B-17 Bomber, its engines salvaged, sits forlornly in a German field. *National Archives*

Two Americans break down a door with rifle butts. Middleton's VIII Corps took Prum on February 12, 1945. On February 28, Eddy's XII Corps took Bitburg, the linchpin of the southern portion of the West Wall in the Eifel region. *National Archives*

An American M8 armored car on patrol. At the same time Patton had Middleton's VIII Corps heading toward Prum, he was planning to aim Eddy's XII Corps at the German town of Bitburg, the other major road center in the western Eifel region. *National Archives*

Bradley began a new offensive on March 1 and assigned Patton the job of crossing the Kyll River, located twelve miles inside Germany. The Rhine River lay some fifty miles east of the Kyll. Once a bridgehead over the Kyll became secure, Patton's forces were to advance and seize the area located between the German cities of Mainz and Koblenz, on the Rhine. If the German defenses in the area were weak, Third Army was to secure a Moselle bridgehead and clear the enemy from the area, then link up with Hodges's First Army.

Patton wasted no time picking up the tempo of Third Army's advance. Two of Patton's divisions captured Trier, Germany, and a bridge across the Moselle River on the night of March 1. The next morning, Patton received a message from Eisenhower's staff telling him to bypass Trier, since it would take four divisions to capture. A bemused Patton sent a message back, "Have taken Trier with two divisions. What do you want me to do? Give it back?"

PATTON'S THOUGHTS ON REST PERIODS

STAFF PERSONNEL, commissioned and enlisted, who do not rest, do not last. All sections must run a duty roster and enforce compliance. The intensity of staff operations during battle is periodic. At the army and corps levels the busiest times are the periods from one to three hours after daylight, and from three to five hours after dark. In the lower echelons and in the administrative and supply staffs, the time of the periods is different but just as definite. When the needs arise, everybody must work all the time, but these emergencies are not frequent; "un-fatigued men last longer and work better at high pressure."

—*War As I Knew It,*
"Letter of Instruction No. 1"

On March 6, the first elements of Third Army crossed the Kyll River. The next day, elements of both First and Third Armies met up a few miles short of the Rhine. By the night of March 7, the 4th Armored Division managed to arrive three miles short of the Rhine, near the city of Koblenz. In the process, Patton's tankers spread havoc throughout the German defenses west of the Rhine River and north of the Moselle River. The 4th Armored Division did not attempt to cross the Rhine River. Instead, it headed southward toward the Moselle. On March 8, Eisenhower ordered Third Army to assist Seventh Army in its southern offensive in the Saar-Palatinate Triangle. This area contained the last sizable German forces still west of the Rhine River. The Saar-Palatinate area itself lay south of the Moselle River and embraced more than three thousand square miles. By March 13, Patton had five of his divisions along the Moselle River and another four located northeast of Trier.

American soldiers hitch a ride on an M4A3(76)WHVSS Sherman medium tank. Despite having Prum and Bitburg, Patton and his Third Army remained some fifty miles west of the Rhine River. The good news was the German West Wall was now behind them and only a miracle would allow the enemy to man and equip another defensive line in the Eifel region. *National Archives*

American soldiers pose with a German 12.8cm (128mm) antiaircraft gun designated the FlaK 40. During February 1945, Walker's XX Corps was busy mopping up the heavily defended Saar-Moselle Triangle, a strip of Germany lying between the Saar and Moselle rivers. On March 1, Walker's XX Corps took the German city of Trier, north of the triangle. *National Archives*

American soldiers cross a small portable bridge under cover of a smoke screen. Elements of Eddy's XII Corps crossed the Kyll River in Germany on March 3, 1945. The 4th Armored Division was pushed through the bridgehead on March 5 with the goal of heading toward the Rhine River and seizing any bridges that might still be standing. *National Archives*

German prisoners are marched across the captured bridge at Remagen, Germany. Even as Patton's Third Army began closing in on the Rhine River in early March, elements of the First Army managed to seize a railroad bridge at the town of Remagen on March 7, 1945, and become the first American soldiers across the Rhine River. *National Archives*

Major General Alexander M. Patch began his Seventh Army's advance on March 15, aided by Patton's forces located north of his position. Third Army armored columns soon swept across the rear of the German defenses in the Saar-Palatinate Triangle. On March 21, elements of Seventh Army linked up with Third Army. By March 25, the Saar-Palatinate Triangle was overrun, and Seventh Army began its preparations for a crossing of the Rhine River.

On March 7, First Army's 9th Armored Division captured a bridge across the Rhine at the town of Remagen. First Army wasted no time trying to expand its bridgehead on the eastern bank of the Rhine. Despite frantic German counterattacks, First Army kept enlarging its bridgehead and pushing deeper into Germany. At the same time, Patton's forces were also crossing the Rhine. Third Army's assault across the Rhine began shortly before midnight on March 22. By the next morning, six battalions of infantry were across the river at a cost of only twenty-eight casualties. Seventh Army first got across the Rhine on March 26. During February and March, Third Army suffered twenty-five thousand casualties, but captured a hundred thousand German prisoners.

An American M4A3(76)W Sherman medium tank has almost been overturned in a large shell crater. *National Archives*

An American soldier looks over a knocked-out German heavy tank destroyer known as the Jagdtiger, which was armed with a powerful 12.8cm (128mm) main gun. On March 8, 1945, Eisenhower directed Patton's Third Army to assist Patch's Seventh Army in taking an area known as the Saar-Palatinate, which contained the only remaining German forces still west of the Rhine River. This mission was completed by March 25. *National Archives*

Patton would later boast of Third Army's Rhine crossing and of beating out the British in that endeavor:

Without benefit of aerial bombardment, ground smoke, artillery preparation and airborne assistance, the Third Army at 2200 hours, Thursday, 22nd March, 1945, crossed the Rhine River.

The 21st Army Group was supposed to cross the Rhine River on 24th March, 1945 and in order to be ready for this "earthshaking" event, Mr. Churchill wrote a speech congratulating Field Marshall Montgomery on the first "assault" crossing over the Rhine River in modern history. This speech was recorded and through some error on the part of the British Broadcasting Corporation, was broadcast. In spite of the fact that the Third Army had been across the Rhine River for some 36 hours.

Patton's disdain for Montgomery knew no bounds, and he took whatever chance he had to criticize the British general and his methods of waging war, as is evident from the following Patton quote: "We never met any opposition because the bigger and better Germans fight Monty. He says so. Also, he advertises so damn much that they know where he is. I fool them."

An American M5 light tank equipped with a public-address system. The loudspeaker could be used for psychological warfare. *National Archives*

An abandoned German Sturmmörser Tiger, armed with 38cm (380mm/14.96 inches) mortar, sits in a small village. *National Archives*

An American truck brings up section of a treadway bridge. Patton wasted no time in arranging for the Third Army to cross the Rhine River in force. The spot chosen for the first crossing was at a place called Oppenheim, ten miles upstream from the city of Mainz. It fell upon 5th Infantry Division, of Eddy's XII Corps, to make the initial crossing. *National Archives*

In one of Patton's most controversial World War II decisions, he ordered a small military rescue mission, known as Task Force Baum, to go deep behind enemy lines to liberate a prisoner-of-war camp near Hammelburg, Germany, on March 24. The camp contained a great number of American military personnel. The mission was not a success, and the majority of the 307 men sent on the mission were captured or killed, as were most of the prisoners liberated by the task force. Many believed that the mission was launched only because Patton was aware that his son-in-law, Lt. Col. John K. Waters, was in the camp.

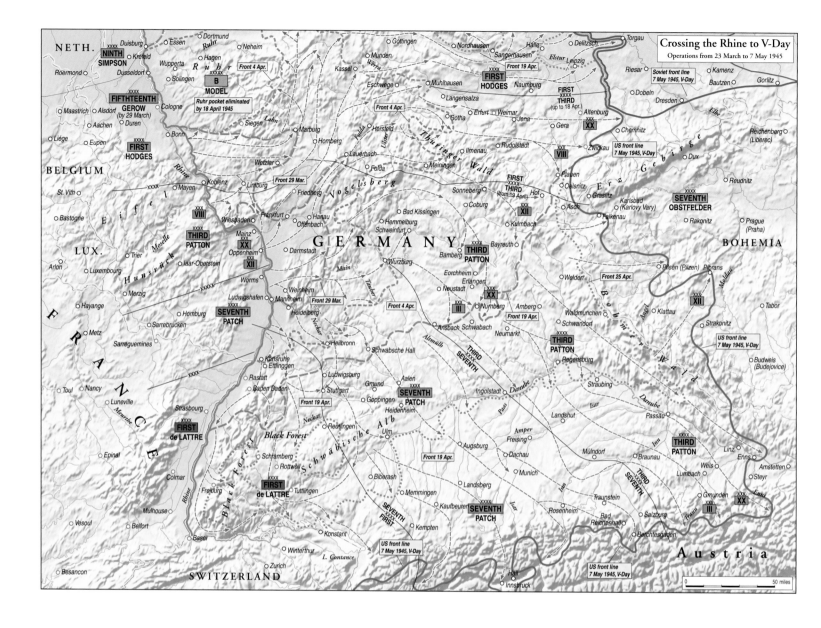

Crossing the Rhine to V-Day
Operations from 23 March to 7 May 1945

At the same time the Allied armies were crossing the Rhine, the Soviet army was encircling the German capital of Berlin. This development forced Eisenhower to rule out Berlin as an Allied military objective. Even the capture of the Ruhr, the industrial heart of Germany, became less important to Eisenhower as his intelligence experts informed him that the Germans were moving important factories out of the area. Despite this, Eisenhower had Montgomery's 21st Army Group and Bradley's First Army advance on the Ruhr. The last organized resistance in the Ruhr ended on April 18 with the capture of 317,000 German soldiers.

A growing concern for Eisenhower were the rumors of a last-ditch stand by remaining German forces deep in the mountains of southern Germany and Austria. The Americans referred to this stand as the German "national redoubt." Later events would show that Eisenhower's and the U.S. Army's fear of a German national redoubt were completely unfounded.

American soldiers drag an assault boat into position. It was March 23, 1945, before the 5th Infantry Division received all the engineering equipment it needed to attempt to cross the Rhine River. However, Patton ordered the river crossing to take place on the night of March 22. Wartime censors have obliterated 5th Division's distinctive diamond-shaped shoulder patches as a security measure. *National Archives*

The crew of a 6x6 amphibious truck, known as a Duck, changes a front tire on their vehicle. While the initial assault waves of 5th Armored Division crossed the Rhine River in small assault boats, reinforcements crossed in Ducks and landing craft operated by the U.S. Navy. *National Archives*

An American two-and-a-half-ton 6x6 truck crosses a pontoon bridge, carrying a load of captured German soldiers and escorted by a military-police Jeep. Despite some limited resistance, 5th Infantry Division's crossing of the Rhine River was a success, and the buildup of American forces on the east side of the river began in earnest on March 23, 1945. *National Archives*

An American M4A1 Sherman medium tank, equipped with an M1 bulldozer blade, clears rubble. *National Archives*

With the Germans in the Ruhr ready to surrender, Eisenhower launched his three army groups eastward toward the Elbe and Mulde rivers on April 11. The Mulde River runs into the Elbe River at Dessau, Germany. On arriving at their objectives, Eisenhower's forces were to halt, because there was an agreement with Soviet leader Joseph Stalin to divide Germany in half. Patton's Third Army now consisted of twelve infantry and six armored divisions divided among four corps. Small patrols from the First Army made contact with the Soviet army along the Elbe and Mulde rivers on April 25. The first formal meetings between American and Russian divisional commanders took place the following day.

A captured German *Volkssturm* (home guard) member, with only an armband instead of a uniform, poses with his rifle. *National Archives*

PATTON'S THOUGHTS ON RECONNAISSANCE

JUNIOR OFFICERS OF reconnaissance units must be very inquisitive. Their reports must be accurate and factual. Negative information is as important as positive information. Information must be transmitted in the clear by radio and at once. The location of the unit giving the information, should, where possible, be in a modified code. The enemy should be located by a magnetic azimuth and range from the point of observation. All members of the reconnaissance unit should know what they are trying to do. The results of all reconnaissance obtained in front of one division must be transmitted to adjacent units.

—*War As I Knew It,*
"Letter of Instruction No. 2"

On April 14, Patton's Third Army approached within ten miles of the western Czechoslovakia border and halted. Patton then received orders to regroup Third Army in preparation for a new mission that would take it into Czechoslovakia and southward into Bavaria and Austria.

From the official, multivolume U.S. Army history of World War II appears this passage describing the situation as Patton's Third Army units rushed through the southern Germany countryside on the way to Austria the last week of April:

The countryside of the Fraenkische Highland was strikingly beautiful with spring. Here a cluster of daffodils, there a farmer turning a damp furrow, cows grazing in green fields. Only in the towns and cities did war seem to have any place. There the streets were dead, sometimes block after block of rubble, or else owed their survival to great white flags of surrender hanging from every building. Almost everywhere during late April, front lines ceased to exist, so that nobody knew when or where the fighting might erupt, at the next hill, ridge, village, stream, whenever a group of Germans with a will to fight took a stand. Sometimes the Germans would let infantry and tanks pass unmolested, then turn sudden, unanticipated wrath on artillery and supply units bringing up the rear. Other times men who had dug in to fight would for some inexplicable reason throw away their weapons to raise hands high in surrender. Everybody knew that the war was over, yet somehow, at one isolated spot or another, the war still went on, real enough for the moment and sometimes deadly for those involved.

A squad of American soldiers carefully advance into a German town. The soldier on the far right carries a Rocket Launcher, Antitank, M9, which weighed fourteen and a half pounds and measured fifty-five inches overall. *National Archives*

British soldiers stand with a captured German Demag D7 unarmored half-track armed with a 2cm (20mm) FlaK 30 (antiaircraft gun). Montgomery's 21st Army Group launched itself across the Rhine River in three places on March 24, 1945. The operation would rival the D-Day landing in Normandy on June 6, 1944, not only in the number of troops involved, but also in the amount of supplies, transport, and special equipment employed. *Tank Museum/Bovington*

A British Comet tank passes by a German roadblock. Once across the Rhine, the goal of Montgomery's 21st Army Group, which included the American 9th Army under Simpson, was the Ruhr, the industrial heartland of Germany. The Ruhr industrial area was fifty miles long at its base along the Rhine River and sixty miles deep. *Tank Museum/Bovington*

An American soldier examines a Walther MKb.42(W) assault rifle in a captured German small-arms factory. By the end of March 1945, the Rhine River, the historical moat that had long guarded Germany from its traditional enemies to the west, was breached in numerous places by the various armies of the Western Allies. The once-mighty German Army was now but a hollow shell on the brink of total defeat. *National Archives*

The Austrian city of Linz, Hitler's birthplace, fell to Third Army on May 4. On that same day various elements of Third Army secured the mountain crossings into Czechoslovakia in case they received orders to take German-occupied Prague, the capital of Czechoslovakia. As events transpired, on May 4, a decision was made by Eisenhower, in conjunction with the Russians, that the Soviet forces would be responsible for the capture of Prague and Third Army would advance only so far into Czechoslovakia.

PATTON'S THOUGHTS ON MAPS

WE ARE TOO prone to believe that we acquire merit solely through the study of maps in the safe seclusion of a command post. This is an error.

Maps are necessary in order to see the whole panorama of battle and to permit intelligent planning.

Further, and this is very important, a study of the map will indicate where the commander should be. In the higher echelons, a layered map of the whole theater to a reasonable scale, showing roads, railways and streams, and towns, is more useful than a large-scale map cluttered up with ground forms and a multiplicity of non-essential information.

—*War As I Knew It,*
"Letter of Instruction No. 1"

Two American soldiers, armed with M1 Garand rifles, take a break from the fighting. The soldier on the left has an M9A1 antitank rifle grenade attached to the muzzle of his weapon. *National Archives*

On May 7, the Germans signed surrender terms that became effective on May 9. May 8, however, became designated as V-E (Victory in Europe) Day, although in some remote areas, fighting continued until May 11. During the period from April 22 to May 7, Third Army took more than 200,000 German prisoners while suffering fewer than 2,400 casualties itself.

At the end of the war, the U.S. Army compiled statistics on its casualties. In 281 days of combat, Third Army saw 21,441 men killed, 99,224 wounded, and 16,200 missing. Nonbattle casualties stood at 111,562. Patton's Third Army managed to seize 81,823 square miles of territory during its brief existence. Estimated casualties among the German forces that faced Third Army in battle accounted for 47,500 killed and 115,700 wounded. In total, Third Army captured 1,280,688 German military personnel between August 1, 1944, and May 13, 1945.

American infantrymen with armor support wait for the order to move out. It became clear to Eisenhower in late March that Montgomery's 21st Army Group would never make it to Berlin before the Red Army. So on March 28, 1945, he shifted the main Western Allied effort from the northern part of Germany to the central part of Germany, which lay in the path of Bradley's 12th Army Group. *National Archives*

A German Tiger B heavy tank sits abandoned in a town. *Patton Museum*

An American soldier looks over a captured German Me 262 jet fighter. As the armored division spearheads of Patton's Third Army began racing across central Germany in early April 1945, they encountered a mixed bag of German defenders; these troops were either diehards who fought to the death, or they offered only token resistance and then surrendered. *National Archives*

American soldiers fire a German 7.5 (75mm) PaK 40 (antitank gun) back at its former owners. *National Archives*

A field full of German prisoners of war reflects the mass surrenders that occurred in the closing stages of the war in Europe. *National Archives*

American soldiers patrol a German town. By the end of April 1945, Patton's Third Army armored spearheads were lined up against the Czech border and deep into Austria and eastern Germany. The fear of a last-ditch defense of the Alpine region in southern Germany and western Austria by the German military proved to be unfounded. *National Archives*

An American soldier cuts a V-E Day cake. On May 7, 1945, the same day elements of Third Army reached the Czech town of Pilsen (or Plzen), the shooting stopped. The next day, V-E Day (Victory in Europe Day), was officially announced. Hitler had committed suicide in his underground bunker in Berlin on April 30. *National Archives*

PATTON AFTER V-E DAY

With the end of the war in Europe, Patton wanted to travel to the Pacific and fight the Japanese. His request was ignored, and he received the appointment as military governor of Bavaria. This job proved ill-suited to Patton's temperament. By the end of September 1945, Eisenhower relieved Patton from his job as military governor and took away his command of Third Army due to an off-the-cuff statement Patton had made during a press conference on September 22. In his remarks, Patton had compared the defunct Nazi Party with the American Republican and Democratic political parties. Patton passed command of Third Army to Gen. Lucian K. Truscott at noon on October 7, 1945. Afterward, Patton received command of Fifteenth Army, whose sole job was writing the history of the war in Europe. There were no corps or divisions attached to the army—only historians and clerks sorting through endless piles of wartime reports.

Patton reviews a tank unit of the 2nd Armored Division near Berlin, Germany, on July 20, 1945, during the Potsdam Conference. Patton stands above the star in the leading M3A1 half-track. At the front of the half-track are Henry L. Stimson, U.S. Secretary of War (a civilian position), and Brig. Gen. John H. Collier, commander of 2nd Armored. Assistant Secretary of War John J. McCloy stands between Patton and Stimson, and Special Assistant to the Secretary of War Harvey H. Bundy is behind them. Maj. Gen. Floyd Parks (on Patton's right) and an unidentified officer stand at the rear of the half-track. Shortly after the war in Europe was over, Patton, in a self-effacing quote, stated, "It was the superior fighting ability of the American soldier, the wonderful efficiency of our mechanical transport, the work of Bradley, Keyes, and the Army Staff that did the trick. I just came along for the ride. I certainly love war." *National Archives*

In these postwar pictures, Patton is shown with his fourth star. Patton would remain commander of Third Army until October 7, 1945, when he handed control over to Gen. Lucian K. Truscott. In place of his beloved Third Army, Patton was given command of the Fifteenth Army, an administrative unit with no combat troops and tasked with writing the official history of the U.S. Army role in the fighting in Europe. *National Archives*

On December 9, 1945, on the way to a day of bird shooting in Germany, Patton was involved in a traffic accident in which he suffered serious injuries, including a broken neck. He lived only eleven more days before passing away in his sleep on December 21. General George S. Patton Jr. was buried with full military honors on December 24, 1945, at the American Military Cemetery in Hamm, just outside of Luxembourg. The next day the *New York Times* ran an editorial in his honor. The editorial said:

History has reached out and embraced General George Patton. His place is secure. He will be ranked in the forefront of America's great military leader. . . . Long before the war ended, Patton was a legend. Spectacular, swaggering, pistol-packing, deeply religious and violently profane, easily moved to anger because he was first of all a fighting man, easily moved to tears because underneath all his manned irascibility he had a kind heart, he was a strange combination of fire and ice. Hot in battle and ruthless too, he was no more hell-for-leather tank commander but a profound and thoughtful military student. He had been compared with Jeb Stuart, Nathan Bedford Forrest and Phil Sheridan, but he fought his battles in a bigger field than any of them. He was not a man of peace. Perhaps he would have preferred to die at the height of his fame, when his men, whom he loved, were following him with devotion. His nation will accord his memory a full measure of that devotion.

The original cross that marked Patton's gravesite. On December 9, 1945, Patton went on a pheasant-hunting trip in Germany. His car collided with a U.S. Army truck that morning, leaving him seriously injured. Patton would succumb to his injuries on December 21, 1945. His wife picked an American military cemetery in Hamm, Luxembourg, for his burial spot. *National Archives*

The current gravesite and marker. Patton's body was moved to the head of the U.S. Army cemetery in Hamm, Luxembourg, near the chapel, on March 19, 1947. *Michel Dieleman*

APPENDIX: WEAPONS AND VEHICLES

PISTOL, AUTOMATIC, CALIBER .45 M1911A1

Martin K. A. Morgan collection

The most widely used handgun in U.S. military service during World War II was typically referred to as the Colt .45 or the .45 automatic. The recoil-operated weapon evolved from the original version, designated the M1911, which saw widespread service in World War I. The A1 version dated from 1922 and featured a host of small improvements over its predecessor. During World War II, the U.S. Army sought to restrict the pistol to officers, troops manning crew-served weapons, and rear-area service troops. However, in specialized units like the airborne, almost everybody received an M1911A1. Also, enlisted military policemen carried it as a sidearm.

Caliber: .45 inch
Overall Length: approximately 8.6 inches
Weight: approximately 3 pounds
Magazine: 7-round box
Muzzle Velocity: 825 feet per second
Maximum Effective Range: 33 yards

RIFLE, CALIBER .30 M1

Martin K. A. Morgan collection

During World War II, this was the standard semi-automatic rifle of the U.S. military. It most often referred to as the Garand after its inventor and designer, John C. Garand. The weapon was the first semi-automatic rifle adopted as standard issue by any military and fired from an integral eight-round box magazine. The first-production Garand came off the assembly line in late 1937. By the end of World War II, over 4,028,375 units of the Garand had been built.

Caliber: .30-06
Overall Length: approximately 44 inches
Weight: approximately 9.5 pounds
Magazine: integral 8-round box
Muzzle Velocity: 2,805 feet per second
Maximum Effective Range: 3,500 yards

CARBINE, CALIBER .30 M1

Martin K. A. Morgan collection

In 1938, the infantry branch of the U.S. Army requested that the Ordnance Department develop a .30-caliber carbine weighing five pounds or less for issue to second-line troops in lieu of pistols. It was the Winchester Company that came up with the successful design of a gas-operated, semi-automatic weapon. Pictured is the M1A1 version of the carbine, with a folding stock, for issue to paratroopers. It was more accurate than the pistol, but fired a less powerful cartridge.

Caliber: .30 inch
Overall Length: approximately 36 inches
Weight: approximately 5.2 pounds
Magazine: detachable 15-round box
Muzzle Velocity: 1,970 feet per second
Maximum Effective Range: 300 yards

BROWNING AUTOMATIC RIFLE, Ml918A2

Martin K. A. Morgan collection

A gas-operated, air-cooled weapon commonly referred to as the BAR, it was originally conceived by John M. Browning at the beginning of the twentieth century. It was adopted by the U.S. Army in 1918 as the Browning machine rifle, model 1918, for use in World War I. The Ml918A2 model, the final production version of the weapon, saw heavy use in World War II, where it established its reputation as a reliable and hard-hitting weapon. It was in great demand by American soldiers. It fired the same ammunition as the Ml Rifle and the Browning .30-caliber machine gun, thus simplifying ammunition supply.

Caliber: .30-06
Overall Length: approximately 48 inches
Weight: approximately 19 pounds
Magazine: detachable 20-round box
Theoretical Rate of Fire: 600 rounds per minute
Muzzle Velocity: 2,650 feet per second
Maximum Effective Range: 3,500 yards

SUBMACHINE GUN, CALIBER .45, M1

Martin K. A. Morgan collection

One of the best known submachine guns to come out of World War II, it was commonly referred to as the Thompson or Tommy Gun, after its inventor and designer, John Taliaferro Thompson. The recoil-operated Ml was the final version of the Thompson and descended from the original model of the weapon, known as the Thompson submachine gun, model of 1921. The U.S. Navy and U.S. Army adopted a modified version of the Thompson, referred to as the M1928Al, before World War II. A simplified Ml version entered service production in 1942 and the improved M1Al version (pictured) entered service in 1943.

Caliber: .45 inch
Overall Length: approximately 32 inches
Weight: approximately 11 pounds
Magazine: detachable 20- or 30-round box
Theoretical Rate of Fire: 700 rounds per minute
Muzzle Velocity: 920 feet per second

SUBMACHINE GUN, CALIBER .45, M3

Martin K. A. Morgan collection

Intended by the U.S. Army to be simpler and less costly than the better-known Thompson, the Submachine Gun, Caliber .45, M3 was authorized for production by General Motor's Guide Lamp division in December 1942. The blowback weapon was nicknamed the Grease Gun, because it resembled the tool used for lubricating automobiles of the era. Over 600,000 Grease Guns came off American production lines. An improved version of the weapon appeared in December 1944 and was designated the M3Al, of which 15,000 were built.

Caliber: .45 ACP
Overall Length with Butt Extended: 29.33 inches
Overall Length with Butt Retracted: 22.44 inches
Weight: 10.25 pounds
Magazine: detachable 32-round box
Cylic Rate of Fire: 450 rounds per minute
Muzzle Velocity: 920 feet per second
Maximum Effective Range: 200 yards

2.36-INCH ROCKET LAUNCHER M1A1

Martin K. A. Morgan collection

The American-designed and -built rocket launcher, popularly known and widely publicized as the bazooka, was, in its original form, the simplest weapon ever produced by the U.S. Army Ordnance Department. It was a smoothbore, breech-loading shoulder weapon of the open-tube type. It could be fired from the standing, kneeling, sitting, or prone position. It could be effective against armored fighting vehicles in certain situations. There were three progressively improved versions of the bazooka: the M1, M1A1 (pictured), and the final model, the M9A1. American factories managed to assemble almost 500,000 units of the bazooka by the end of World War II.

Caliber: 2.36 inch
Overall Length: 4 feet 6.5 inches
Weight: 13.25 pounds
Muzzle Velocity: 270 feet per second
Effective Range: 100 yards

KARABINER 98K

Martin K. A. Morgan collection

The standard bolt-action rifle used by the German military during World War II, it was a shortened and modified version of the Gewehr 98 bolt-action rifle employed by the German military during World War I. The "k" in the weapon's designation stood for "kurz" (short); the Gewehr 98 was over 5 inches longer than the Kar98k. The 98k could be fitted with a grenade launcher or modified into a sniper rifle.

Caliber: 7.92x57mm
Overall Length: 43.7 inches
Weight: 9 pounds
Magazine: integral 5-round box
Muzzle Velocity: 2,100 feet per second
Maximum Effective Range: 800 yards

GEWEHR 43

Martin K. A. Morgan collection

A gas-operated, semi-automatic rifle that evolved from an earlier model, designated the Gewehr 41, which proved a slight disappointment in service. The product-improved Gewehr 43 featured a new gas-operating system based on a Russian design and began appearing in German military use in 1943. Many of these weapons appeared in service with a sighting telescope and were employed as sniper rifles.

Caliber: 7.92x57mm
Overall Length: 44 inches
Weight: 10 pounds
Magazine: detachable 10-round box
Muzzle Velocity: 2,546 feet per second
Maximum Effective Range: 1,365 yards

MP40

Martin K. A. Morgan collection

A blow-back (recoil) operated submachine gun referred to by the Germans as a maschinenpistole (machine pistol), the MP40 was developed from an earlier model designated the MP38, which first appeared in German military service in 1938. Distinctive features of both weapons were a folding stock and an all-metal-and-plastic construction.

Caliber: 9x19mm
Overall Length: 33 inches
Weight: 10 pounds
Magazine: detachable 32-round box
Theoretical Rate of Fire: 500 rounds per minute
Muzzle Velocity: 1,200 feet per second
Maximum Effective Range: 219 yards

MASCHINENGEWEHER 34 (MG 34) GENERAL-PURPOSE MACHINE GUN

Chun-Lsu Hsu

The MG34 was the world's first general-purpose machine gun, and it could be readily adapted to a variety of roles, such as an infantry squad weapon fitted with a bipod, an antiaircraft weapon on a dual mount, or a heavy machine gun, with an indirect sight, mounted on a four-leg carriage. The air-cooled machine gun had a quick-change barrel to allow for sustained rates of fire. The weapon could be fed either from a belt or by a saddle drum magazine containing seventy-five rounds. The biggest problem with the M34 was that it was too expensive and time consuming to build, and it was replaced in 1942 by the simpler, but equally effective, MG42. However, the MG34 would survive in German military service until the end of the war in Europe.

Caliber: 7.62mm (0.31 inch)
Length: 48 inches
Weight with Bipod: 26.5 pounds
Weight with Tripod: 42 pounds
Theoretical Rate of Fire: 900 rounds per minute
Muzzle Velocity: 2,475 feet per second
Maximum Effective Range: 2,500 yards

PANZERFAUST

Martin K. A. Morgan collection

The scourge of Allied tankers for the last two years of World War II was the German, mass-produced Panzerfaust (tank fist). It was a single-shot, throw-away, recoilless, rocket-propelled grenade that took a fearsome toll of any tanks that got within its short radius of action. Development of the first version of the Panzerfaust began in 1942, and the first production units were delivered in late 1943. A continuous series of improved versions of the Panzerfaust, more powerful and with longer ranges, appeared up until the war in Europe ended. A Panzerfaust 60 (pictured) was the most common version in service; its production started in late 1944.

Weight: 13 pounds
Range: 66 yards
Projectile Diameter: 5.91 inches
Muzzle Velocity: 150 feet per second
Armor Penetration: 7.9 inches

105MM HOWITZER M2A1

Michael Green

As early as World War I, some far-sighted individual in the U.S. Army saw a need for a 105mm howitzer as a divisional support weapon. Nothing came of the observation until 1934, when the U.S. Army Ordnance Department developed a successful 105mm design based on a German 105mm howitzer design from World War I. It was not until June 1940 that the weapon was placed into production as the 105mm howitzer M2A1. By the end of World War II, American factories had built 8,536 units of the field-artillery piece, which saw action around the globe.

Height: 5 feet 7 inches
Length: 19 feet 5inches
Width: 7 feet 3 inches
Weight: 4,260 pounds
Maximum Effective Range: 12,500 yards

15CM NEBELWERFER 41

Michael Green

The 15cm Nebelwerfer 41 was a six-barrel, 150mm (5.9-inch) rocket launcher mounted on a simple two-wheeled carriage with a split trail. The German term *Nebelwerfer* translates to "smoke throwing." The weapon was originally intended to fire poison gas or smoke rockets. During World War II, it fired only high-explosive and smoke rounds. To prevent the launcher unit and carriage from turning over while firing, the rockets were fired one at a time in a fixed sequence of about ten seconds. Due to the very loud howling noises the rockets made in flight, American soldiers nicknamed them the Screaming Meemies.

Length of Barrels: 51 inches
Weight: 1,195 pounds
Traverse: 30 degrees
Elevation: 44 degrees
Maximum Range (firing high explosives): 7,330 yards
Weight of Rocket (high explosive): 75.3 pounds
Velocity: 1,120 feet per second

88MM FLAK 36

Michael Green

The legendary German 88mm FlaK (antiaircraft gun), feared by all Allied bomber crews, was developed in secret during the 1920s by the well-known German armament firm of Krupp in cooperation with the Swedish arms builder Bofors. By the time Hitler came to power in 1933, the towed weapon was ready for production. The first version was designated the FlaK 18. The FlaK 36 (pictured) was an improved version introduced in 1939. While the weapon is best known as an antitank weapon during World War II, it was an impressive antiaircraft gun and lasted in German military service to the end of the conflict.

Length of Gun Tube: 16 feet 1.8 inches
Weight in Towed Configuration: 7.1 tons
Weight in Firing Configuration: 5.49 tons
Maximum Effective Ceiling: 32,500 feet
Practical Rate of Fire: 12 to 15 rounds per minute
Muzzle Velocity (High Explosives): 2,690 feet per second
Traverse: 360 degrees
Elevation: minus 3 degrees to plus 85 degrees

7.5CM PAK 40 (75MM ANTITANK GUN)

Christophe Vallier

P-47 THUNDERBOLT FIGHTER

U.S. Air Force

P-51 MUSTANG

U.S. Air Force

The German army quickly discovered, during the early stages of their invasion of the Soviet Union, in the summer of 1941, that their standard towed antitank guns were having difficulty penetrating the armor on the Soviet army's T34 medium tank and KV heavy tank. To redress this inferiority, the Germans rushed into service the 7.5cm PaK 40, which had been under development since 1939. Like its predecessor, the 5cm (50mm) PaK 38, the 7.5cm PaK 40 was towed into action on a two-wheel mount by either a wheeled or half-track vehicle. German industry built approximately 23,500 units of the 7.5cm PaK 40 by the time the war in Europe ended. The gun could also be employed as a field-artillery piece with indirect sights.

Total Length of Weapon: 20 feet 3 inches
Length of Gun Tube: 11 feet 4 inches
Height: 4 feet 1 inch
Width: 6 feet 6 inches
Weight: 3,136 pounds
Maximum Muzzle Velocity: 2,530 feet per second
Maximum Effective Range with Direct Sights: 1,969 yards

The largest fighter to see service in World War II, the P-47 Thunderbolt, nicknamed the Jug, was best known to most GIs in Europe as a premier ground-attack aircraft. The prototype of the P-47 Thunderbolt was flown in May 1941, and the first production version saw combat in April 1943. The aircraft would go on to see combat in every active-duty combat theater with the American military and also serve with various Allied air forces. By the time production of the P-47 Thunderbolt ended, 15,579 units had come off the assembly lines.

Crew: 1 man
Wingspan: 40 feet 9 inches
Height: 14 feet 1 inch
Length: 36 feet 1 inch
Wing Area: 300 square feet
Weight, Empty: 10,000 pounds
Weight, Combat Loaded: 19,400 pounds
Maximum Speed: 428 mph
Service Ceiling: 42,000 feet
Armament: 8 machine guns, plus miscellaneous bombs and rockets

The American P-51 Mustang was a single-seat, long-range fighter initially used by the British Royal Air Force. It first saw action with the RAF on May 10, 1942. While effective below 15,000 feet, it did not perform well above that until a British supercharged Merlin 61 engine was installed. The new engine allowed it to operate up to almost 42,000 feet. Production of the P-51 for the U.S. Army Air Force began in early 1943. A total of 15,586 units, in different versions, rolled off American assembly lines during the war. The AAF primarily used it as a fighter escort over Europe, but it doubled as a ground-attack aircraft.

Crew: 1 man
Wingspan: 37 feet 4 inches
Height: 11 feet 1 inch
Length: 33 feet 4 inches
Wing Area: 235 square feet
Weight, Empty: 7, 040 pounds
Weight, Combat Loaded: 11,500 pounds
Maximum Speed: 487 mph
Service Ceiling: 41,600 feet
Armament: 6 machine guns plus provisions for an assortment of bombs and rockets

B-17 FLYING FORTRESS

U.S. Air Force

The B-17 was a four-engine, heavy bomber primarily employed by the U.S. Army Air Forces (USAAF) in the daylight bombing campaign over Europe during World War II. The first flight of a B-17 prototype took place in 1935. By the time production of the B-17 series of bomber ended in May 1945, a total of 12,731 aircraft had come off the assembly lines of various companies.

Crew: Up to 10 men
Wing Span: 103 feet 9 inches
Height: 19 feet 1 inch
Length: 74 feet 9 inches
Wing Area: 1,400 square feet
Weight, Empty: 36,135 pounds
Weight, Combat Loaded: 72,000 pounds
Maximum Speed: 287 mph
Service Ceiling: 35,600 feet with a 6,000-lb bomb load
Armament: up to 13 machine guns

M8 ARMORED CAR

Michael Green

The open-topped M8 was originally envisioned as a wheeled tank destroyer. However, it entered U.S. Army service as a reconnaissance vehicle. Production of the vehicle began at Ford in March 1943 and continued until May 1945, with a total production run of 8,523 vehicles. The biggest problem with the M8 was its lack of an independent suspension system, which limited its off-road mobility. There was also a serious breakage problem with its front leaf springs. Another problem with the M8 was its very thin floor armor, which made it very vulnerable to antitank mines.

Crew: 4 men
Length with Gun Forward: 16 feet 5 inches
Height: 7 feet 4.5 inches
Width: 8 feet 4 inches
Weight: 8.7 tons
Engine Type: gasoline-powered Hercules JXD 6-cylinder
Thickest armor: 1 inch
Primary Armament: 37mm gun
Secondary Armament: 2 machine guns

M5 LIGHT TANK

Christophe Vallier

Combat in North Africa against the German military in 1942 and 1943 had quickly shown the U.S. Army that its light tanks were badly suited for frontline duties against German tanks and armored fighting vehicles. Many in the army wanted to replace all the thinly armored and undergunned light tanks with medium tanks. This was not possible, and the light tanks were used by the U.S. Army until the end of the war in Europe in secondary roles, such as reconnaissance and rear area security duties. Production of the M5 light tank began in April 1942 and continued until December of the same year, with a total production run of 2,074 vehicles.

Crew: 4 men
Length with Gun Forward: 14 feet 6 inches
Height Over Cupola: 8 feet 5 inches
Width: 7 feet 4 inches
Weight: 16.6 tons
Engine Type: gasoline-powered twin Cadillac V-8s
Thickest Armor: 2 inches
Primary Armament: 37mm gun
Secondary Armament: 3 machine guns

M4A3 MEDIUM TANK

Michael Green

Of the six different versions of the first-generation M4 series of medium tanks built between 1942 and 1945, the M4A3 model was the preferred type by the U.S. Army due to its liquid-cooled V-8 engine's high output, compactness, and excellent power-to-weight ratio. Due to insufficient numbers of M4A3 tanks, the army also used the M4 and M4A1 versions powered by air-cooled radial engines. All versions of the vehicle are best known as the Sherman.

Crew: 5 men
Length with Gun Forward: 19 feet 4.5 inches
Height Over Cupola: 9 feet 6 inches
Width: 8 feet 7 inches
Weight: 33.6 tons
Engine Type: liquid-cooled gasoline V-8
Thickest Armor: 3.5 inches
Primary Armament: 75mm gun
Secondary Armament: 3 machine guns

M18 TANK DESTROYER

Michael Green

The open-topped M18 was a highly mobile tank destroyer riding on a torsion bar suspension system. Top speed of the vehicle was sixty miles per hour, making it the fastest tracked armored vehicle of World War II. American factories built 2,507 units of the M18 between July 1943 and October 1944. The vehicle's suspension system utilized torsion bars, with five road wheels per side (each having a shock absorber) and four-track return rollers.

Crew: 5 men
Length with Gun Forward: 21 feet 10 inches
Height: 8 feet 5 inches
Width: 9 feet 2 inches
Weight: 20 tons
Engine Type: air-cooled gasoline radial
Thickest Armor: 1 inch
Primary Armament: 76mm gun
Secondary Armament: 1 machine gun

75MM HOWITZER MOTOR CARRIAGE M8

Christophe Vallier

To provide armored cross-country mobility to the 75mm pack howitzer, the U.S. Army designed an open-topped turret that mounted on the modified hull of the M5 light tank. In this configuration, the weapon became the 75mm howitzer motor carriage M8. Production of the M8 began in September 1942 and continued through January 1944. A total of 1,788 M8s were built. Power for the M8 came from two Cadillac car engines, each of which was connected to a Hydra-Matic transmission, providing six forward speeds and one reverse speed. When firing a high-explosive (HE) shell, the 75mm howitzer on the M8 could reach a maximum range of 9,610 yards.

Crew: 4 men
Length with Gun Forward: 14 feet 6.75 inches
Height: 7 feet 6.5 inches
Width: 7 feet 4.25 inches
Weight: 17.3 tons
Engine Type: liquid-cooled gasoline
Maximum Speed: 40 mph
Thickest Armor: 2.5 inches
Primary Armament: 75mm howitzer
Secondary Armament: 1 machine gun

JAGDPANZER IV

Andreas Kirchhoff

THE HETZER

Michael Green

PANTHER AUSF. A

Ground Power Magazine

To deal with more heavily armored Red Army tanks, the Germans decided to mount the long-barreled, 75mm main gun of the Panther medium tank on the turretless armored chassis of a Panzer IV medium tank. Production difficulties made this plan impossible at first, so the shorter, less powerful 75mm main gun on the StuG III was utilized instead. The modified vehicle was designated the Jagdpanzer IV and went into production beginning in January 1944. Production ended in November 1944, with 769 units built. Traverse for the main gun, mounted in the front superstructure plate, was limited to 20 degrees in either direction. Elevation for the main gun on the Jagdpanzer IV was minus 5 degrees to plus 15 degrees.

Crew: 4 men
Length: 6 feet 7 inches
Height: 9 feet 5 inches
Width: 10 feet 4 inches
Weight: 28 tons
Engine Type: liquid-cooled gasoline
Thickest Armor: 3.15 inches
Primary Armament: 75mm gun
Secondary Armament: 2 machine guns

The Hetzer was an example of the German ability to retain obsolete tanks in service by doing away with the tanks' existing turrets and superstructures and replacing them with a low-profile, turretless, armored superstructure. The new superstructure was armed with a fixed forward-firing main gun with limited traverse and elevation. The Hetzer was based on the chassis of the Czech-designed and built Panzer 38(t), originally armed with a turret-mounted 37mm main gun. Production of the Hetzer began in April 1944 and continued to the end of the war in Europe, with 2,584 units completed.

Crew: 4 men
Length: 21 feet
Height: 7 feet
Width: 8. feet 6 inches
Weight: 16 tons
Engine Type: liquid-cooled gasoline
Thickest Armor: 2.36 inches
Primary Armament: 75mm gun
Secondary Armament: 1 machine gun

Production of the replacement for the Panther Ausf. D medium tank (the first model) began in September of 1943. The new Panther Ausf. A (Sd.Kfz. 171) consisted of a Panther Ausf. D chassis fitted with a redesigned turret. By the time production of the Panther Ausf. A ended in May 1944, German industry had produced 2,200 units. The final production version of the Panther tank series was the Ausf. G model, which began coming off the assembly lines in March 1944. The highest level of armor protection was found behind its well-sloped front armor plate.

Crew: 5 men
Length with Gun Forward: 29 feet 1 inch
Height Over Cupola: 9 feet 8 inches
Width: 10 feet 7 inches
Weight: 50 tons
Engine Type: liquid-cooled gasoline V-12
Thickest Armor: 4.7 inches
Primary Armament: 75mm gun
Secondary Armament: 3 machine guns

TIGER AUSF. E

Richard Cox

The Tiger Ausf. E heavy tank, commonly referred to as the Tiger I, had extremely thick armor for its time and a powerful main gun. For most of World War I, the vehicle dominated the battlefields it was committed to. Time consuming and expensive to build, German industry constructed only 1,350 units between August 1942 and August 1944. It was eventually replaced on the assembly lines by the Tiger B, otherwise known as the Tiger II.

Crew: 5 men
Length with Gun Forward: 27 feet 8 inches
Height Over Cupola: 9 feet 5 inches
Width: 12 feet 1 inches
Weight: 63 tons
Engine Type: liquid-cooled gasoline V-12
Thickest Armor: 4.3 inches
Primary Armament: 88mm gun
Secondary armament: 3 machine guns

TIGER B HEAVY TANK

Dave Marian

To replace the original Tiger E heavy tank, the Germans ordered a new, larger heavy tank in January 1943, armed with a more powerful version of the 88mm main gun that was mounted on the Tiger E. The new heavy tank first came off the production line January 1944 and was designated the Tiger B; it remained in production until March 1945. By the time production of the Tiger B ended, a total of 489 units were produced. Instead of having the flat, vertical armored plates found on the hull of the Tiger E, the Tiger B featured a hull with sloped armor plates like the Panther medium tank.

Crew: 5 men
Length with Gun Forward: 33 feet 8 inches
Height Over Cupola: 10 feet 1 inch
Width: 12 feet 3 inches
Weight: 77 tons
Engine Type: liquid-cooled gasoline
Maximum Speed: 24 mph
Thickest Armor: 7.09 inches
Primary Armament: 88mm gun
Secondary Armament: 3 machine guns

STURMGESCHUTZ III G ASSAULT GUN

Michael Green

Originally intended as an infantry-support vehicle equipped with a low-velocity 75mm howitzer, the Sturmgeschutz (StuG) series eventually evolved into a very successful self-propelled tank destroyer. The StuG Ausf. G version (pictured) was the last production model of the 7,720 units built between December 1942 and the end of the war in Europe. Turretless assault guns proved popular with the German military, as tanks with these guns were cheaper and faster to build than conventional turreted tanks. On the battlefield, the tanks' low height made them easier to conceal from attacking enemy forces.

Crew: 4 men
Length: 18 feet 2 inches
Height: 6 feet 4 inches
Width: 9 feet 8 inches
Weight: 27 tons
Engine Type: liquid-cooled gasoline
Thickest Armor: 3.15 inches
Primary Armament: 75mm gun
Secondary Armament: 2 machine guns

ONE-QUARTER-TON, 4X4, TRUCK

Michael Green

Popularly referred to as the jeep, the one-quarter-ton 4x4 truck was the world's first mass-produced four-wheel-drive small vehicle. It would climb a 60 percent grade and ford a stream eighteen inches deep while fully equipped and loaded. The vehicle could also tow a 37mm antitank gun or a two-wheel trailer. Various American companies built a total of 639,245 units by the time World War II ended. In addition to being widely used by the American military, the extremely reliable vehicle would see service with a number of Allied armies.

Crew: 2 men
Length with Winch: 11 feet .25 inch
Height: 5 feet 9.75 inches
Width: 5 feet 2 inches
Weight: 3,253 pounds
Engine Type: liquid-cooled gasoline
Maximum Speed: 65 mph
Maximum Range: 300 miles
Primary Armament: 1 machine gun

2½-TON, 6X6, AMPHIBIAN TRUCK (DUKW-353)

Christophe Vallier

Best known by its nickname, the Duck, this amphibious truck with a boat-type hull was based on the standard 2½-ton GMC 6x6 truck chassis. Commissioned in 1940, it first appeared in service in late 1942. On land, the vehicle uses six driving wheels and a conventional steering-gear assembly. In water, it is moved by a propeller at the rear of the vehicle. Steering in the water is done with the combined use of the front wheels and rudder, which are interconnected to and operated by the steering-gear column. On land, the Duck could carry twenty-five troops or 5,350 pounds of cargo. A total of 21,147 Ducks came off American assembly lines during World War II.

Height (Top Up): 8 feet 9.5 inches
Length: 31 feet
Width: 8 feet 2.88 inches
Weight: 19,570 pounds
Maximum Speed on Land: 45 mph
Maximum Speed in Water: 6.3 mph
Engine: 6-cylinder liquid-cooled gasoline
Cruising Range (Land): approximately 220 miles
Cruising Range (Water): approximately 50 miles

MODEL CCKW CARGO TRUCK

Christophe Vallier

The model CCKW cargo truck was most produced truck during World War II, and over 800,000 of all different versions came off American assembly lines. Best known by its most common names—the Two and a Half, the Jimmy, the Deuce-and-Half, or the GMC—the six-wheel-drive vehicle had a rated payload of two and a half tons, which meant it was a medium-duty truck. Having evolved from civilian trucks, the vehicle came with either an open or closed cab and could be fitted with a wide variety of rear-body configurations.

Height: 7 feet 3.19 inches
Length, Long Wheelbase: 21 feet 3 inches
Length, Short Wheelbase: 19 feet 2.5 inches
Width: 7 feet 4 inches
Weight: 6,000 pounds
Maximum Speed on Road: 45 mph
Engine: 6-cylinder liquid-cooled gasoline
Cruising Range: approximately 220 miles

M3A1 HALF-TRACK	M26 TRACTOR TRUCK	M29 WEASEL

Christophe Vallier

Michael Green

Michael Green

Capable of serving in many different roles—such as an ambulance, command vehicle, engineer vehicle, or prime mover—the open-topped M3A1 half-track was primarily employed by the U.S. Army as an armored personnel carrier during World War II. There were three seats in the vehicle's driving compartment with five additional seats on either side of the rear crew compartment. The ten men in the vehicle's crew compartment entered and exited by a door in the rear of the crew compartment. Besides the crew's own weapons, there was a .50-caliber machine-gun ring mount over the driving compartment. The U.S. Army fielded over 4,000 units of the M3A1 half-track by the time World War II ended.

Crew: 13 men
Length with Winch: 20 feet 9.62 inches
Height: 8 feet 10 inches
Width with Mine Racks: 7 feet 3.5 inches
Weight: 10 tons
Engine Type: liquid-cooled gasoline
Maximum Speed: 40 mph
Thickest Armor: .5 inch
Primary Armament: .50-caliber M2HB machine gun

The M26 tractor truck was a large and impressive 6x6 vehicle intended to supply the power and equipment needed for a variety of recovery and wrecking operations. To undertake these roles in combat, the vehicle had an armored cab that would protect its crew from small-arms fire and assorted battlefield fragments. Armament on the vehicle consisted of a roof-mounted .50-caliber machine gun on a ring mount. There were three winches on the M26 tractor truck, one in the front and two in the rear. The M26 tractor truck normally towed an eight-wheel semitrailer, which could carry a payload of 80,000 pounds. Together with an attached semitrailer, the M26 tractor trailer was over sixty-one feet long.

Crew: 7 men
Height: 10 feet 4 inches
Length: 25 feet 4 inches
Width: 10 feet 10.75 inches
Weight: 24 tons
Maximum Speed on Road: 26 mph
Engine: liquid-cooled gasoline
Cruising range: approximately 250 miles

A small, full-tracked, light cargo carrier originally designed for use over snow and ice, this vehicle had very low ground pressure, which made it useful in a variety of terrain where wheeled vehicles would have difficulties moving around. The engine was located on the right front of the vehicle, and the driver on the left front. Behind the driver's compartment were seats for the assistant driver and two passengers. A modified version of the vehicle was made amphibious and designated the M29C.

Height: 5 feet 11 inches
Length: 10 feet 5.34 inches
Width: 5 feet 6 inches
Weight: 5,425 pounds
Maximum Speed on Road: 36 mph
Engine: liquid-cooled gasoline
Approximate Cruising Range: 175 miles
Payload: 1,200 pounds

TANK RECOVERY VEHICLE M31 SERIES

Christophe Vallier

In order to allow the U.S. Army to recover its tanks from the battlefield, a number of surplus M3 medium tanks—models M3, M3A3, and M3A5—were converted into armored recovery vehicles (ARVs) during World War II. For camouflage purposes, the normal appearance of the tank was retained as far as possible. In the case of the M31B1 ARV (pictured), a dummy 75mm gun was mounted in the hull. The gun opened as a door, giving access to the crew compartment. A 60,000-pound winch was installed on the lower front hull. A total run of 296 units of the M31 series was completed between October 1942 and December 1943.

Crew: 6 men
Height: 9 feet 9 inches
Length: 26 feet 5 inches
Width: 8 feet 4 inches
Weight: 30 tons
Maximum Speed: 25 mph
Engine Type (M3IBI): liquid-cooled diesel
Cruising Range: approximately 110 miles

TYPE 82 KÜBELWAGEN

Christophe Vallier

Based on a modified chassis of the original Volkswagen Bug, designed by Ferdinand Porsche as a car for the German working class in the 1930s, the Kübelwagen was an open-topped military version. Performing a role similar to the American jeep, the Kübelwagen proved to be a popular and reliable vehicle with the German military. It featured rear-wheel drive, in contrast to the four-wheel drive of the jeep, and thus had significantly worse cross-country performance. Early preproduction models saw service during the German military invasion of Poland in September 1939. Full series production of the Kübelwagen for the German armed forces began in February 1940. By the time the war in Europe ended, over 50,000 units of the Kübelwagen had rolled off German factory floors.

Crew: 2 men
Height: 4 feet 5 inches
Length: 12 feet 3 inches
Width: 5 feet 3 inches
Weight: 1,400 pounds
Maximum Speed on Road: 62 mph
Engine: air-cooled gasoline
Cruising Range: approximately 215 miles

SCHWIMMWAGEN TYPE 166

Christophe Vallier

The Schwimmwagen was an amphibious, four-wheel-drive, off-road vehicle that used some components of the Type 86 Kübelwagen. The vehicle body was made of thin, welded steel and could seat four men. The engine in the Schwimmwagen was of slightly larger capacity than the engine mounted in the Kübelwagen and gave better all-around performance. The Schwimmwagen's crankcase was extended to the rear of the vehicle's body and engaged the rear-mounted propeller shaft by means of a dog clutch. German factories built about 15,000 units of the vehicle between 1940 and 1944.

Crew: 2 men
Height: 5 feet 3.6 inches
Length: 12 feet 6.6 inches
Width: 4 feet 10.3 inches
Weight: 1,992 pounds
Maximum Speed on Road: 50 mph
Engine: air-cooled gasoline
Cruising Range: approximately 280 miles
Payload: 958 pounds

SELECTED BIBLIOGRAPHY

Allen, Robert S. *Patton's Third U.S. Army: Lucky Forward.* New York: Manor Books, 1974.

Blumenson, Martin. *Breakout and Pursuit.* United States Army in World War II. Washington, D.C.: U.S. Army, Office of the Chief of Military History, 1961.

————. *The Patton Papers,* 2 vols. New York: Houghton Mifflin, 1974.

Bradley, Omar N. *A Soldier's Story.* New York: Rand McNally, 1951. Reprint, New York: Rand McNally, 1978.

Cole, Hugh M. *The Ardennes: The Battle of the Bulge.* United States Army in World War II. Washington, D.C.: U.S. Army, Office of the Chief of Military History, 1965.

————. *The Lorraine Campaign.* United States Army in World War II. Washington, D.C.: U.S. Army, Office of the Chief of Military History, 1950.

D'Este, Carlo. *Patton: A Genius for War.* New York: Harper Collins Publishers, 1995.

Ellis, John. *The Sharp End: The Fighting Man in World War II.* New York: Charles Scribner's Sons, 1980.

Essame, H. *Patton: A Study in Command.* New York: Charles Scribner's Sons, 1974.

Forty, George. *U.S. Army Handbook.* London: Ian Allan, 1979.

————. *The Armies of George S. Patton.* London: Arms and Armour Press, 1996.

Greenfield, Kent R., Robert R. Palmer, and Bell I. Wiley. *The Organization of Ground Combat Troops.* United States Army in World War II. Washington, D.C.: U.S. Army, Office of the Chief of Military History, 1947.

Harrison, Gordon A. *Cross-Channel Attack.* United States Army in World War II. Washington, D.C.: U.S. Army, Office of the Chief of Military History, 1950.

Hastings, Max. *Overlord: D-Day and the Battle for Normandy.* London: Pan Books, 1985.

Irving, David. *The War Between the Generals: Inside the Allied High Command.* New York: Congdon & Lattes, 1981.

MacDonald, Charles B. *The Last Offensive.* United States Army in World War II. Washington, D.C.: U.S. Army, Office of the Chief of Military History, 1973.

————. *The Siegfried Line Campaign.* United States Army in World War II. Washington, D.C.: U.S. Army, Office of the Chief of Military History, 1950.

Palmer, Robert R., Bell I. Wiley, and William R. Keast. *The Army Ground Forces: The Procurement and Training of Ground Combat Troops.* United States Army in World War II. Washington, D.C.: U.S. Army, Office of the Chief of Military History, 1948.

Patton, George S., Jr. *War As I Knew It.* Boston: Houghton Mifflin, 1947. Reprint, New York: Bantam Books, 1981.

Pogue, Forest C. *The Supreme Command.* United States Army in World War II. Washington, D.C.: U.S. Army, Office of the Chief of Military History, 1954.

Province, Charles M. *The Unknown Patton.* New York: Hippocrence, 1983.

————. *Patton's Third Army.* New York: Hippocrence, 1991.

————. *Patton's One-Minute Messages.* Novato, Calif.: Presidio Press, 1995.

Weigley, Russell. *Eisenhower's Lieutenants.* Bloomington: Indiana University Press, 1981.

Whiting; Charles. *Patton.* New York: Ballantine Books, 1970.

Wilmot, Chester. *The Struggle for Europe.* New York: Carroll & Graf Publishers, 1986.

INDEX

Military Units and Materiel

American Units

1st Army Group, 14, 27

I Armored Corps, 189, 215

4th Observation Squadron, 113

IV Armored Corps, 71

IX Tactical Air Command (TAC), 66

12th Army Group, 31, 36, 42, 63, 88, 98, 115–117, 119, 123, 126, 146, 147, 151, 156, 161, 163, 168, 171, 176, 215, 217, 244, 248, 263

  11th Armored Division, 217, 221, 222, 238

    41st Cavalry, 238, 239

12th Observation Squadron, 113

XVIII Airborne Corps, 178, 232

  82nd Airborne Division, 17, 18, 166, 178

  101st Airborne Division, 17, 18, 166, 178, 179, 181, 192, 200, 202, 207, 211, 212, 214, 222, 225, 227, 233, 238

    326th Engineers, 207

  106th Infantry Division, 167, 170, 175

    14th Cavalry Group, 167, 170, 175

  506th Parachute Infantry Regiment, 227

XIX Tactical Air Command (TAC), 27, 66, 86, 112, 113, 144, 146, 171, 189, 207, 209, 212

21st Army Group, 15, 25, 33, 34, 65, 99, 110, 112, 115–117, 119, 126, 130, 137, 146, 147, 168, 176, 183, 190, 216, 229, 241, 244, 248, 254, 256, 260, 261, 263

84th Fighter Wing, 113

106th Mechanized Cavalry Group, 84

Central Command (CENTCOM), 1

Coalition Forces Land Component Command (CFLCC), 1

Eighth Army, 71

Fifteenth Army, 1st Cavalry Division, 215

First Army, 2, 5, 18, 19, 21, 22, 24, 25, 27–31, 33, 34, 36–40, 42–44, 46, 49–51, 53, 56, 61, 83–85, 87, 90, 96, 98, 108, 111, 118, 119, 143, 146, 151, 155, 162, 176, 190, 214–216, 222, 229, 232, 235, 236, 238, 239, 242, 248, 249, 252, 256, 258

  V Corps, 18, 19, 21, 23, 156, 165, 166, 232, 246

    2nd Infantry Division, 13

  VII Corps, 18, 19, 21, 22, 24, 32, 43, 44, 46, 47, 50, 51, 56, 84, 85, 112, 214, 222, 232, 236, 238

    1st Infantry Division, 18, 46

    2nd Armored Division, 46, 51, 189, 238, 267

    3rd Armored Division, 46, 71, 236

    4th Armored Division, 50, 54, 57–59, 67, 69, 71–74, 76, 77, 80, 88, 111, 128, 129, 131, 132, 134–136, 140, 142, 143, 145, 171, 185, 187–190, 192, 193–195, 197, 199–202, 204, 206–212, 214, 218, 223, 224, 240, 250, 251

      37th Tank Battalion, 192, 201, 205

    4th Infantry Division, 18, 46

    6th Armored Division, 50, 54, 56–58, 67, 75, 77–80, 118, 135, 136, 139, 161, 225–227, 232, 233

      9th Armored Division, 172, 211, 218, 220, 222, 252

      9th Infantry Division, 46, 79

      30th Infantry Division, 30

      82nd Reconnaissance Battalion, 51

      90th Infantry Division, 83, 107, 118, 150, 151

  VIII Corps, 21, 40, 47, 53, 162, 164, 217

  XIX Corps, 21, 34, 47, 99

  29th Infantry Division, 18, 28

  30th Infantry Division, 30, 46

First U.S. Army Group (FUSAG), 2, 29

Ninth Army, 116, 118, 145, 146, 151, 158, 176, 190, 242

  84th Infantry Division, 239

Seventh Army, 3, 36, 130, 151, 159, 215, 250, 252, 253

  6th Army Group, 130, 151, 152, 168, 216

  30th Infantry Regiment, 3

  45th Infantry Division, 159

Signal Corps, 63, 138, 141, 203

Third Army, 1–3, 5–7, 9, 10, 13, 21, 26–28, 30, 31, 36, 38–40, 42, 53, 54, 56, 60, 63, 65–68, 71, 75, 77, 83–86, 88–91, 94, 98, 99, 101, 103–105, 108, 111–113, 115–119, 121–123, 125–134, 136–138, 143, 145–147, 149, 151–153, 158–160, 162, 164, 168, 171, 172, 175, 176, 179, 181–183, 188, 193, 211, 212, 214–218, 221, 222, 224, 229, 233–236, 238, 239, 241, 242, 245, 246, 248–250, 252–255, 258, 259, 261, 262, 264–266, 268

  2nd Infantry Division, 13

  43rd Reconnaissance Squadron, 134

  87th Infantry Division, 217, 221, 222

  VIII Corps, 6, 51, 54, 56–59, 67–71, 73, 75, 77, 80, 83, 84, 86, 91, 118, 155, 156, 158, 159, 165, 176, 178, 179, 185, 217–219, 221, 222, 225, 227, 233, 238, 239, 246, 249

    2nd Cavalry Group, 71

    13th Infantry Regiment, 71

    17th Airborne Division, 221

    83rd Infantry Division, 77, 83, 118

  XII Corps, 6, 27, 79, 88, 94, 105, 111, 112, 118, 125, 127, 129, 132, 134, 138, 139, 142, 149–152, 187, 198, 216, 228, 234, 239, 246, 249, 251, 255

    26th Infantry Division, 149, 161, 187, 190–192, 195–197, 228, 229, 233

  XV Corps, 6, 13, 27, 67, 83–87, 90, 95, 96, 98–102, 104, 106–108, 111, 112, 118, 125, 246

    5th Armored Division, 83, 96, 100, 107, 108, 110, 257

    79th Infantry Division, 107, 108, 112, 118

    85th Infantry Division, 67

XX Corps, 6, 27, 71, 85, 86, 89–91, 94, 96, 104, 105, 111–114, 118, 123, 125, 132, 138–142, 144, 146, 149–153, 164, 234, 246, 251

3rd Cavalry Group, 146

5th Infantry Division, 85, 90, 91, 111, 113, 114, 139, 142–145, 147, 150, 151, 255, 257, 258

6th Infantry Division, 91

7th Armored Division, 111–114, 125, 139, 140, 142, 143, 149, 158, 166

10th Armored Division, 150, 158, 164, 166

28th Infantry Division, 109, 175, 217

35th Infantry Division, 85, 88, 90, 111, 125, 128, 131, 132, 134, 136, 140, 143, 149, 198, 224, 225, 227, 228, 232

80th Infantry Division, 127, 128, 131, 132, 139, 143, 149, 171, 187, 190, 191, 193, 197, 198, 200, 228

318th Infantry Regiment, 197, 212

95th Infantry Division, 150

British Units

3rd Division, 25

Eighth Army, 25

Second Army, 18, 29, 43, 44, 65, 96

Canadian Units

First Army, 65, 95, 96, 101, 102, 106

French Units

French Forces of the Interior (FFI), 37, 63, 72, 74, 79, 108, 121

Free French 2nd Armored Division, 85, 90, 91, 96, 100, 108, 118, 151

Free French First Army, 151

German Units

Army Group B, 229

Fifth Panzer Army, 91, 95, 96, 98, 111, 134–136, 145, 157, 176, 181, 200, 223–225, 229, 236

1st SS Panzer Division, 88, 223

2nd Panzer Division, 88

2nd SS Panzer Division, 88

3rd Panzer Grenadier Division, 224

9th SS Panzer Division, 224

12th SS Panzer Division, 224

15th Panzer Grenadier Division, 212, 224

26th Volksgrenadier Division, 224

XXXIX Panzer Corps, 223

XLVII Corps, 176, 223

116th Panzer Division, 88

167th Volksgrenadier Division, 223

340th Volksgrenadier Division, 224

Army Group Luettwitz, 223, 224

First Army, 134, 142

Luftwaffe, 14, 28, 84, 183

II Parachute Corps, 28

Panzer Lehr Division, 34

Seventh Army, 27, 56, 59, 76, 88, 91, 95, 96, 98, 111, 157, 179, 181, 193, 197–199, 210, 211, 228, 229, 233

LXXXV Corps, 198

Sixth Panzer Army, 157, 169, 236, 238

Weapons

FG42 rifle, 27

FlaK 30, 53, 260

FlaK 36, 41, 60

FlaK 38, 5, 34

FlaK 40, 251

Granatenwerfer 34, 23, 105

Granatenwerfer 36, 132

Granatenwerfer 42, 158

M1 antitank gun, 29, 59, 112, 166, 196, 212, 226

M1 Garand rifle, 11, 55, 139, 165, 181, 196, 201, 262

M1 howitzer, 80, 81, 128, 154, 221

M1 mortar, 165, 175

M1 rocket launcher, 171

M1A1 bazooka, 24, 37, 51, 85, 117

M1A1 flamethrower, 83

M1A1 howitzer, 178

M2 Browning machine gun, 38, 83, 144, 165, 186, 190, 195

M2 mortar, 13, 68, 88

M2A1 artillery piece, 77

M2A1 howitzer, 46, 177, 232

M2HB machine gun, 40, 213

M3 submachine gun, 31, 137, 156, 198

M5 antitank gun, 187

M7 howitzer, 153, 180, 222

M7A1 rocket, 117

M8 howitzer, 42

M9 antitank gun, 260

M9A1 antitank rifle, 262

M9A1 bazooka, 37, 185

M15 antiaircraft unit, 195

M18 howitzer, 232

M42 machine gun, 221

M51 machine gun carriage, 75

M1917A1 machine gun, 125, 157, 199, 214

M1917A4 machine gun, 146, 204, 242

M1919A4 machine gun, 141, 192

M1919A6 machine gun, 223

M1928A1 Thompson submachine gun, 30

Mk II fragmentation rife grenade, 35

Nebelwerfer 41, 144

PaK 40, 6, 264

PaK 43, 140, 160, 216

Raketenwerfer 43, 111

Aircraft

B-17 bomber, 16, 44, 248

C-47 transport, 26, 122

Focke-Wulf Fw 190 fighter, 14

L4 light observation plane, 179

P-47 fighter, 26, 66, 128, 229

Ground Vehicles

Demag 7 half-track, 53

Demag D7 half-track, 260

FT-17 light tank, 56

M3 half-track, 157

M3A1 half-track, 59, 142, 267

M4 Sherman tank, 9, 28, 32, 42, 46, 100, 103, 104, 110, 133, 169, 205, 220, 236

M4A1 Sherman tank, 14, 28, 38, 162, 211, 258

M4A2 Sherman tank, 27, 91

M4A3 Sherman tank, 58, 69, 76, 99, 115, 123, 130, 145, 149, 163, 172, 206, 207, 214, 217, 227, 229, 238, 250, 253

M4A3E2 Sherman tank, 209, 233

M4A4 Sherman tank, 65

M5 light tank, 106, 247, 254

M7 carriage, 153, 180

M8 armored car, 167, 225, 249

M10 tank destroyer, 39, 87, 181, 210, 235

M16 antiaircraft half-track, 116

M18 tank destroyer, 133

M24 light tank, 248

M29 cargo carrier, 167, 216

M32 tank-recovery vehicle, 200

M36 tank destroyer, 183

M41 light tank, 71

Panther Ausf. A tank, 26, 33, 49, 91, 92; D tank, 96; G tank, 142, 145, 227

Panzer IV tank, 73, 92

Puma armored car, 133

Sd.Kfz. 2 Kleines Kettenkrad, 99

Sd.Kfz. 8 half-track prime mover, 35

Sd.Kfz. 167 StuG IV, 95

Sd.Kfz. 231, 61

Sd.Kfz. 250 half-track, 177

Sd.Kfz. 250 Neu, 127

Sd.Kfz. 251 Ausf. D, 97, 157, 205, 234

StuG IV Ausf. G assault gun/tank destroyer, 48

Tiger B tank, 156, 202, 234, 254, 263

Tiger E tank, 72, 87

General

Abrams, Creighton W., 201, 202, 205

Alencon, 86, 92, 96

Amiens, France, 116

Angers, France, 90

Antwerp, Belgium, 116, 156, 158, 160, 169, 180, 181

Ardennes, the, 115, 116, 153–160, 162, 163, 165–172, 175, 176, 178, 181, 183, 185, 186, 188, 193, 194, 208, 209, 212, 215–218, 224, 225, 229, 233–239, 241

Argentan, France, 91, 95, 98, 100–102, 104, 106, 107

Arlon, France, 171, 183, 185, 188–190, 193, 195, 206, 211, 224, 225

Arloncourt, France, 226

Armagh, Northern Ireland, 13

Arnaville, France, 142, 149

Arracourt, France, 131, 134, 135, 142

Assenois, France, 202, 205, 206, 211, 223

Avranches, France, 50, 53, 56–60, 66, 68, 77, 84, 85, 88–91, 93, 98

Baade, Paul W., 198

Bain-de-Bretagne, France, 72

Bastogne, France, 158, 166, 168, 172, 176, 179–183, 185–195, 197–202, 204–212, 214, 216–220, 222–226, 228, 229, 233–236, 238

Battle of the Bulge, 2, 153–155, 186, 198, 209, 220, 224, 229, 236, 239, 241

Beauchamps, France, 84

Bercheux, France, 201, 202

Bernard, Lyle, 3

Bettembourg, Luxembourg, 134

Bigonville, France, 192, 193, 195, 206, 207

Bitburg, Germany, 249, 250

Bizory, France, 227

Blanchard, Wendell, 192, 202, 205

Boggess, Charles Jr., 207

Bois de Fragotte, France, 220

Bourcy, France, 226

Bradley, Omar, 5, 18, 24, 25, 27–31, 34, 36–38, 40–44, 46, 49, 50, 54, 59, 61, 63, 66–68, 71, 81, 87–91, 93, 97–102, 104, 106–108, 110, 111, 117, 118, 130, 132, 137, 143, 145–147, 156, 158, 163, 164, 171, 176, 187, 188, 215–218, 234, 239, 241, 242, 244, 246–249, 267

Brandenberger, Erich, 211, 229

Brehal, France, 58

Brest, France, 67, 75, 77–81, 83, 116

Brittany, France, 5, 21, 28, 30, 33, 38, 40, 53, 54, 56, 60, 62, 63, 66–70, 72, 75–78, 83, 86, 91, 118, 146

Brolo, Sicily, 3

Brul, France, 221

Buron, France, 189, 204

Cadman, Charles R., 175

Caen, France, 29, 29, 43, 44, 92, 95

Chartres, France, 105, 112, 113

Château-Salins, France, 131, 134

Chaumont, France, 189, 192, 204, 207

Chenogne, France, 219, 221

Cherbourg, France, 19, 22, 27

Churchill, Winston, 4, 25, 254

Clochimont, France, 202

Collins, Joseph Lawton, 18, 32, 43, 44, 46, 47, 50, 51, 56, 214, 219, 232

Connaughton, George W., 200

Cook, Gilbert R., 88, 105

Cotentin Peninsula, France, 15, 19, 22, 33, 38, 40, 53

Coutances, France, 28, 30, 32, 34, 38, 43, 47, 50, 51, 53, 56

Crerar, Henry D. G., 95

Cross, Leslie H., 134, 135

Cullen, Curtis G. Jr., 28

Dager, Holmes, 129, 188

Darmstadt, Germany, 147

Dempsey, Miles C., 18, 43, 44

Derval, France, 72

Dessau, Germany, 258

Devers, Jacob L., 151

Dietrich, Josef, 98

Dinan, France, 75, 77, 78

Dornot, France, 141, 142, 149

Dover, England, 14

Dreux, France, 104, 105

Dunkirk, France, 25

Eddy, Manton Sprague, 79, 88, 111, 112, 118, 125, 127–129, 131, 132, 134–136, 138–140, 142, 143, 149–152, 216, 249, 251, 256

Eisenhower, Dwight D., 2, 7–10, 14–17, 19, 20, 25, 27, 29, 33, 36–38, 40–42, 49, 53, 71, 81, 84, 91, 92, 102, 104, 108, 115, 117–119, 123, 126, 127, 130, 132, 137, 143, 145–147, 151, 152, 156, 158, 162, 163, 166, 170–173, 175, 176, 178, 182, 183, 185, 188, 190, 214–217, 239, 241, 242, 244, 248–250, 253, 256, 258, 261, 263, 266

Falaise, France, 91, 92, 95, 96, 100–104, 106, 108, 110

Flers, France, 98

Forgeres, France, 63, 68, 84

Forrest, Nathan Bedford, 268

Fort Driant, 144, 145

Fox Red beach, 20

Frankfurt, Germany, 147

Gaffey, Hugh J., 90, 103, 129, 136, 139, 145, 188, 189, 192, 194, 195, 197, 200, 202, 207, 208, 211

Gardner, Glenn H., 201

Gay, Hobart R., 13, 164, 215

Geraud, Henri, 123

Gerow, Leonard T., 18, 165, 166

Granville, France, 58

Grow, Robert W., 75, 77–80, 136, 225, 227

Haislip, Wade H., 13, 67, 83, 84, 86, 87, 90, 95, 96, 98, 100–102, 104, 106–108, 111, 112, 118, 125

Harlange, Luxembourg, 227, 229

Harrold, Thomas L., 219

Hart, Liddell, 129

Hines, John L. Jr., 225

Hitler, Adolf, 6, 29, 31, 35, 59, 63, 65, 88, 96, 98, 126, 127, 140, 142, 155, 156, 159, 160, 183, 186, 198, 216, 223, 224, 229, 233, 236, 238, 239, 241, 261, 266

Hodges, Courtney H., 31, 40, 42, 61, 83–85, 87, 90, 96, 98, 99, 119, 146, 151, 176, 190, 215, 216, 229, 235, 236, 238, 239, 242, 248, 249

Hompre, France, 201, 211, 212

Houffalize, Belgium, 216, 217, 222, 232, 233, 235, 236, 238, 239

Houmont, France, 221

Huelgoat, France, 79

Jodl, Alfred, 31

Kluge, Guenther von, 31, 31, 88, 96, 98

Koblenz, Germany, 249, 250

Koch, Oscar W., 160, 161, 164

Laval, France, 86, 87

Lavaselle, France, 221

Le Havre, France, 15

Le Mans, France, 86, 87, 90, 92, 96, 99

Leclerc, Jacques Philippe, 85, 96

Liege, France, 116

Linz, Germany, 261

Livarchamps, Belgium, 212

London, England, 7

Longvilly, France, 226

Lorient, France, 72–74, 76, 77, 80

Lorraine, France, 123, 125, 127, 130–133, 138, 149, 153

Luettwitz, Freiherr V., 223, 224

Luneville, France, 135

Lutrebois, Belgium, 223, 224, 226, 227

M1 bulldozer blade, 28, 217, 258

MacArthur, Douglas, 8

Maddox, Halley G., 164

Mageret, Belgium, 233

Mainz, Germany, 147, 249, 255

Manbeuge, France, 116

Mande-Saint-Etienne, Belgium, 229

Mantes-Gassicourt, France, 112

Manteuffel, Hasso von, 176, 223, 229

Marche, Belgium, 220

Marigny, France, 32

Marshall, George C., 8–10, 36, 71, 92, 152, 162

Martelange, Belgium, 188, 189, 191, 193, 195, 204

Marvie, Belgium, 229

Maultier, 102, 232

Mayenne, France, 86, 87

McAuliffe, Anthony C., 179, 212

McBride, Horace L., 143

McNair, Lesley J., 50

Messerschmitt Bf 109, 245

Metz, France, 116, 118, 125, 138, 140–144, 146, 147, 150, 151

Middleton, Troy H., 51, 54, 56, 58, 59, 67, 69, 71, 73–75, 77, 78, 80, 83, 84, 118, 155, 156, 158, 159, 165, 166, 172, 176, 178, 179, 185, 217, 218, 221, 222, 227, 239, 249

Millikin, John, 171, 183, 185, 187, 190, 191, 193–195, 198, 211, 212, 214, 217, 224–227, 229, 233

Model, Walter, 127, 229

Montgomery, Bernard, 15, 25, 27, 29, 33, 38, 43, 44, 65, 91, 97, 99, 101, 102, 106, 110, 112, 115–119, 123, 126, 130, 137, 145–147, 176, 183, 190, 216, 229, 235, 239, 241, 242, 244, 248, 254, 256, 260, 261, 263

Montgomery, Bradley, 41

Morris, W. H. H., 150

Mortain, France, 88, 90–93, 95–99

Nancy, France, 116, 118, 125, 127, 128, 131, 132, 138–140, 142, 143

Nantes, France, 74, 90

Neffe, Belgium, 225, 226

Neufchâteau, Belgium, 185, 195, 201, 211, 218, 219, 225

Nogent-sur-Seine, France, 114

Normandy, France, 1, 2, 5, 12, 15–18, 21, 23–31, 33–35, 37–39, 41, 42, 56, 61, 63, 65, 70, 76, 79, 83, 87, 88, 90, 97–101, 112, 117, 119, 129, 260

Noville, Switzerland, 238

Oliver, Lunsford E., 83

Omaha Beach, 11, 18–22, 26

Oppenheim, Germany, 256

Orleans, France, 103–105, 111, 112

Oubourcy, Belgium, 233

Paris, France, 27–30, 33, 66, 85, 87, 89, 94, 103, 105–109, 111, 112, 114, 173

Paris-Orleans Gap, 103, 111, 112

Pas de Calais, France, 12, 14, 27

Patch, Alexander M., 252, 253

Patton, George S., 1–3, 5–7, 9–11, 13, 14, 16, 18, 25–27, 29, 31, 34, 36, 37, 40, 43, 50, 53, 54, 61–63, 66, 67, 70, 71, 73, 75–79, 81, 84–90, 92, 95, 96, 98, 99, 102–107, 111–115, 117–119, 121–123, 125–127, 129–131, 134, 135, 137, 139, 143–147, 149, 151, 153, 158, 160–164, 168, 171–173, 175–177, 183, 185, 187–192, 194, 195, 197, 198, 201, 204, 205, 208, 211, 214–218, 220, 225, 226, 228, 233, 234, 237–239, 242, 246, 248–250, 254, 255, 257, 259, 262, 266–269

Pearl Harbor, Hawaii, 71, 215

Polk, James, 134

Pontaubault, France, 58, 63, 68, 69, 75

Prum, Germany, 215, 216, 239, 241, 248–250

Quatre-Vents, France, 193

Quiberon Bay, France, 69, 72

Remagen, Germany, 252

Remichampagne, Belgium, 202

Remoiville, France, 195, 202

Rennes, France, 63, 67–69, 71, 72, 76

Rochefort, France, 229

Rommel, Erwin, 16, 129

Roosevelt, Franklin D., 4, 8

Rotterdam, the Netherlands, 116

Rundstedt, Karl Rudolf Gerd von, 224, 236

Saarbrilcken, Germany, 162

Saarburg, Germany, 150, 152

Saarlautern, Germany, 150, 152

Sainlez, Belgium, 212

Schwere Granatenwerfer 34, 23

Senonchamps, Belgium, 220

Sheridan, Phil, 268

Sibret, Belgium, 202, 205, 218, 219, 223, 224

Simpson, Alan, 145, 146, 151, 158, 176, 190, 242, 261

Simpson, William H., 118

St. Gilles, France, 32

St. Hilaire-du-Harcouet, France, 85–87, 90

St.-Lô, France, 23, 28–30, 33, 38, 53

St. Malo, France, 67, 77, 80

St. Vith, Belgium, 158, 166, 168, 191, 214, 216, 217, 225, 227, 239

Stalin, Joseph, 4, 258

Strong, Ken, 156, 158

Stuart, Jeb, 268

Sylvester, Lindsay M., 111

Taylor, Maxwell, 212, 222, 227

Tehran, Iraq, 4

Thionville, France, 125, 140, 142

Tintange, Belgium, 200

Trier, Germany, 162, 248–251

Troyes, France, 112

Truscott, Lucian K., 266, 268

Utah Beach, 19–21

Vannes, France, 72, 73, 76, 80

Vaux-lez Rosières, Belgium, 202

Verdun, France, 139, 171–173, 185

Villeroux, Belgium, 219, 220

Villers-la-Bonne-Eau, Belgium, 227, 229

Vitre, France, 90

Walker, Walton Harris, 71, 85, 86, 89, 90, 96, 104, 105, 111–114, 118, 123, 125, 132, 138–142, 144, 147, 150–153, 251

Wardin, Belgium, 225, 233

Warnach, Belgium, 191, 192, 200, 205, 207

Waters, John K., 256

Werbomont, Belgium, 178

Weyland, Otto P., 27, 66, 86, 106, 112, 113, 144, 146, 207, 209

Wood, John Shirley, 69–74, 128, 129